What Every Manager Needs to Know About FINANCE

What Every Manager Needs to Know About FINANCE

Hubert D. Vos, Editor

Excerpted from the
AMA Management Handbook, Second Edition,
William K. Fallon, General Editor

amacom

American Management Association

This book is available at a special
discount when ordered in bulk quantities.
For information, contact Special Sales Department,
AMACOM, a division of American Management Association,
135 West 50th Street, New York, NY 10020.

Library of Congress Cataloging-in-Publication Data

What every manager needs to know about finance.

  "Excerpted from the AMA management handbook, second
edition, William K. Fallon, general editor."
  Includes index.
  1. Business enterprises--Finance. 2. Corporations--
Finance. I. Vos, Hubert D. II. AMA management handbook.
2nd ed.
HG4026.W48 1986   658.1'5   86-47626
ISBN 0-8144-7667-8

Printing number

10 9 8 7 6 5 4 3 2

Publisher's Note

The revised and expanded second edition of the *AMA Management Handbook*, originally published in 1983, is the single most comprehensive source of information on management available today. Over 1,600 pages long, the handbook contains 163 chapters, which are divided into fourteen major sections. Every conceivable management and business topic is covered.

Now, in response to numerous requests to make discrete sections of the handbook available to managers and executives with interests in specific fields, AMACOM Books takes great pleasure in publishing this excerpt, the complete section on finance, as it originally appeared in the *AMA Management Handbook*.

This comprehensive volume provides indispensable information on every aspect of financial management—from the responsibilities of the chief financial officer to the role of an investor relations program. It is our hope that this volume will prove as valuable as the original handbook has been to its thousands of readers.

Robert A. Kaplan
Publisher
AMACOM Books

Contents

The Role of Finance in General Management   **5**

Responsibilities of the Chief Financial Officer   **6**

        Setting Financial Policies / 6
        Financial Administration / 12

Planning, Budgeting, and Forecasting   **17**

        Scope of Financial Planning, Budgeting,
          and Forecasting / 18
        The Planning and Budget-Development Process / 19
        Business-Direction Planning / 22
        Strategy Development / 25
        Annual Planning / 30
        Performance Reporting / 43
        Data Relationships / 49
        Conclusion / 51

1

Acquisitions and Divestitures   **53**

> Organization / 53
> Strategy / 54
> Planning to Implement the Merger Strategy / 55
> Evaluating the Acquisition / 56
> Structuring the Transaction / 56
> Afterword / 57

Capital Expenditures and Return on Investment   **57**

> Requirements of a Capital Expenditure Program / 58
> Methods of Evaluating Capital Expenditures / 61
> Cost of Capital / 65
> Capital Rationing / 67
> Risk Analysis / 68
> Central Considerations / 69

Financing Corporate Requirements   **69**

> Short-Term Financing / 70
> Intermediate-Term Financing / 71
> Long-Term Financing / 74

Cash Management and Bank Relations   **78**

> Objectives of Cash Management / 79
> Cash-Management Techniques / 80
> Bank Selection Criteria / 97

Accounts Receivable: Credit Collections   **98**

> Current Receivables Trends / 98
> Function of the Credit Manager / 99
> Value of Information / 99
> Evaluation of Risk and Credit Control / 100
> Reporting Results / 103
> Planning Receivables Collections / 103

General Accounting and Financial Statements **105**

      General Accounting / 105
      Financial Statements / 110

Cost Accounting and Analysis **115**

      Process Cost Accounting / 117
      Job-Order Cost Accounting / 120
      Standard-Cost Accounting / 121
      Direct Costing and Absorption Costing / 125
      Cost Accounting for Defense Contracts / 128

Inventory Valuation and Control **133**

      Inventory Valuation and Performance
        Measurement / 134
      Inventory Management and Control / 139
      Physical Inventory / 147
      Summary / 148

Federal Income Tax Responsibilities **148**

      Management's Limitations / 149
      Management's Options / 149
      Business Growth / 152
      The Tax Department in the Large Corporation / 152
      Becoming Tax-Oriented / 155

State and Local Taxes **155**

      Types of Taxes / 156
      Administration / 159

Presentation and Interpretation of Operating Results **159**

      Role of Management / 160
      Operating Results versus Performance Results / 160
      Source of Data for Operating Results / 161
      Presentation Methods / 161
      Interpretation of Operating Results / 168
      Summary / 171

Internal Auditing   **171**

        Foreign Corrupt Practices Act / 172
        Responsibilities of the Audit Department / 172
        Operational Audits / 173
        Data Processing Audits / 174
        Fraud / 175
        Reporting Relationships / 176
        Staffing / 176
        Audit Plans and Reports / 177
        Year-End Audit / 178
        Audit Committee / 178
        Evaluating the Audit Function / 179

The External Audit   **179**

        Financial Statements / 180
        The Auditor / 183
        Generally Accepted Auditing Standards / 183
        Internal Control / 184
        Evidential Matter / 186
        The Auditor's Report / 186
        Supplementary Financial Information / 187
        Additional Services by the Independent Auditor / 188

Management of Pension Funds   **188**

        The Employee Retirement Income Security Act
          of 1974 / 189
        Setting Investment Policy to Meet Objectives / 189
        Investment Strategy Formulation / 191
        Selecting External Managers / 192
        Measuring Investment Performance / 194

Investor Relations   **195**

        Goals and Objectives of an Investor Relations
          Program / 196
        The Place of Investor Relations in the
          Organization / 198
        Basic Elements of an Investor Relations Program / 199
        Costs versus Benefits / 201

Index   **203**

THE ROLE OF FINANCE IN GENERAL MANAGEMENT

The role of finance in general management for a particular company at a particular time will be partly determined by variables such as the type and size of the business, its financial health, and the personalities and backgrounds of the senior executives and directors of the company. The material in this section explores in depth the various functional activities usually included under the broad umbrella of the financial organization, although not all financial organizations include all the functions described. From the viewpoint of general management, a number of those functions may be considered internal "mechanical" activities of the finance department. Management's concern with these functions will tend to be limited to wanting satisfaction that they are carried on accurately, efficiently, effectively, and reliably. For instance, the general accounting function may be so viewed in a company manufacturing consumer products, but may be seen in a totally opposite way in an enterprise that depends heavily on large numbers of transactions with individuals, such as a bank or a multioffice consumer loan company.

Similarly, the tax function may not loom large in general management's concern once management is satisfied that tax returns are always filed promptly and correctly, with only the minimum legal tax being paid. Yet, in the same company, the tax considerations involved in selecting a site for a new plant can propel the tax function to the center of management attention.

The role of the financial function in general management will depend on what management perceives to be important at a particular time. But two aspects of the financial function dictate the minimum part it must play in any enterprise.

First, the language of finance provides a common denominator for the discrete functions that make up the business. The head of manufacturing may manage his responsibilities best by physical measures (such as production per man-hour and raw-materials yields) rather than by dollar-oriented ones. The same can be true for other components of the organization—marketing, personnel, and so on. But ultimately, all the separate measures must be harmonized into a single language. It is the finance function which does this, providing information on the health, direction, and progress of the company. In performing this role as translator and thus combiner and commentator, the finance function will assume a role in general management.

The second general basis for finance's role in management lies in the special ingredient it administers for the company—money. For a business, money is the blood in the circulatory system. If its money is not properly managed, the enterprise faces commercial death. If its money is correctly managed, the enterprise may survive, although other tests—products, marketing, and so on—obviously must be met. As the administrator of the company's money—the function of the company that raises money and supervises its use—finance almost automatically assumes a role in general management.

At a minimum, the service of these two elements—common language and stewardship of money—involves the financial function with general management. How far beyond the minimum the financial function should go in any company cannot be prescribed. Personalities, relative competence, and the critical needs of the company will be the key determinants. The minimum role is demanded and unavoidable; a larger role is available for those capable of applying financial skills thoughtfully and cooperatively to the broader context of the total business, current and future, which is the arena in which general management operates.

The emphasis in the foregoing material has been on the financial function, as opposed to the financial organization. The distinction is necessary, because in a small company, the function can be lodged in the person of the founder or chief executive; in larger environments, the responsibility may in fact reside in the person to whom the chief financial officer reports, rather than truly inside the finance organization.   □ *Shepard P. Pollack*

RESPONSIBILITIES OF THE CHIEF FINANCIAL OFFICER

In recent years, the role of the chief financial officer (CFO) has grown considerably in American corporations. This is due in part to the growing amount of financial reporting required by government agencies and the investing public. The more significant reason, however, is the fact that, with the recent acceleration of inflation, the advent of fluctuating exchange rates, and the resulting sharp increases and decreases in economic activity and interest rates, corporate managements have had to turn increasingly to the chief financial officer for evaluation and recommendations of the alternative courses of action open to the corporation. As a result, the chief financial officer has become a broad-gauged executive in the senior ranks of management who is responsible for bringing the financial point of view to bear on most of the important decisions a company has to make. He is normally directly responsible to the chief executive officer of the company, and he is with increasing frequency a member of the board of directors.

His responsibilities can be analyzed under two main headings. On the one hand, he is responsible for setting a great number of financial policies. On the other hand, he is also responsible for the administration of the financial departments that report to him.

Setting Financial Policies

Although establishing and maintaining a system of internal controls and reports are not necessarily the most important responsibilities of the CFO, without an adequate system of internal controls and reports the CFO cannot carry out any of his other responsibilities. A company of any significant size must have a documented system of internal controls if it is to avoid financial chaos. In addition, under recent federal legislation, the Foreign Corrupt Practices Act, corporations are legally required to have an adequate and documented system of internal controls throughout their operations, including their overseas operations.

To monitor the adherence to the system of internal controls, financial management develops a system of accounting policies, procedures, and reports. Policies and procedures are contained in instruction manuals, which are disseminated to all key locations. Many accounting reports are issued monthly, but some may be issued weekly, quarterly, semiannually, or annually. These accounting reports supply information, in a rigorous format, that indicates to the reviewer whether operations are under proper control. Regular review of accounting reports to ensure that operations are under control, and to highlight and quickly investigate problems that may appear, is one of the fundamental responsibilities of financial management. The usual internal controls are those that apply to the handling of cash, the recognition of sales, the authorization and disbursement of expense items, the method of cost accounting and inventory valuation, and the procedures for the approval of capital expenditures.

The usual financial reports consist of income statements, balance sheets, statements of sources and uses of funds, and more detailed reports supporting the line items in each of these principal statements. Internal control procedures and accounting reports have to be tailored to each business. Although certain summary statements are common to most businesses, particular industries require special procedures and special statements. In ordering his priorities, the chief financial officer must first make sure that an adequate system of controls and reports is in place. If it is not, his first task is to implement an adequate system.

Provision of Measurements

It is not enough for the financial organization to provide financial reports that indicate the status of various aspects of the corporation. It is necessary for an adequate financial organization to develop concepts of measurement that are to be used by corporate employees in evaluating the adequacy of the information contained in the financial statements. The specific measurements will vary according to industry, but the following are found in many companies. *Gross profit percentage* is a useful measurement to indicate the spread between selling price and cost of goods sold. A shrinking of gross profit percentage may indicate either a problem in manufacturing costs or inadequate selling prices. Another useful measurement is showing *general and administrative expenses as a percentage of sales*. Frequently, each expense item is measured as a percentage of sales. *Pretax income as a percentage of sales* is also frequently used, as is *net income after taxes as a percentage of sales*. The latter ratio is frequently called *return on sales* and is a prime indicator of the profitability of the company.

There are other ratios that emphasize various aspects of the balance sheet. *Days-sales-of-receivables-outstanding* is a measure to determine whether collections are happening in accordance with company policy or whether they are later, which can be a harbinger of lower profit, poor customer relations, and bad debts. *Days-sales-of-inventory-on-hand* is a measure that indicates the general health of the company. For each industry and company there is an adequate level for inventories, which sometimes changes according to a seasonal pattern, and which represents a favorable balance between the ability to meet customer needs and avoidance of excessive investment in inventories. When inventories step out of pattern, it is usually an indication that something significant is happening to the business that senior management needs to analyze quickly and react to with serious consideration. *Turnover-of-fixed-assets* is a measure that divides total sales by total fixed assets. It is usually calculated annually and is an indication of the capital-intensiveness of the business. Because of the higher replacement cost of fixed assets under inflationary conditions, this ratio decreases when new capital expansion programs are undertaken. It is useful, however, to view the long-term implications of a change in the ratio as an indicator of a possible change in the financial characteristics of the company. *Turnover-of-net-assets,* which is sales divided by total assets with a deduction for current liabilities other than debt, is another measure used to evaluate the financial characteristics of the company. When turnover of net assets declines, it is necessary to have a corresponding increase in the return-on-sales ratio to maintain a given level of profitability. Return on investment is the final measure of the profitability of any business. The relationships can be seen in the following equations:

$$\text{Return on investment} = \frac{\text{net income}}{\text{net assets}}$$

$$= \frac{\text{net income}}{\text{sales}} \times \frac{\text{sales}}{\text{net assets}}$$

$$= \text{return on sales} \times \text{turnover of net assets}$$

Uncompensated decline in either return on sales or turnover of net assets leads to a decline in return on investment and company profitability. With high inflation and increasing asset values, the chief financial officer must emphasize programs that permit lower asset investment or higher returns for a given level of sales.

The measurements mentioned so far are all of an operational nature. In addition, there are measurements of a financing nature. Financing provides the capital in addition to the equity in the business to fuel its growth. Financing measurements will be discussed more fully in the section "Setting Financing Policy." Suffice it to say here that there is a relationship between operational measurements and financing measurements that determines the sustainable rate of growth of an enterprise. This concept is important because it ties together the principal financial measurements with what is today the key objective of most companies: to have a certain acceptable rate of earnings growth. There are a number of sustainable earnings-growth-rate formulas, some of which involve sophisticated mathematical formulation. We will illustrate one here that is simple yet adequate for most purposes:

$$\text{Sustainable growth rate} = \frac{NI}{NA} \times (1-D)(1+R_1+R_2)$$

where NI = net income for current year

NA = net assets employed at end of previous year; net assets are defined as total assets less: cash, short-term investments, and all current liabilities except any short-term debt

D = fraction of earnings paid out in dividends

R_1 = allowable debt-to-equity ratio

R_2 = ratio of deferred taxes to equity

If a company is growing at a rate slower than its sustainable growth rate, then opportunities are passing the company by; it is not using its financial resources for the best return to the shareholders. In such cases, the chief financial officer should point out this underutilization of financial resources so that management can organize programs to improve their utilization. In other cases, the recent growth rate in earnings may be substantially greater than the sustainable growth rate. In such cases, the chief financial officer should point out to others in management that if such an actual growth rate continues, the company will run out of money and, since it will have exhausted its debt capacity, will be forced to either reduce its rate of growth or issue more equity-oriented securities to the public to increase its equity base.

There are other measurements, but our purpose here was to clearly indicate how important it is for a chief financial officer to ensure that adequate measurements appropriate to his company and industry are in place and that their meaning is well understood by the other members of management.

Annual and Long-Range Plans

Most modern companies have long-range plans, sometimes called strategic plans, which cover a period of four to five years, and an annual plan, sometimes referred to as a profit plan or budget, which covers the current year.

Long-range plans should delve deeply into questions of company strategy, such as stage of industry maturity, competitive positions, product innovations, and demographic changes. Inevitably, however, these strategic plans also include financial schedules, which summarize the expected financial performance of the company if all the strategies adopted in the plan are met. The chief financial officer and his staff play a major role in evaluating the adequacy of such financial long-range operational plans.

The financial staff should be particularly adept at modeling alternative solutions so that management can have a set of clearly defined and analyzed options to select from. Financial modeling frequently centers on the allocation of resources between product lines and includes the impact of divestments and acquisitions. Sensitivity studies showing the effects of possible changes in volumes, selling prices, costs, and so forth, are also useful. Computer programs are available to assist in the clerical work involved in financial planning.

The annual plan requires even more detailed analysis on the part of financial management. Plans should have an element of stretch in them, and yet be attainable. It is important to ensure that the financial measurements in the plan are clearly understood and that progress against the plan will be monitored periodically during the year, usually monthly.

In addition to attending to the annual plan, it is the financial management's responsibility to see that there is in place a regular system of forecasting that will indicate the likely month-end, quarter-end, and year-end results and how they deviate from plan. Inputs for forecasts must come from operating management personnel, but it is the financial staff's responsibility to put the forecast together and to establish a review process that ensures sufficient accuracy of the forecast.

Evaluation of Major Expenditures

The chief financial officer should recommend to the chief executive officer and to the board a schedule of authorization limits for capital expenditures, depending on the level of management. Normally, division management has authority to approve capital expenditures up to a stated amount per expenditure. A higher limit is set for the chief operating officer or the chief executive officer. Projects above that amount have to go to the board of directors for approval. In addition, the chief financial officer needs to ensure that there are rigorous methods of presenting and evaluating capital expenditures. Normally, these include such measurements as payout in years, return on investment, discounted cash flow, and internal rate of return.

In addition to setting the framework for the presentation and approval of capital expenditures, the financial staff should ensure that a system of post-completion audits is in place for major capital expenditures. Such audits tell management whether the actual performance of the project is according to the levels indicated in the approval process. In processing capital expenditures, the financial staff also needs to review accounting, making sure that items that should be capitalized are in fact capitalized, and that those which should be expensed are expensed. In addition, tax implications must be carefully evaluated to ensure that the investment tax credit and other credits are taken if applicable and, in the case of operations in foreign countries, that any capital expenditure grants from the government are taken advantage of.

It is usual for the chief financial officer to also play a key role in evaluating acquisitions, whether they be acquisitions of assets or of total companies. It is more difficult to establish a definite format for such evaluations. The chief financial officer should carefully evaluate the nature of the acquisition and prescribe the appropriate analyses for that acquisition. There may be common denominators to all the acquisition analyses, but it is good not to overlook the special analyses required in specific instances.

Evaluation of Economic Trends

This heading would probably not have appeared in a description of the chief financial officer's role written a decade or so ago. With the considerable inflation that has persisted since then, and with the serious internal dislocations that have affected multinational companies and also domestic companies as a result of the energy shortage, fluctuating interest rates, foreign competition, and so on, the chief financial officer is the best person in senior management to follow these economic phenomena and advise on their financial consequences to the firm.

In particular, the effect of inflation on the operations of the company and on the meaning of its financial statements are his responsibility. Recently, the SEC and the Financial Accounting Standards Board have required companies to present in the notes to their annual financial statements an analysis of the effects of inflation on the year's operations. This is an external reporting requirement, but it is important for the finance staff to go beyond these summary statements and to evaluate in depth the effect of inflation on the adequacy of the company's pricing policy, the trends in its manufacturing costs due to the increases in raw materials, labor, and equipment costs, the replacement cost of new plants that will be required, and the trend that changing exchange rates will have on foreign competition.

The chief financial officer keeps abreast of these situations by being in touch with banks that supply him with economic analyses and forecasts, reading financial magazines and reviews that evaluate techniques for analyzing the impacts of economics on a company, and keeping in contact with related trade associations as well as with his own operating people. He must be aware of changes in government tax policy, depreciation rules, the likelihood of price controls, and other such eventualities.

Setting Financing Policy

The number of companies that can finance their operations without external debt is far smaller than it used to be. Moreover, with the advent of high inflation, it has become increasingly questionable whether sound financial management is compatible with an absence of debt on the balance sheet. A well-managed company can earn so much more on the operating assets it uses in its business than the after-tax interest cost of money borrowed that it has become a generally accepted axiom that it is sound policy to have a reasonable amount of external debt. The chief financial officer, in coordination with the board of directors, must determine what is a reasonable amount of debt.

The debt management policy of a company is usually expressed in terms of a series of ratios. For many years the ratio of debt to equity has been used as a guide for companies to measure their indebtedness. Companies have expressed themselves as having a policy of maintaining their total debt-to-equity ratio at 1 to 2 or 1 to 1, and so on. In recent years, a more sophisticated key ratio has been developed, which is called the total-debt-to-capitalization ratio. Capitalization is defined as total debt plus deferred taxes plus equity. Thus a company will state that its goal for total debt to capitalization is 30 percent or 40 percent. The inclusion of deferred taxes in capitalization is a realization that with the permanence of accelerated depreciation as a means of calculating depreciation for tax purposes, deferred taxes have become a permanent and growing item in most company balance sheets and represent, in effect, the equivalent of an interest-free loan. Having settled on a debt-to-capitalization ratio, a company then needs to determine how much of its debt it wishes to be of a short-term nature and how much of a long-term nature. Normally, long-term debt is used to finance fixed assets, and short-term debt is used to finance accounts receivable and inventory. Some companies establish that short-term debt should not be more than X percent of long-term debt. Other companies establish other ratios. Frequently, the ratio of short- to long-term debt will depend on the trend in interest rates. At times companies anticipate their long-term funding requirements because rates are particularly attractive, and they will at that time have a reduction in short-term debt. At other times, short-term debt will increase to higher proportions because long-term rates are deemed at an inappropriate level for funding. It is important to have some guideline for determining at what point a company should fund with longer-term debt to avoid having a balance sheet that is over-weighted in short-term debt. This is especially true since most long-term debt has fixed rates, whereas most short-term debt carries fluctuating rates.

The chief financial officer must also establish policies for the company on when it will lease assets instead of buying them. There should be policies on foreign financing, taking into account the effect that foreign financing has on reducing the net asset exposure in foreign currencies. There is a need for a dividend pol-icy, which is usually expressed as a percentage of earnings. Growth companies tend to have a high retention of funds because they need their resources to con-tinue to fuel their above-average growth. Mature companies tend to have a lower earnings retention because they operate at a lower level of growth and, therefore, have lower financial requirements.

Setting Cash Investment Policies

The chief financial officer is, in most cases, also the chief investment officer of the company. The major source of investment funds is normally represented by the company's pension funds. Most funds are managed by outside advisers, and there are therefore the tasks of selecting the outside advisers, determining how they will be measured, and actually monitoring their performance. There are also funds from savings plans that need to be invested. In some companies, there are times when there is a heavy accumulation of short-term funds. In such cases, the finance department must determine the best method of investing those funds so as to obtain the highest return possible while ensuring the safety of the funds and their availability at the time the company will require them. Finally, em-ployee benefit plans increasingly have features that help executives build capital. These plans may be insurance-based, or they may be tied to stock options or other incentives. The finance department must assist the personnel department in doing a rigorous financial analysis of these plans so that they are fully under-stood and are in the best interests of both the executives and the company.

Financial Administration

Figure 2-1 shows the chief financial officer's reponsibilities in a typical medium-size to large company. In a small company, one would frequently find a doubling up of functions, with the positions of director of taxes, director of management information systems, and director of financial personnel disappearing. It is the functions on this chart, not the titles, which are meaningful. In some cases the chief financial officer's subordinates are vice presidents; in other cases they are directors. These titles are meaningful for the individuals concerned but do not change the nature of the functions. It is imperative that the chief financial officer establish a clear chart of organization for his responsibilities. It is also important that he set the content of each major function and that it be in keeping with the appropriate principles of internal control. Let us examine the issues he must re-view in setting up each key function.

Figure 2-1. Organization chart for the financial function.

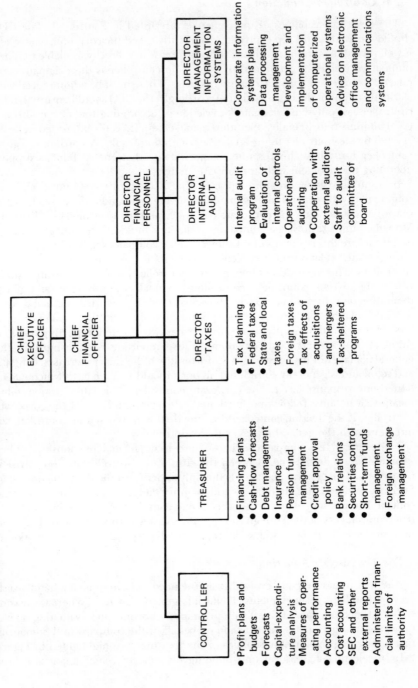

CHIEF EXECUTIVE OFFICER

CHIEF FINANCIAL OFFICER

DIRECTOR FINANCIAL PERSONNEL

CONTROLLER

- Profit plans and budgets
- Forecasts
- Capital-expenditure analysis
- Measures of operating performance
- Accounting
- Cost accounting
- SEC and other external reports
- Administering financial limits of authority

TREASURER

- Financing plans
- Cash-flow forecasts
- Debt management
- Insurance
- Pension fund management
- Credit approval policy
- Bank relations
- Securities control
- Short-term funds management
- Foreign exchange management

DIRECTOR TAXES

- Tax planning
- Federal taxes
- State and local taxes
- Foreign taxes
- Tax effects of acquisitions and mergers
- Tax-sheltered programs

DIRECTOR INTERNAL AUDIT

- Internal audit program
- Evaluation of internal controls
- Operational auditing
- Cooperation with external auditors
- Staff to audit committee of board

DIRECTOR MANAGEMENT INFORMATION SYSTEMS

- Corporate information systems plan
- Data processing management
- Development and implementation of computerized operational systems
- Advice on electronic office management and communications systems

The Controller's Function

The key responsibilities of the controller are listed in Figure 2-1. The CFO should ensure that his top controller, frequently called the corporate controller, is well versed in accounting theory and practice or has directly available to him a number of trained accountants who are. The controller is the originator and guardian of the company's accounting policies. These must be administered with clarity throughout the organization. Accordingly, the CFO should ensure that his controller not only has adequate knowledge of accounting theory but also is a good administrator. Finally, operating management is keenly interested in being assisted by the controller in the analysis of operating results. Accordingly, a good controller must have interests and a personality that enable him to support operating management with appropriate analyses.

In a multidivisional organization, a further decision the CFO must make, in conjunction with general management, is the determination of the relationship that will exist between the corporate controller and the controllers of divisions. Most medium-size to large companies today are multidivisional organizations, and therefore this is an important subject. Some companies have what is called a "straight-line" relationship between the corporate controller and the division controllers. This means that the corporate controller is the administrative superior of the division controllers, controlling their salary and benefits and giving them direction. In most companies, however, there is only what is called a "dotted-line" relationship between the corporate controller and the division controllers. This means that the division controller has two different reporting relationships. He has a straight-line or administrative reporting relationship with the general manager of his division, who informs him of his salary increases, benefits, and so on and is generally considered his boss. In addition, he has a functional or dotted-line responsibility to the corporate controller. This latter responsibility means that he must follow the functional orders and guidance of the corporate controller. If the division controller does not do this, the corporate controller can intervene with the general manager to obtain remedy.

There are a few companies where there is no formal relationship, either straight-line or dotted-line, between the corporate controller and the division controllers. The general manager is the only superior to the division controller. Such organizations are, in today's world, in grave danger of going out of financial control. It is questionable whether they are in compliance with the internal-control requirements of the Foreign Corrupt Practices Act. In addition, such a situation can lead to substantial financial-reporting discrepancies between divisions.

The Treasurer's Function

The treasurer's function evolved from the need to have someone handle cash receipts and bank disbursements. Today it is a major function. Whereas the controller's function concerns itself with planning, reporting, and evaluating operations, the treasurer takes direct action on behalf of the company in the financial marketplace. Specific responsibilities of the treasurer are highlighted in Figure 2-1. In selecting a treasurer and defining his role, the chief financial officer should make sure that his candidate has a good understanding of how to control cash receipts and cash disbursements and is proficient in performing credit analysis. Having assured himself of this basic knowledge, he should seek out a treasurer who will understand the debt markets, the equity markets, the investment markets, insurance practices, foreign-exchange management, and real estate financing. In addition, the treasurer must be good at coordinating these items of knowledge into a long-range financing plan for the corporation as well as an annual plan. Finally, the treasurer should have a good personality to handle relationships with commercial and investment bankers and other outside organizations he comes in contact with.

In today's world, a good treasurer can add greatly to the bottom line.

The issue of straight-line subordinates versus dotted-line subordinates does not arise frequently in the treasurer's function. The normal practice is to centralize the treasurer's function in the company's head office. Thus few activities in the divisions are part of the treasurer's overall functions. For those few that are, the procedures are usually laid down for the division personnel, who take their direction from the central treasurer's office.

Tax Planning

In many corporations, the tax department has become a separate department answering directly to the chief financial officer. This is in recognition of the enormous importance of taxes to the bottom line. When nearly 50 percent of pretax profits are paid out in taxes, they are one of the most significant expenditures in the company. Tax planning helps ensure that the company conforms with all relevant tax laws while taking advantage of all legal opportunities. Especially for multinational corporations, the need for a tax planning function is great. There are real opportunities for legal tax sheltering overseas, and there are also great penalties in taxes to be paid if certain transactions are not structured in the best manner.

Another reason that the tax planning function is becoming a separate department relates to the knowledge required for an effective modern tax function— essentially, knowledge of tax law and of financial accounting. Numerous individuals have now become both accountants (frequently certified public accountants) and lawyers. This combination of backgrounds in an individual is helpful in a tax function and distinct from the typical background of either the controller or the treasurer.

Internal Audit

The role of the director of internal audit has grown considerably in most companies in recent years. In part, this is due to the growth of companies, which entails far-flung operations and the need to ensure that company policy and basic accounting controls are observed at all locations. It is also due to the growth in government regulations, such as the Foreign Corrupt Practices Act, and the increased stature and responsibility of the audit committee of the board of directors under the influence of the Securities and Exchange Commission. In a typical company, the internal auditor will answer directly to the chief financial officer, but he will have a dotted-line responsibility to the audit committee of the board of directors. The audit committee will be composed of outside directors only, and they will, in the course of the year, meet privately with the director of internal audit to assure themselves of the adequacy of the controls throughout the corporation and of the conduct of the financial department.

In many companies, the internal audit function has gone beyond its internal control role and moved into operational auditing. This means that when the internal auditors do an audit of an operating plant or division, they not only try to ascertain that basic financial controls are in place and company policies followed, but also observe actual operations and make recommendations if they see opportunities for significant improvement as a result of their audit work. Carefully done, operational auditing is a cost-effective way of getting a higher return from the audit function by making it helpful to operating management.

The director of internal audit also links up with the external auditors in agreeing to the plan for the audit of the company's operations for the fiscal year. Increasingly, there will be cooperation between the external and internal auditors to avoid duplication of the work they do during the course of the year. Such cooperation, while increasing efficiency of audit work, in no way diminishes the independence of the external auditors.

Management Information Systems

The management information system is not always under the control of the chief financial officer. In some companies it answers directly to the chief executive officer or to an administrative officer. In those cases where the management information systems function does answer to the chief financial officer, he must ensure that it seeks as clients for its services all departments and groups within the company. The time has long passed when the computer was considered solely an accounting tool. Data processing applications today encompass management of sales forces, the control of manufacturing plants, the provision of communication systems to all company locations, long-range planning models, and others, in addition to accounting processing. The chief financial officer should consider himself the host to the management information systems function and should encourage it to take a very broad view of the total company and to produce for the company a long-range management information systems plan. This plan should be reviewed and accepted by general management. There should be a steering committee or advisory committee from numerous departments within the company, which should meet directly with the management information systems department to be kept up to date on the latest computer trends and to discuss their applicability to operations of the company.

Financial-Personnel Administration

Although this function will not be found within the financial departments of small companies, it is becoming increasingly necessary in medium-size and large companies. Good accounting and finance personnel are in short supply. An important responsibility of the chief financial officer is to ensure that there is a steady and appropriate flow of accounting talent entering the company, usually in the lower ranks as trainees, and that these employees are appropriately trained in the policies and procedures of the company. In addition, since accounting and finance personnel form a common professional group within the company, it is important to establish a system of salary grades for them and to follow a regular procedure of evaluation. A strong financial organization is one in which key financial managers have handled many different jobs as they developed in the organization. Such evaluation and job rotation programs do not occur by accident. They need to be planned, and it is only through such planned programs that one can develop the kind of financial managers who will be able to take over top positions within the company in finance and, frequently, in operating management. To the extent he feels the need, the chief financial officer should have a personnel director to coordinate training programs, evaluation systems, and job rotation and promotion for him.

Relating to External Groups

One of the reasons it is important for the chief financial officer to have good subordinates is that he normally spends a good portion of his time relating to groups both within the company and outside the company.

Within the company he not only spends considerable time assisting general management, but he frequently has to make presentations to committees of the board of directors, such as the finance committee, the pension funds committee, and the audit committee. He is also called upon to explain the company's financial policies to meetings of operating management and to join in the deliberations of major company decisions.

His external relationships encompass his role with the external public auditors, for whom he is the principal management contact. He is also in touch with both the company's commercial and investment bankers, frequently with security analysts, and, increasingly, with government agencies that pass regulations affecting the financial requirements of the company. These external relationships can have an important impact on the health and reputation of the company.

□ *Hubert D. Vos*

PLANNING, BUDGETING, AND FORECASTING

The basic objectives of financial planning, which includes annual budgeting and forecasting, are (1) to increase the intrinsic value (shareholder wealth) of the organization; (2) to provide a basis for improved management decisions; and (3) to identify developing business problems in time for effective action. Although these objectives have changed little over the years, the scope of activities that comprise financial planning and the available tools and techniques to support those activities have broadened considerably.

Scope of Financial Planning, Budgeting, and Forecasting

Financial planning, budgeting, and forecasting have traditionally been concerned with the problems of annual operations, resulting in an annual plan comprised of the operating plan, the capital budget, the cash forecast, and the consolidated corporate annual plan. The objective of the annual plan is to translate operating plans into financial statements. The plan is most often the responsibility of line management, and one of its principal uses has been to make period-to-period evaluations of line managers.

The long-range focus of financial planning has in the past been on special studies such as merger and acquisition analysis and capital expenditure analysis. These areas involved major commitments of capital for uncertain returns, which made them a natural testing ground for new concepts and techniques that promised to improve the decision process or reduce the risks of specific decisions. The emphasis on extensive analysis and the unique nature of each study made this area of financial planning the natural province of staff departments. As the frequency of these special studies increased and as the environment became more turbulent and unpredictable, there was increased pressure to remove the tag of "special" and integrate these forward-looking studies into the ongoing process of financial planning.

Strategic planning is the term that has been applied to the process of actively managing the future direction of the organization. It is an emerging discipline whose focus is the fundamental economics of the company and the relation of the organization to the broader economic environment. As strategic planning has developed as a discipline, it has begun to shift its focus from a staff-oriented activity to a line-management responsibility.

The emerging recognition of the linkage between strategic and annual planning has created the need for an integrated analytical framework that can be used to evaluate and monitor both the long-term and short-term financial results of alternative business strategies. The material presented here explores such a framework under the broad title of financial planning. It presents a methodology along with the tools and techniques necessary to answer the following key financial planning questions:

- What are the firm's business opportunities?
- What are the capabilities of this firm for exploiting those business opportunities?
- What risk and return posture is the firm willing to assume toward these business opportunities?
- At a given risk/return posture, will a new opportunity or an existing operation create additional wealth for the firm?
- How would an investment or divestiture decision affect the overall risk of the firm's business?
- What impact would the investment have on the firm's cash flow and return on investment during each accounting period of its projected life?

□ What are the limits and best uses of the firm's internal and external financial sources?

□ How much cash can and should the firm pay out in dividends?

□ How does the firm prioritize, reconcile, pursue, and monitor these objectives over the strategic and annual planning horizon?

The remainder of this discussion develops an approach to help managers answer these key questions for strategic and annual planning. It also suggests how to monitor results through performance reporting. Specifically, it explains the financial planning process and activities in six sections: (1) the planning and budget-development process, (2) business-direction planning, (3) strategy development, (4) annual planning, (5) performance reporting, and (6) data relationships.

The Planning and Budget-Development Process

As shown in Figure 2-2, the plan development and monitoring process is divided into four major phases: (1) establishing the business direction, (2) strategy development, (3) annual planning, and (4) performance reporting.

The overall *business direction* is established by conducting a review of both the external environment in which the company operates and the organization's internal capabilities to exploit the business opportunities identified. This analysis provides the context in which business objectives are defined and translated into financial objectives. For example, a multiyear business objective such as a target market share can be translated into an associated time-phased impact on financial results, such as ROI or cash flow. The translation could also have been reversed if the business objective had been stated as the achievement of a specified ROI by a certain year.

During the *strategy development* phase, the organization must determine the risk/return posture it is willing to assume toward the various business opportunities previously identified. Specifically, it must establish a cost of capital for evaluating the individual investments. The business strategies identified during internal and external analysis are further expanded and tested for financial feasibility by evaluating the profitability of proposed investments (or divestitures), using inflation-adjusted dollars at the marginal-cost-of-capital rate. The calculations involved in such an evaluation include the investment's net cash flow, net present value, and payback period. Various combinations of ongoing operations and incremental investments (and/or divestitures) can then be evaluated for their contribution to the overall business mission, which is usually a combination of market growth, portfolio balance, and financial targets (such as consistent earnings growth and dividend payout). After an overall investment and operating strategy has been agreed on, it is reviewed for its impact on internal or external funding requirements. If funding constraints are not exceeded, the strategic plan is adopted. The strategic plan is usually documented in a multiyear, high-level profit and loss statement, investment plan, cash-flow projection, and balance sheet.

Figure 2-2. Financial planning and monitoring process.

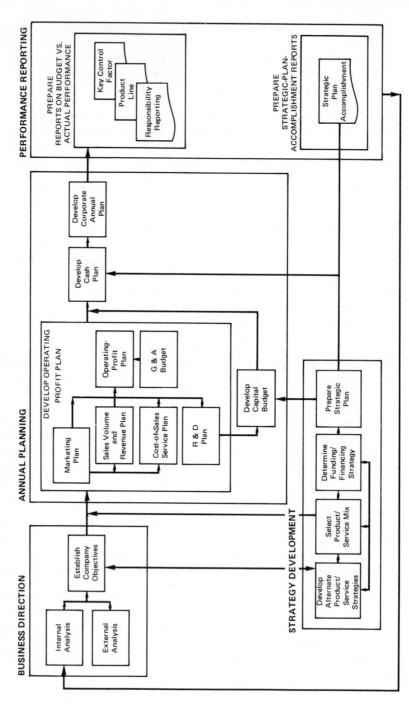

The first year of the strategic plan is then used to provide the operating targets for *annual planning*. The annual plan is typically composed of an operating-profit plan, a capital budget, a cash-flow projection, and a consolidated balance sheet.

The operating-profit plan is developed by multiplying the sales volume projected by the marketing plan by planned prices to calculate projected sales revenue. From this are subtracted (1) the cost of sales, which is based on the inventory and production (or service delivery) plan, (2) research-and-development expenses, and (3) selling, general, and administrative expenses, to derive an operating profit for each product (or service) line. These profit and loss statements for each product (service) line are then consolidated to summarize total operating profit for the company.

The annual capital budget is developed by identifying and summarizing the portion of the multiyear investment plan that is to be expended during the plan year. The cash-flow statement is constructed by deducting investment and operating cash disbursements from projected monthly operating and nonoperating cash receipts.

The corporate annual plan is then developed by consolidating operating and nonoperating profit plans into a consolidated profit and loss statement and completing the corporate balance sheet by including changes in equity, debt, and dividends projected for the plan year.

Performance reporting monitors the achievement of both annual and strategic objectives. Annual performance reporting typically focuses on key control factors (such as weekly unit sales, inventory turnover, utilization ratios, and so on) and variances between planned and actual performance in product lines, responsibility centers, and legal entities. This reporting provides the basis for short-term corrective action by operating management. Strategic performance reporting typically focuses on progress toward the achievement of multiyear objectives.

Planning Horizon

The individual components of the overall financial plan vary in the length of time covered by a plan and in the plan revision frequency. Figure 2-3 graphically shows the planning horizons of various products of the planning process. The different horizons can usually be divided into five categories:

1. Long-range-planning horizon—5-year to 25-year net-cash-flow projection of investments, discounted to determine net present value.
2. Strategic-planning horizon—five-year operational (volumetric) and financial planning.
3. Annual-planning horizon—twelve-month operational (volumetric) cash and profit planning.
4. Forecast horizon—twelve-month projection extending beyond the length of the formal annual plan.
5. Outlook horizon—projection of current year-end results based on actual results incurred to date and the latest forecast data for the months remaining in the fiscal year.

Figure 2-3. The planning and budget-development process.

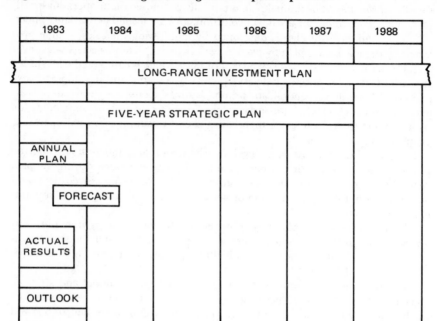

Business-Direction Planning

Establishment of a business direction provides a context in which management can operate. This context consists of goals and objectives, constraints, and financial resources, most visibly expressed as a series of financial plans that management is responsible for achieving. Figure 2-4 is a schematic representation of the strategic resource-conversion cycle.

The task of management is to convert the most general type of resource—financial—into increasingly more specific resources, which ultimately meet some market need, at which point they are reconverted into new financial resources. Accomplishment of this task is a complex process necessitating an objective assessment of the company's strengths and weaknesses and a thorough understanding of the competitive threats and opportunities facing the company. Both the overall social and economic environment in which the company operates and the underlying values of management will affect the process and thus must be explicitly considered.

The development of each key component of the business-direction plan (external analysis, internal analysis, and company objectives) is described in more detail in the next few pages.

Figure 2-4. The strategic resource-conversion cycle.

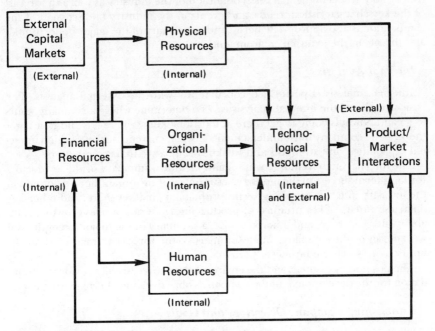

Source: Strategy Formulation: Analytical Concepts, by Charles Hofer
and Dan Schendel. St. Paul, Minn.: Wash Publishing, 1978.

External Analysis

Since the external environment is in constant change, business decisions based on the current external environment alone (or those that simply ignore the external environment) run a high risk of being ineffectual. Management must recognize which external factors could most substantially affect the business and attempt to forecast those factors. In this way, management can make business decisions that take advantage of external opportunities and diminish the impact of external threats.

Specifically, to complete the external analysis, management must (1) identify factors in the external environment that will affect the business during the planning horizon; (2) identify the external factors that will be key to the company's business decisions; (3) analyze, evaluate, and forecast the key factors; (4) identify opportunities and threats in the external environment; and (5) prepare the environmental forecast.

The major components of the environmental forecast are a forecast of the key economic, regulatory, and political variables that will affect the business; a forecast of the key technological changes that will affect the business; a forecast of the size and growth rate of the market, including a forecast of key characteristics, trends, and events in the market; a definition of the industry as well as a forecast of the key characteristics, trends, and events in the industry (a discussion of the competition is also appropriate here); and a summary of the major opportunities and threats in the external environment.

Internal Analysis

Internal analysis is performed concurrently with the external analysis. The basic premise of the internal analysis is: "To determine where a company wants to go and how it is going to get there, it must first know where it is and how it got there." The company must understand its history, current market position, internal capabilities, and strengths and weaknesses relative to its competitors.

The internal analysis must focus on and include a summary of the key factors for long-term success in the industry; a summary of the organization's position in the industry in terms of sales growth, profitability, market share, and other key data; a summary of key products or product lines in terms of sales growth, profitability, market share, and other key data; a summary of the major strengths and weaknesses of the company; and a summary of the forecast attractiveness of the industry in which the business operates.

The position assessment and the environmental forecast will provide the foundation for the development of the company's objectives and alternative strategies.

Establishing Company Objectives and Goals

Objectives are defined as general statements of what the organization must do to accomplish its business mission. A business mission identifies the purpose of the company and the limits—markets, product lines, geographic areas, and distribution channels—within which it will operate. Goals are defined as statements of specifics that quantify objectives. That is, goals are the specific things that must be accomplished in a certain time to achieve business objectives.

For example, a company's objective may be to enter a new market, and the corresponding goal may be to achieve a 15 percent average return on investment over the next five years in that new market.

The process of developing objectives and goals will differ from company to company, depending on the organizational structure of the company and the degree of decentralization. It is, however, an iterative process that incorporates feedback from subsequent stages of the planning process, as demonstrated by the following example.

A company has set an objective of marketing a new product that will involve high research-and-development costs during the next two years, and high marketing costs during the subsequent year to introduce the product. Company management has set a financial goal of an average annual return on investment of 15 percent over the next five years. The new-product investment is then evaluated, and the impact of the investment on company performance shows that the business objective and the financial goal are inconsistent. Management must now analyze the expected profitability (net present value) of the new-product investment, accept or reject the decision to develop the new product now, and, if necessary, revise the return-on-investment goal to a level that is feasible.

Generally, a company's financial objectives and goals must be feasible given (1) the available product/market opportunities and problems and (2) any capital constraints or other resource constraints.

The end result of this step in the financial-planning process is a memorandum identifying specific financial and nonfinancial objectives and goals.

Strategy Development

Armed with the financial and nonfinancial objectives and goals of the previous phase, management in this phase seeks to determine how financial, technical, human, and organizational resources will be allocated among competing business strategies. The major product from this phase is the strategy memorandum.

The financial projections contained in this memorandum are developed in three steps:

1. Evaluation of alternative product/service strategies—the capital investment components of the strategy are screened against minimum-return-on-investment criteria.
2. Product/service mix selection—individual strategies are analyzed for their impact on overall company portfolio balance and projected operating results.
3. Funding/financing strategy development—company plans are evaluated and approved for internal or external funding, and the debt, equity, and dividend decisions required to support these plans are made.

Before alternative strategies can be evaluated, the company's cost of capital must be determined. A company obtains its funds from two basic sources: debt and equity. Both debt holders and stockholders require a level of return commensurate with the degree of risk that has been undertaken. Debt holders receive a stream of fixed interest payments as a return. Stockholders receive the company's residual cash that remains after all other payments are made (dividends). The weighted average cost of capital of a company is the return required by both these parties, weighted by the relative market value of the debt and the equity the company holds. Therefore, the weighted average cost of capital is the same as the market-determined opportunity cost of funds provided to the company.

It is important to note that when determining the average cost of capital of a company for investment analysis purposes, the proper measure to use is the average *marginal* cost of capital. The marginal cost of capital is the cost of an additional increment of capital.

Developing Other Product/Service Strategies

In this step, particular investments or divestitures, or groups of them, are chosen from a list of potential product/market opportunities that are believed to meet the company's objectives and goals. Product/market investments could include purchase of new plant and equipment, acquisition of an existing company, introduction of a new product line, expansion of an existing facility, replacement of existing plant and equipment, and/or lease-or-purchase decisions.

Once an investment or divestiture has been selected for further evaluation, the associated financial assumptions must be stated. A complete financial description of the investment or divestiture requires projection of the initial cash outlay, the expected cash inflows, and the expected cash outflows.

The initial cash outlay is the initial cost of the investment. For example, if the investment is to build a chemicals plant, the cash outlays would be the funds necessary to buy or build the plant, not the funds necessary to maintain the plant operations. These outlays could all be in the initial time period or be staggered throughout the life of the project.

The expected cash inflow or outflow represents the estimated after-tax net cash flow from the operation of the new investment. The data necessary to derive net cash flow are projected annual cash sales at various unit prices, projected annual operating-cash costs, corporate marginal tax rate, and depreciation from the new investment. Tax rate and depreciation are necessary to obtain the net cash benefit from the depreciation tax deduction.

The financial assumptions made about the investment or divestiture are then analyzed to determine if the investment is profitable; which investment from a list of mutually exclusive investments is most profitable; if divesting is more profitable than retaining; and if the investment is more profitable than other investments when a capital constraint is present.

There are several quantitative measures that can be used to evaluate an investment or divestiture decision. Usually, more than one of the following measurements is included in the analysis:

- payback period—the number of years required to recover the initial investment.
- net present value—the present value of the cash flows discounted at the cost of capital, minus the initial outlay.
- internal rate of return—the interest rate that equates net cash flows to the initial investment outlay.
- profitability index—the present value of expected returns discounted at the cost of capital divided by the initial investment outlay. It is a benefit/cost ratio.

Inflation is a major factor in evaluating alternatives, and it must be accounted for in either the cost of capital or the estimated cash inflows and outflows over the life of a project.

Selecting a Product/Service Mix

The objectives of this segment of strategy development are to select from a mix of recommended investments (divestitures) those that best contribute to achieving overall company objectives; define the overall operating and capital resources required to achieve company objectives; and revise, as required, any unattainable company objectives.

The process begins with the ranking of investment alternatives according to one of the previously listed profitability measures. The combined financial results of the company are then estimated for various investment mixes.

To determine the effect of each proposed investment on the time-phased key financial control factors (such as net cash flows and ROI) over the strategic horizon, each investment must be individually analyzed (either included in or left out of the operating plan) to determine its effect on overall profit contribution. In other words, this is an iterative process in which a variety of investment combinations are applied to the operating plan to produce a number of scenarios for management to select from.

Although profitability should be management's primary criterion for selection of alternative investments, other factors must also be considered:

- *Portfolio balance.* Management should consider product/service-line investment plans in a portfolio perspective. Management must analyze the investment plans of each product/service line to determine the level of industry-specific risk the corporation will incur from undertaking the proposed investments.

- For example, two investment plans from separate product/service lines might both be very profitable. However, if both investments will direct each product or service line heavily into a specific market, this might contribute more industry-specific risk to the corporation than is desired. Therefore, diversification is an important factor to be considered.

- *Accounting earnings.* Although theoretically not a valid criterion by which to evaluate investments, accounting earnings are an important factor to the investment community, and corporate management should therefore at least examine the impact that product/service-line investment plans will have on earnings.

- *Merger and acquisition plans.* Although investment plans submitted by product/service-line management are profitable, corporate management also has the option to consider acquisitions of outside firms in order to achieve the corporate objectives and goals. This could well be a more profitable strategy than many of the investments approved by product/service-line management. (Acquisitions can be analyzed using the same capital budgeting techniques used for internal investments.)

- *Corporate guidelines.* It is important that corporate management ensure that the investment plans of all product/service lines will direct the corporation toward the desired corporate goals and objectives while staying within corporate policy guidelines.

After management selection and approval of the alternative investments, both a combined strategic operating plan and a capital investment plan are prepared. The process begins by adjusting the previous operating and capital plan for any effects that a newly approved investment is expected to have on other current investments. For example, a newly approved investment might have an adverse impact on the projected revenue of an existing investment.

The *strategic operating plan* should include cash revenues, cash expenses, depreciation and other noncash charges, operating profit, net cash flows from operations, net assets employed, and key control factors such as ROI.

The *capital investment plan* should include time-phased capital outlays from each investment over the strategic-planning horizon; time-phased net cash inflows from each investment over the strategic-planning horizon; and total capital outlays for each time period. It is important to note that the investment plan includes data from newly approved investments as well as from prior investments still under development that affect the strategic-planning horizon.

If some of the goals of the company are unattainable once all investment opportunities have been considered (for example, if the original goals are unrealistic), the goals should be revised to reflect the projected outcome of the anticipated operations over the strategic-planning horizon. This will ensure that operating management is not held accountable for results that do not meet unrealistic goals.

Determining the Funding/Financing Strategy

The objectives of this segment of strategy development are to determine consolidated corporate financing requirements; develop a corporate strategic financial plan that best achieves corporate objectives within business and financial constraints; and revise (as required) any unattainable corporate objectives.

After consolidation of the strategic operating plans and capital investment plans for all strategic business units (product lines or service lines) within the overall company, the financing plan can be determined, beginning with the analysis of funding sources.

Internal sources. One source of funds is from operations. These funds could be shifted from one product/service line to another to finance the approved investments of the latter, or a product/service line could be generating enough cash flow independently to support investments approved for that same product/service line.

External sources. Assuming that internal funds are not sufficient to support the proposed investment plans, the corporation must resort to outside financing. This financing may take one or more of three basic forms: common stock, preferred stock, and long-term debt. The choice of external financing methods can be critical to the corporation because of its effect on the firm's cost of capital and capital structure.

Often the internal and/or external sources of funding are limited by dividend restrictions. If the corporation has a predetermined dividend policy, the amount of dividends required would be a major constraint on the availability of internal funds. If the corporate dividend plan is not predetermined, then the financing plan must be analyzed concurrently with the dividend plan. The analysis involves tradeoffs between the desirability of paying dividends to stockholders and the advantages of retaining the funds for investment purposes.

The following is a summary of the basic factors to consider when developing a corporate dividend policy.

▪ *Legal considerations.* Foremost among these are some state laws: (1) The net-profits rule provides that dividends may be paid only from past and present earnings; (2) the capital-impairment rule protects creditors by forbidding the payment of dividends from capital; and (3), the insolvency rule provides that corporations may not pay dividends while insolvent. Long-term debt contracts also frequently restrict a firm's ability to pay cash dividends. Furthermore, the tax position of stockholders greatly influences the desire for dividends. For example, a corporation that is closely held by a few individuals in high income-tax brackets might not desire dividends, since capital gains are taxed at a lower rate. Finally, tax regulations applicable to corporations provide for a special surtax on improperly accumulated income.

- *Past dividend payout policy.* Many corporations maintain a "stable" dividend policy by keeping their dividends at a relatively steady dollar amount. There are several reasons for a stable dividend policy. First, investors might be expected to value more highly dividends they are more sure of receiving, since fluctuating dividends are riskier than stable dividends. Second, many stockholders live on income received from dividends. Finally, one of the criteria for placing a stock on the legal list is that dividend payments be maintained. Legal lists are lists of securities in which mutual savings banks, pension funds, insurance companies, and other fiduciary institutions are permitted to invest.

- *Earnings.* If earnings are relatively stable, a firm is better able to predict future earnings. Therefore, a firm with stable earnings might be able to pay out a higher percentage of its earnings than a firm whose earnings are relatively unstable.

- *Growth requirements.* As was mentioned previously, unless the dividend plan is predetermined (that is, unless there is a stable dividend policy), the dividend plan and financing plan should be developed concurrently. For example, if the corporation has many good investment opportunities that require financing, the dividend paid might be reduced to provide as much internal financing as possible. Also, smaller companies might be forced to retain earnings because they do not have easy access to the capital markets to support their investment plans.

- *Cash-flow position.* By far the most important consideration is the availability of cash to pay dividends. Technically, dividends should not be paid out of cash earnings until a deduction is made for the current cost above traditional depreciation deductions for replacing plant and equipment. The result is often called discretionary cash flow—the amount of cash available for dividends and growth.

- *Affordable dividends.* This is the maximum amount of dividends that can be paid, given various constraints such as sales growth rate, debt-equity ratio, and capital expenditure requirements.

Another important factor in the analysis of funding sources is the amount of growth in assets (or sales) that the corporation can sustain without altering its current capital structure. Called affordable growth, this determines the maximum amount of sales or asset growth that can be achieved through retained earnings plus new debt required to maintain the current debt-equity structure.

Developing the Strategic Plan

As a final step, all approved operating and capital investment plans for the different product/service lines are consolidated with corporate data to produce the corporate strategic plan and strategy memorandum. The strategy memorandum lists the selected products/services to be funded over the strategic planning horizon, the consolidated corporate profit and loss statement, the balance sheet, the cash-flow plan, and the capital investment plan. The corporate financing plan and dividend plan are also finalized as part of the strategic plan.

Linkage to Annual Planning

All this strategic planning is useless unless it is integrated with the annual plan. If the financial decisions that come out of the strategic planning do not result in positive rewards for operating managers from the control and reward systems of the organization, then the strategic-planning process is a waste of resources. The most frequent failure of earlier strategic-planning approaches was to ignore the linkage to day-to-day operations. From a financial perspective, this means that annual budgets and financial plans must be directly linked to the strategic finan-cial-planning process. Figure 2-5 is an example of the integration necessary to make strategic financial management a success.

Annual Planning

Annual planning is the process by which management, within the context of its long-range strategic plan, plans in financial terms for next year's operations. Annual planning is also known as budgeting, operating planning, or, in institutions operated for a profit, profit planning.

The annual-planning process starts with the first year's operating targets and financial projections of the five-year strategic plan, along with the overall business direction as set by senior management. The business objectives, operating targets, and financial projections are refined and linked to the day-to-day operations and monitoring process. The annual plan is documented in the following four components, each of which is concerned with the coming plan year:

- *The operating-profit plan.* This is based on the volumetric data developed during business-direction and strategy development. It includes revenues and operating expenses and is used as a basis for planning operating profit.
- *The capital budget.* This is based on the capital investment plan developed during the strategic-planning process. It excludes all expenditures that are to be expensed during the year and, therefore, affects the year's profit and loss. It includes all types of capital investment, from major construction projects to research-and-development projects or major systems and development projects.
- *The cash forecast.* This is based on both the operating plan and the capital budget and represents the plan of managing cash flow. It includes a forecast of both cash revenues and cash disbursements, taking into account various timing considerations.
- *The consolidated corporate plan.* This is based on all the other plans and accounts for various consolidation considerations, such as intercompany transactions, corporate overhead allocations, nonoperating-income (investment) plans, and so on. Also, to make the financial plan complete, a balance-sheet plan and a funds-flow plan should be developed at this time.

In order for the annual plan to be an effective management tool, it must present financial and operating budget data by month for use in performance reporting. The analysis of variances between the budget and actual results, which

Figure 2-5. Framework for strategic financial planning.

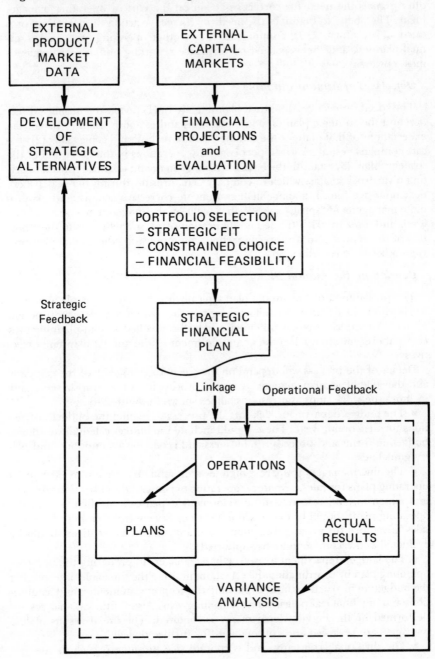

highlights problems or potential problems in implementing the annual plan, often signals the need for corrective action on the part of operating management. The ability to highlight the need for corrective action in marketing, production, inventory, R&D, administrative, and other operating areas makes annual planning and the associated performance reporting one of management's most powerful tools.

Objectives of Annual Planning

The specific objectives of annual planning are to (1) review the business direction and the strategic plan on an annual basis and establish whether or not the expectations of that plan for the coming year are realistic and achievable; (2) allocate company resources to support company operations in the execution of the strategic plan; (3) establish the basis for management and financial control by setting a yardstick against which to compare actual results during the year (where deviations are found, management can initiate corrective action); and (4) promote management "spirit," specifically a habit of planning and goal setting at all levels and a teamwork attitude and motivation of personnel to attain their portion of the annual plan. In this connection, communicating the annual plan provides a basis for coordination.

Developing the Annual Plan

The preparation of the annual plan typically involves many people at several levels within the organization, all working together over a relatively short period of time. An orderly, well-documented, and well-controlled annual-planning process is therefore essential to the accomplishment of the annual planning objectives.

Details of the process will depend on the size and complexity of the company and the style of its management. A typical process for a medium-size company includes the work steps and responsibilities shown in Figure 2-6.

■ The budget department kicks off the process by issuing the budget instructions for the coming year. These should include the budget calendar/deadlines, budgeting forms and procedures, business and economic assumptions, and policy guidelines.

■ The line managers prepare a high-level or summary version of next year's operating plans for sales, inventory, operating expenses, administration and general expenses, and research-and-development expenses. The first pass at the operating plans should be expressed in terms of key control factors such as unit sales, inventory turnover, production rates, and so on. Alternatives should be evaluated and recommendations supported.

■ The budget department assists the line managers in preparing the first-pass operating plan by coordinating the effort, monitoring the timetable, interpreting the budgeting instructions, and explaining the economic guidelines and assumptions and any financial policies for the coming year. Also, historical analyses are performed by the budget department, as required. The initial results of line managers are reviewed and consolidated for further review.

■ The divisional, company, and corporate vice presidents, such as the vice

Figure 2-6. The annual planning process.

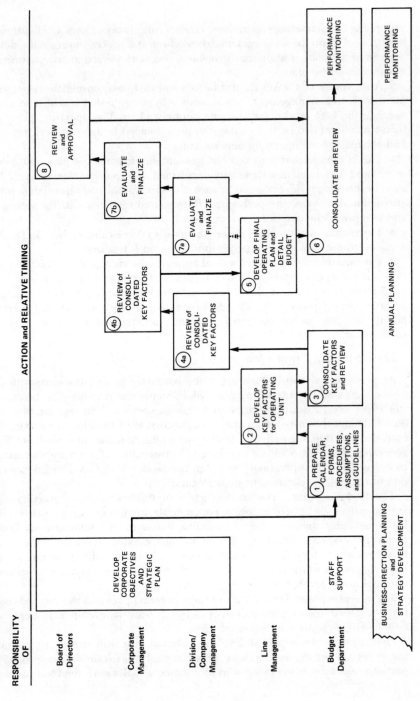

presidents for marketing, operations, engineering, finance, personnel, administration, and so on, provide guidance throughout the process, oversee the development of the plan, test for reasonableness, and work toward interdepartmental integration of the plans.

■ After review of the key control factors and first-pass consolidated operating plans with top management, adjustments and/or requested modifications are made to the high-level departmental operating plans. The operating plans are then further refined by line managers into a detailed budget for both revenue and expense by the operating department.

■ The budget department consolidates and summarizes the plans. Accuracy checks and reasonableness checks are performed. If a computer system is used to assist in the budget-development process, the appropriate coding and data preparation and correction are performed. Reviews and revisions with line managers and vice presidents are done as required.

■ Top management reviews the annual plan, evaluates alternatives, and makes revisions to the plan as appropriate until the plan is finalized.

■ The board of directors reviews and approves the annual plan. This will form the basis for its evaluation of management's performance during the year.

When the process is complete, the annual plan is made available to the management reporting process. Actual results are then compared with the current-month and year-to-date budgets for variance analysis and corrective management action.

The Operating-Profit Plan

As previously shown in Figure 2-2, the operating-profit plan starts with the marketing plan. The marketing plan will influence the revenue plan because it will affect sales. Also, it will affect marketing expenses. The revenue plan will then influence the cost-of-sales plan, because costs are a function of the sales volume. Finally, the research-and-development plan and the administrative-and-general-expenses plan will be developed. At this point, all the components are completed and the operating-profit plan can be developed. A detailed description of each of the component steps follows.

The marketing plan.   The marketing plan establishes how the marketing goals and objectives will be accomplished. For example, to meet certain growth or market-penetrating objectives, certain spending levels for the following marketing factors must be set: advertising, promotion, sales, product development, and customer service. These discretionary spending items have different impacts on sales volume. A sensitivity analysis for each one would be required to set optimum spending levels.

The revenue plan.   On the basis of the marketing plan and the implied sensitivity of sales to the various marketing factors, a realistic revenue plan can be established. This is done in two steps.

First, a sales-volume plan is developed, showing the unit sales being planned under certain pricing assumptions. This is typically based on data developed as part of a sales forecasting process. In such a process, sales personnel forecast sales by product, often down to the customer level. When summarized, this plan would be presented as shown in Figure 2-7.

As can be seen from the exhibit, the sales plan (or budget) identifies the products to be sold, the price to be charged, and the dollar volume expected to result.

The second step is price determination. An analysis of sales sensitivity to price must be performed to help establish the optimum price for each item. This is an iterative process, because pricing decisions have to be coordinated with marketing factors and production constraints. After the prices are set and a final sales plan is approved, the next step in the process can be initiated.

The cost-of-sales/service plan. The cost-of-sales plan (or service plan for a service company) is developed to support the sales plan already developed. This is done in two steps. First, the production and inventory plan is developed. In the manufacturing environment, for example, operating personnel can plan production on the basis of the planned sales level as well as planned inventory levels. If the current levels of inventory are excessively low, production rates will tend to

Figure 2-7. Sales plan.*

Description	Unit of Measure	Number of Units	Unit Price	Unit Gross Sales
Product Line A				
Item 1	DZ	630	100	63,000
Item 2	DZ	710	100	71,000
Item 3	DZ	420	100	42,000
Item 4	DZ	930	100	93,000
Item 5	DZ	1,000	100	100,000
Item 6	DZ	540	100	54,000
Item 7	DZ	220	100	22,000
Total		4,450		445,000
Product Line B				
Item 91	EA	300	1,000	300,000
Item 92	EA	213	1,000	213,000
Item 93	EA	55	1,000	55,000
Total		568		568,000
Service Parts				82,000
Total				1,095,000
Sales Adjustments:				
Cash Discounts				(10,000)
Outbound Freight				(20,000)
Net Sales				1,065,000

* Monthly data omitted for simplicity.

exceed sales levels. If planned inventory at the end of the budget year is to be reduced significantly in comparison to current levels, then production levels will generally be lower than sales.

A very important aspect of production planning is the material requirements, established by exploding the bill of materials for an item by the volume for that item. A material requirements planning (MRP) system is typically employed for this purpose.

The second step in the development of the cost-of-sales/service plan is to convert the production and inventory *plan* into a production *budget*. This will typically have three components: labor, materials, and overhead. An example of such a budget is shown as Figure 2-8. This production budget is based on volumes established in the production plan. However, since not all items produced will be sold, the changing levels of inventory have to be planned for. Also, certain financial costs not directly related to production need to be planned for. Both of these items are included in the cost-of-sales budget. An example is shown as Figure 2-9.

Figure 2-8. Annual production budget.

	Unit of Measure	Number of Units	Standard Cost	Budget
A. Direct Labor				
Item 1	DZ	1,000	20	20,000
Item 2	DZ	1,000	30	30,000
Item 3	DZ	2,000	30	60,000
Total				110,000
B. Direct Materials				
Item 1	EA	1,000	210	210,000
Item 2	EA	1,000	120	120,000
Item 3	EA	2,000	15	30,000
Total				360,000
C. Manufacturing Overhead				
Production VP's Office				9,000
Manufacturing Superintendent's Department				49,000
Industrial Relations				5,000
Production Control				8,000
Purchasing				3,000
Receiving and Stores				6,000
Plant Engineering and Maintenance				32,000
Inspection				7,000
Methods Engineering and Tools				19,000
Total Manufacturing				138,000
Grand Total—Production				608,000

Figure 2-9.   Cost-of-sales plan for a manufacturing company.

Description		Budget
Standard Manufacturing Overhead		
Production Departments Overhead		$138,000
Costs Not Charged to Departments		
Depreciation	$15,000	
Property taxes	5,000	
Insurance	5,000	
Payroll taxes, pension, vacations, etc.	20,000	45,000
Total		183,000
Total Labor at Standard Cost		110,000
Total Materials at Standard Cost		360,000
Total Standard Costs Incurred		653,000
Plus Inventory Decrease		47,000
Standard Cost of Sales		$700,000

As can be seen from the figure, certain costs not charged to departments have to be planned for at the company level. These include depreciation, property taxes, insurance, payroll taxes, and benefits (pensions, vacations, and so on). Also, an adjustment is made to the production costs for the planned decrease in inventory.

The marketing plan (follow-up). The marketing plan must be finalized at this stage of the operating-profit-plan development. At the outset it was developed as a basis for developing the revenue plan. At this point it needs to be finalized so that all marketing expenses can be carefully planned. This is particularly important since the final pricing decisions, which followed the sensitivity analysis and review of production constraints, may have necessitated a change in volume and product mix.

The research-and-development plan. The research-and-development plan has two components: the capital portion and the expensed portion. Only the expensed portion is planned at this point, since it directly affects the profit plan. Such a plan would typically consist of several components: (1) salaries—professional and nonprofessional employees, college recruits, factory labor, and so on; (2) contracted research—consultants, private laboratories, universities, clinical tests, and so on; (3) operating expenses—experiment materials, laboratory chemicals, scientific literature, scientific exhibits, and so on; (4) building and equipment costs—depreciation, outside equipment rental, mechanical services, fuel, and the like; and (5) overhead transfers—for example, nonresearch transfers to R&D from overhead expenses (benefits, occupancy, and so on) and nonresearch services to other departments (materials storage, quality control, computer usage, and so on).

The administrative-and-general-expenses plan. The administrative-and-general-expenses plan represents the plans of the various staff departments and of the offices of senior management. For example, the controller's department would develop a budget as follows:

BUDGET OF THE CONTROLLER'S DEPARTMENT

Description	Amount
Controller's office	$16,000
General accounting	15,000
Cost accounting	34,000
Budgets and procedures	20,000
Total	$85,000

This could then be summarized in a summary budget called the administrative-and-general-expenses budget, as follows:

A&G BUDGET

Description	Amount
President's office	$ 62,000
Controller's department	85,000
Secretary-treasurer's department	48,000
Total	$195,000

When all the areas have developed their budgets, the final step in the process can be initiated.

The final operating-profit plan. The operating-profit plan shows how profit can be generated directly as a result of operations. An example is shown in Figure 2-10. As can be seen from the figure, the gross margin has to be reduced by the marketing, R&D, and A&G budgets to arrive at the planned operating profit. It should be noted that items such as interest and taxes also have to be planned and deducted from operating profit to arrive at the net profit plan.

The Capital Budget

Capital expenditures generally provide continuing long-term benefits or profit potential primarily in periods after the planning year. Such expenditures include the following categories: land, plant, and equipment (acquisition or construction); research and development; major systems development; and significant manpower development programs.

Control over these expenditures is very important because they involve sizable long-term commitments of company funds and because the use of these funds is generally under management's discretion. The primary control exercised over these capital expenditure projects is generally in the management approval process carried out during the capital budgeting segment of annual planning.

The annual capital budget is developed within the context of the long-range capital investment plan. The major distinction between the two processes is as follows: The long-range planning process is designed to evaluate the feasibility of each capital project from the investment analysis point of view and, also, to com-

Figure 2-10. Operating-profit plan for a manufacturing company.

Net Sales	$1,065,000
Cost of Sales	700,000
Gross Margin	365,000
Expenses:	
Development Engineering (R&D)	11,000
Selling and Shipping (Marketing)	93,000
General and Administrative (A&G)	196,000
	300,000
Operating Profit	65,000
Other (Income) Expense:	
Interest Income	2,000
Interest Expense	3,000
	1,000
Net Profit Before Taxes	64,000
Provision for Income Taxes	34,000
Net Profit	$ 30,000

pare the rate of return between projects and time-phase the various projects over the long term. The annual capital plan assumes that a long-range plan exists, and is used for planning the execution of the long-range plan over the short term (the year).

The specific objectives of the annual capital plan are to plan for (1) the allocation of funds for the next year's portion of the capital plan; (2) the execution of each project in the plan at a level of activity consistent with the project's annual budget; and (3) the monitoring and control of the project activity during the year.

During capital budgeting, management must evaluate the cost to completion and the effect of each proposed project on long-range company activities. Specific programs or projects are identified and individually justified. A typical long-term capital budget may look as follows:

Project	Internal Rate of Return	Payback	Net Present Value	Date of Completion	Estimated Total Cost
Project 1	21%	5 Years	$2,500,000	1/1/XX	$4,700,000
Project 2	19%	3 Years	2,000,000	8/1/XX	3,200,000
Total					$7,900,000

The attractiveness of the investment, the completion date, and the total cost have to be part of the long-term view of the capital plan.

The next part of capital budgeting involves expanding the overall capital investment plan to include more detailed cost data. Here is an example of the resulting capital budget (figures in thousands of dollars):

Project	Inception to Date	Budget for Current Year	Estimate for Future Years	Estimate of Total Costs at Completion	Original Cost	Project Variance
Project 1	$1,800	$600	$2,300	$4,700	$4,200	$500
Project 2	2,700	100	400	3,200	3,000	200
Total	$4,500	$700	$2,700	$7,900	$7,200	$700

Annual budget amounts are identified in the second column entitled "Budget for Current Year."

Finally, the capital budget for the current year is broken down by month to match the schedule of the work and serve as a basis for monitoring monthly progress.

Since the annual capital budgeting process is a major control tool for the long-range capital investment plan, it should also include a review of the following components of the long-range plan for each project: proposal initiation/assumptions; technical review/changes; economic evaluation/assumptions; risk evaluation/changes; and intangible considerations.

The Cash Forecast

A major element of annual planning is the cash forecast. This forecast is generally the responsibility of the chief financial officer. It will be a natural by-product of the annual profit plan and the capital budget. The objective of annual cash forecasting is to identify periods of cash shortages and/or periods when excess cash is accumulated. A seasonal business may have both of these conditions. For example, cash shortages may develop as inventory is accumulated prior to the peak period, and excess cash may result as collections are made from peak-season sales. On the other hand, a growing business may have a continual cash shortage because cash is constantly tied up in increasing inventories and receivables.

A brief look at the cash cycle within a business may help clarify the process of cash forecasting. This cycle can briefly be illustrated as follows:

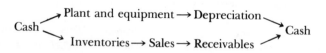

Knowing what a company's cash needs are for the coming year allows management to plan for needed funds. Short-term lines of credit can be arranged in an orderly fashion to cover temporary cash shortages or to allow time to arrange for permanent financing. If additional funds from the security markets are necessary, planning increases the chance for a company to issue securities under advantageous market conditions. Conversely, if excess funds will be available during the year, a direct contribution to profit can be earned by investments in short-term securities.

In order to analyze cash flows, the income statement may be adjusted to the cash basis to form a *cash-flow statement*. Typical side captions of such a statement would include the following:

Cash provided by:
  Net book income
  Noncash charges
    Depreciation
    Amortization
    Depletion
  Net decrease (increase) in assets
    Accounts receivable
    Inventories
    Marketable securities
    Other assets
  Net increase (decrease) in liabilities
    Accounts payable
    Other current liabilities
    Sale of fixed assets
    Bank loans and other borrowings
    Sale of common stock

Cash expended for:
  Plant, property, and equipment
  Dividends
  Debt retirement
  R&D programs
  Computer systems development
  Manpower development
  Other investments
Net cash provided (expanded)
Beginning cash balance
Ending cash balance

The columns across the top of such an analysis would, of course, identify cash flow by month.

There are usually several key factors that have a primary influence on a company's cash position. These factors will vary between companies and, therefore, must be identified as an initial part of annual planning. Most of the analysis work in cash forecasting will, therefore, be concentrated on these key factors.

The Consolidated Corporate Plan

As discussed previously, each functional area of the business is responsible for a section of the annual plan. At some point, these plans must be pulled together and finalized into an overall annual plan. Staff or budget personnel will be responsible for compiling the annual plan and preparing an analysis indicating conflicts, alternatives, and so on. Top management is responsible for resolving these conflicts and making sure that the annual plan is a coordinated whole, consistent with long-range objectives.

The first step in finalizing the annual plan is to verify that the operating plans are reasonable, acceptable, and consistent. If sales are too low, new promotion programs may be required. If production costs or inventories are too high, adjustments will be required. If available cash is short, a revised capital budget may be required.

Also, there must be a balance between sales, production, and inventories. Sales should not be planned to exceed production capacity. Inventory levels should be adequate to support the market plan and projected delivery dates; however, they should not be planned at such a high level that excessive financial carrying costs are incurred. Excess plant capacity should be absorbed by additional production activities.

The second step in finalizing the annual plan is to verify that the annual plan is consistent with long-range objectives. A balance should be reached between spending for current needs and spending for future requirements. For example, some spending on new-product development may be necessary to perpetuate the business. Also, the specific features of the annual plan must be examined to make sure that they are not in conflict with stated long-range objectives. For example, long-range objectives may call for a compound growth rate of 10 percent per year, to be achieved by continuing growth in plant capacity. On the other hand, the annual plan may call for a high dividend payout from current earnings. This situation could present a direct conflict if funds for plant investment were to come at least partly from current operations. On the other hand, investment funds raised from outside sources may increase interest charges, increase risk, or dilute earnings to shareholders. Top management obviously must resolve this type of policy conflict.

Finally, the annual plan must represent a desirable allocation of company resources between functions and/or subsidiary divisions. Functional plans may reflect the fact that lower-level managers feel their particular area is the most important area of the company's operations. Top management must verify that funds and management attention are being directed in the most desirable manner.

Several revisions of the initial annual plan may be required before all these conflicts are resolved. However, as stated earlier, much of the benefit of annual planning is in the planning process itself. The process of refining and finalizing the annual plan will communicate problems and company objectives across functional and departmental lines. It will also help crystallize company strengths and weaknesses as well as alternative courses of action open to top management. Finally, without annual planning, the conflicts pointed out during the planning process might otherwise have gone unnoticed until serious damage had been done.

Typically, in larger organizations, a consolidation step is required to consolidate the plans of the various divisions at the corporate level. Such consolidation at the corporate level would concentrate on financial and capital expenditure considerations.

Approval and Communication of the Annual Plan

The finalized annual plan, consisting of the operating-profit plan and the capital budget for each major area of the business, along with the consolidated plan and consolidated cash forecast, should be presented to the board of directors for formal approval. It should then be distributed throughout the top-management ranks. Distribution as appropriate by major business area should be made to the lower levels of the organization. The finalized plan then serves as the overall company guide for the coming year.

Performance Reporting

In order for the financial-planning process to be effective in an organization, it is necessary to report actual results of operations against the annual plan. The reporting of performance against the plan must be timely and accurate and represent controllable items. Effective management control of operations is then achieved by reporting actual results, identifying the variations from plan and analyzing their causes, and responding to the problems identified. Performance reporting is, therefore, an integral part of planning and budgeting.

Responsibility Reporting

Performance reporting should be tailored to the organization and encompass the activities of each manageable business unit defined to exist within the company. The performance of each business unit is reported to the individual responsible for accomplishing the annual plan. The reporting is characterized by organizational as well as functional groupings and typically identifies responsibility, accountability, and profitability. The focus on key performance indicators—monetary and statistical amounts—is also an important attribute.

Once the budget is organized by organizational entity, actual costs and revenues must be assigned to the appropriate cost or profit center. "Roll-up" reporting communicates performance results to all levels of management. Problem areas are isolated by highlighting significant variances from plan. Therefore, the keys to effective management control are performance reporting by responsibility area and good variance analysis.

An example of responsibility reporting in a manufacturing company is shown in Figure 2-11.

The key reporting design concepts that should be used in constructing the responsibility reports include:

- Organize by logical business unit/line of service.
- Report actual revenues and expenses against budgeted revenues and expenses.
- Direct the report to the individual responsible for performance.
- Clearly identify controllable and noncontrollable costs.
- Include performance indicators, including key factors and productivity measures, on certain responsibility reports.
- Ensure that the reports contain an outlook (actual to date plus forecast for remaining months of the fiscal year).
- Design exception reports and/or indicators to focus management's attention on exception areas.
- Ensure that summaries of lower-level responsibility reports will be available for the next management level.

Figure 2-11. Roll-up structure for responsibility reporting.

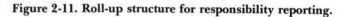

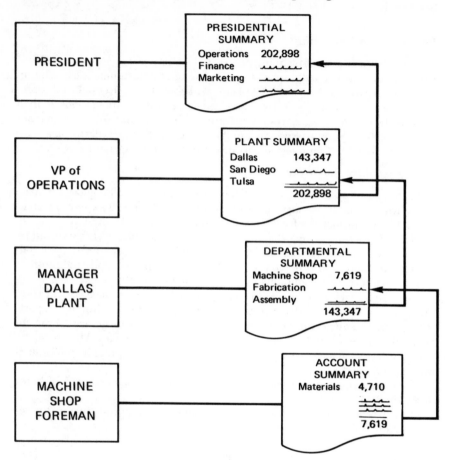

- Present statistical data along with financial data.
- Make sure that both fixed and variable budgets are available for comparison with actual cost.

Variable Budgeting

Variable budgeting (also known as flexible budgeting) is an important tool to help management separate spending from volume variances. Since costs are generally fixed, variable, or semivariable, a fixed budget has limited value when the expected volume changes. A variable budget, in contrast, is designed to change with changes in volume.

Variable budgeting, therefore, seeks to determine the factors or activity measures that correlate an increase or decrease in cost with a change in volume. A good budget factor must be a direct measure of the cost-incurring activity. It must be affected only by volume and be sensitive to changes in the activity level. Examples of budget factors or activity measures for use in developing variable budgets are units of output, man-hours, machine hours, number of shifts, and cost-center days or hours.

Naturally, more than one factor could be used in developing a variable budget. The type of expense or revenue will usually suggest the type of factor or activity measure to use. For example:

Type of Expense	*Variable Budget Factor*
Raw material consumed	Actual units of production by product
Manufacturing labor	Days operated, or units of production

The use of flexible budgeting allows a much more meaningful interpretation of variances in performance against plan. Volume variances, which result solely from operating at a different current volume from that anticipated during annual planning, can be easily segregated from spending variances. The major reason for separating these variances is for responsibility reporting. Through variable budgeting, the operations department can be measured in its ability to meet standard unit cost projections (irrespective of volume, which is a marketing/sales responsibility). The marketing/sales department can be measured in its ability to generate the volume of sales anticipated in the annual plan.

Product-Line Reporting

Performance reporting should also include profitability reporting for product lines. A profitability reporting roll-up structure is shown in Figure 2-12.

The key reporting design concepts for profitability reporting include the identification of sales, expenses, and contributory profit by product and product line/line of service; a comparison of actual expense with what cost should be at actual level of activity; a focus on comparative reporting for multiple locations or departments performing the same or similar functions; and the use of both dollars and statistics to report the performance of the product line.

Key-Factor Reporting

Key factors are measures of the vital signs of a business. They may be either financial or statistical numbers or ratios that can tell management about the health of the business. Some key factors—for example, sales revenues, orders received, and shipments—measure the movement of a business toward its goals. Other key factors measure the stability of the business. Examples include inventory turnover, days of sales in accounts receivable, and liquidity.

Forecast values of key factors provide the best early warning for management control.

Key factors are generally simple, straightforward measures of performance. Although many examples of key factors can be identified, there are usually only a few important key factors in any business.

Figure 2-12. Roll-up structure for product-line reporting.

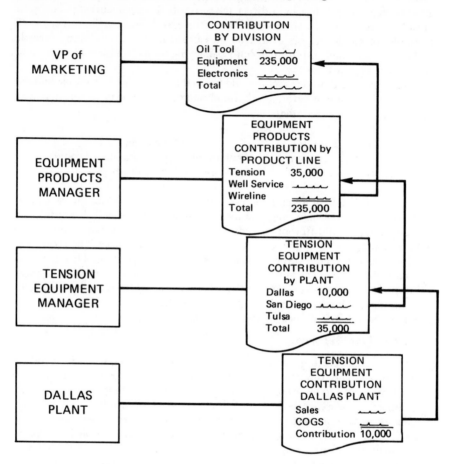

Key-factor reports should be brief, containing only the few key factors, and yet give as complete a picture as possible. The timeliness of information is also very important for successful key-factor reporting. Key factors should be reported to the responsible individual who can exercise the most direct control. Those reported to lower-level responsibility areas should be summarized and reported to higher-level responsibility areas.

The frequency of key-factor performance reports is determined by the availability of the data required to calculate the key factors. Daily and weekly flash reports may be appropriate for certain key factors that are readily available. Weekly and monthly reports would include key factors whose components cannot economically be made available more frequently. Monthly key-factor flash reports should be a preview of the final monthly profitability reports.

Figure 2-13. Weekly key-factor report for a chemicals company.

Division		Current Week		Month to Date		Next Week		Current-Month Outlook		
		Actual	Target	Actual	Target	Current Outlook	Target	Current	Prior	Original
Electrochemical										
Gross sales	($)	35	30	65	60	30	45	150	130	148
Order backlog	($)	10	20	22	38	10	15	40	40	40
Tons produced	(tons)	45	50	70	100	50	50	200	180	220
Specialty Chemical										
Gross sales	($)	100	90	220	200	70	100	400	410	370
Production % of schedule		90	96	90	95	100	100	96	97	99
Chlorine consumption	(tons)	30	20	70	40	20	29	140	150	130
Finished-goods inventory	($)	1,375	1,490	1,375	1,490	1,400	1,490	1,450	1,490	1,490
Montez										
Gross sales	($)	1,300	1,500	2,600	3,000	1,000	1,200	5,000	6,000	5,500
Gross sales	(lbs.)	1,930	2,000	3,800	3,900	2,200	2,100	8,000	9,500	9,000
Salable production	(lbs.)	2,200	2,100	4,300	4,000	1,800	2,000	9,000	9,500	10,000
Finished-goods inventory	($)	5,530	6,000	5,530	6,000	5,000	5,300	5,000	6,300	6,500

Figure 2-14.   Strategic financial-analysis report for a manufacturing company.

| | | | Cash Outflows | | Net Cash Inflows | |
| | | | Initial Expenditure* | | Realized Cash-Flow Return Actual-to-Date* | |
Investment	Year Initiated	Expected Duration	Actual	Variance from Plan	Actual	Variance from Plan
Cleburne Plant	1980	8	$500,000	$100,000	$330,000	$30,000
Greenville Smelting	1980	8	250,000	50,000	120,000	(8,000)
Dallas Plant Upgrade	1981	10	300,000	(25,000)	176,000	10,000
Fredricksberg Plant	1982	10	400,000	60,000	112,000	(14,000)
Upgrade Dallas Plant						
CAD/CAM Project	1983	5	180,000	30,000	35,000	5,000
Paint shop Addition	1983	10	90,000	(10,000)	20,000	—

* Adjusted to current dollars.
† Discount rate (hurdle rate) = 10 percent.

Actual results should be compared against operational targets. Accumulations and comparisons—for example, month-to-date data and comparisons to the previous key-factor report—should be provided to facilitate simple analysis. An outlook to month-end and year-end should also be provided to indicate whether the budget can be met. In addition, some key factors might be reported only on an exception basis.

An example of a weekly key-factor report is shown in Figure 2-13. It makes user-defined key factors available to operations management. The key indicators listed for each division were identified as the best performance indicators available by each division. Adjusted financial data are not available until month-end. Therefore, this report focuses on gross-sales statistics and other nonfinancial operating data maintained by the divisions during the month.

An important component of the report is the current-month outlook. This shows the current-month outlook based on the current projections, the prior projection, and the original projection.

Monitoring the Strategic Plan

Strategic financial-analysis reporting provides management the information to evaluate performance of past strategic decisions. The reports provide the critical feedback on the success or failure of the strategic plan.

The objectives of strategic financial-analysis reporting are to complement the planning function and to monitor the accomplishment of the strategic plan. The sophistication of how strategic decisions are monitored should correspond to the level of sophistication used to analyze and make the strategic decisions. Therefore, a specific strategic decision should be monitored against the same factors that were used for its justification. The reporting allows management to determine whether or not to continue with the strategy. Reporting and analysis of ex-

| Net Cash Inflows | | | | Net Return | | | |
| Expected Discounted Future Cash Flows† | | Net Cash Return | | Average CAP to Date | | Average Expected CAP to Completion | |
Revised	Variance from Original Plan	Actual	Variance from Plan	Actual	Plan	Revised	Original
$320,000	$20,000	$150,000	$(50,000)	16.5%	18.8%	16.0	18.8%
140,000	12,000	10,000	(46,000)	12.0%	16.0%	14.0%	16.0%
399,000	12,000	275,000	47,000	19.6%	17.0%	19.0%	17.0%
475,000	(28,000)	187,000	(102,000)	14.0%	18.5%	16.0%	18.5%
115,000	(5,000)	(30,000)	(30,000)	19.4%	20.0%	16.0%	20.0%
162,000	(18,000)	92,000	(8,000)	22.2%	20.0%	20.0%	20.0%

isting strategic plans should be performed on a regularly scheduled basis, usually quarterly, semiannually, or annually.

Strategic financial-analysis reporting allows subsequent evaluation of strategic decisions, based upon the comparison of realized cash flows to date and the re-evaluated expected cash flows, versus the originally expected cash flows used to justify the investment.

An example of a strategic financial-analysis report is shown in Figure 2-14. It examines the past performance of the investment versus its planned performance, as well as the expected future performance versus the originally planned performance.

The average cash asset percentage (CAP) earned per year for the investment is calculated by dividing the realized cash-flow return by the number of years the investment has been in existence and by the initial expenditure. The average expected CAP to completion is the expected discounted future cash flows divided by the number of years remaining in the investment and by the initial expenditure.

Data Relationships

A major prerequisite to effectively integrating strategic and annual planning is the ability to define and enforce a *single* analytical framework (or model) that decomposes strategic objectives into manageable and interrelated components that can be (1) tested *before* adoption for reasonableness and consistency and (2) monitored *during* execution from year to year, as well as month to month.

Figure 2-15 provides such a framework which relates the impact of investment, operating, financing, and dividend decisions to overall financial performance. This schematic demonstrates the relationship between the strategic components and the operational components of a strategic plan.

Figure 2-15. Relationships between factors affecting financial performance.

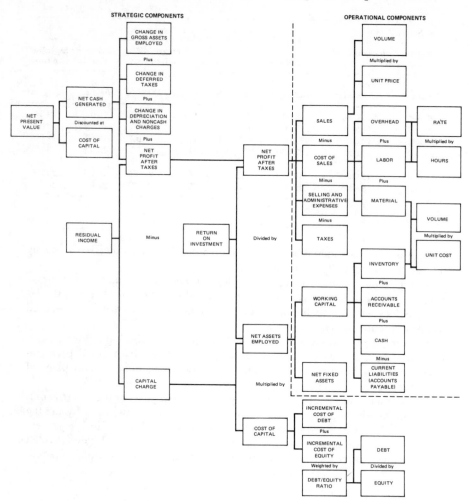

The *strategic components* of the plan relate to the investment decision. An investment should be analyzed on the basis of its discounted cash flows and the net present value of those cash flows. The responsibility of managing and controlling the strategic components is generally that of senior management.

The *operational components* of the plan relate to the implementation of the plan. The responsibility for the management and control of these components is that of operations management and financial management.

The time frame to be used in this schematic varies. The components of net present value must be considered for the duration of the investment, whereas the components of earnings may be considered for the duration of the investment or for only a single period.

The various components are defined by the boxes on the schematic. The relationships of the components are defined by the terms between them. For example:

Net present value = net cash generated discounted at the hurdle rate
Hurdle rate = incremental cost of debt plus the incremental cost of equity

By incorporating the same model logic into the responsibility reporting system, management can monitor monthly, quarterly, and annual progress toward achievement of strategic objectives already tested for reasonableness. The model logic can also identify the source and interrelationships of major variances.

Conclusion

As shown in Figure 2-2, business-direction planning, strategy development, annual planning, and performance reporting are all related through a feedback mechanism that compares the accomplishment of strategic goals to the strategic plan. Similarly, the business-planning and financial-planning process is a closed loop in which all factors affecting financial performance and strategic and annual planning are related. Figure 2-16 illustrates the closed-loop nature of the factors affecting the planning process.

External analysis provides current market values for the company's present lines of business. These market values can then be compared with management's projection of the present value of the same businesses to determine if any should be divested to free funds for more profitable opportunities.

External and internal analyses identify the market-share opportunities and sales-growth capabilities that can be exploited by alternative business strategies. Each strategy can then be translated into projected financial results.

Investment analysis is then used to eliminate strategies that do not earn a return exceeding the cost of capital for that line of business.

Operations analysis is then used to determine which combination of investments, divestitures, and ongoing operations best achieves the company's overall business and financial objectives.

Financing and dividend analysis are performed concurrently to determine the amount and timing of internal and external funding required to support the strategic and annual plans.

Finally, both the proposed strategic and annual plans are reviewed to ensure consistency among the objectives of market penetration, sales growth, cash flow, return on investment, earnings-per-share growth portfolio balance, capital structure (debt/equity ratio), and dividend payment. For it is the interplay between all these factors that ultimately determines the company's overall cost of capital, which, in turn, affects the basic investment decisions of the strategic plan.

☐ *A. Mark Dalton, Byron A. Tsinikas, and Richard S. Wasch*

Figure 2-16. Closed-loop business and financial planning.

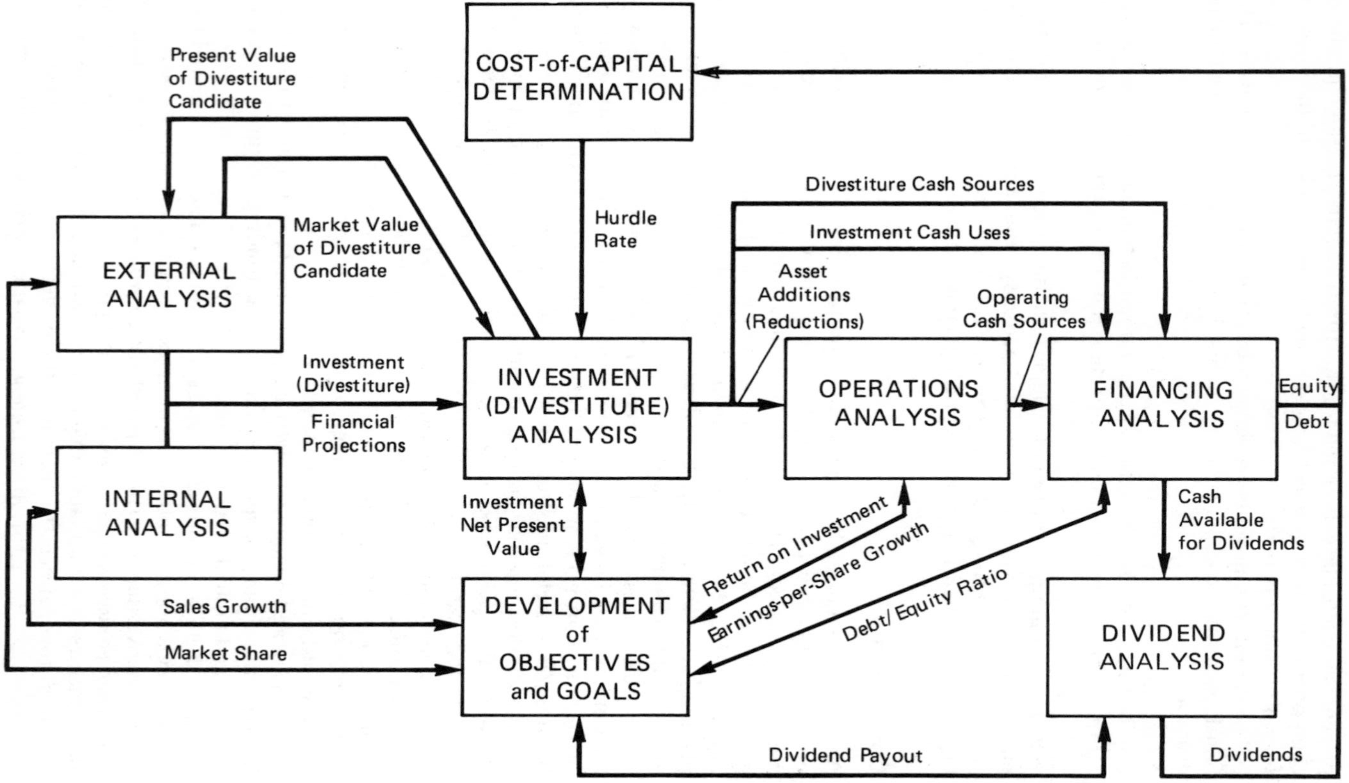

ACQUISITIONS AND DIVESTITURES

Recent multibillion-dollar contested acquisitions signal that the merger market has changed. These changes have important strategic implications for nearly all U.S. corporations.

The corporate raid has become common practice. Large size no longer assures protection. Virtually all companies are vulnerable in the takeover game. Low stock prices and high inflation rates make many companies cheaper to buy than to recreate. These factors also have caused many companies to be worth more dead than alive.

The pressure for short-term stock-price performance, as well as the desire to continue "running the show," remains a driving force for most managements. In an era of swallow or be swallowed, some aggressive corporate managements have stepped up the search for acquisition candidates. At the same time, other managements, with an eye on near-term stock prices, have cashed in on undervalued assets by making significant divestitures part of their capitalization reduction plans.

Merger participants are not without recourse to a variety of intelligent strategies. But one thing is certain: knowledge of existing merger market conditions and of the rules of the game are essential to formulating strategy. Unsolicited takeover offers have created an opportunistic merger environment. The company that was not for sale yesterday on a voluntary basis may be seeking a friendly haven today because of an unsolicited offer. In today's environment, negotiated mergers run a greater risk of having unwanted interlopers. Buy and sell decisions often have to be made within a limited amount of time. To operate successfully in these volatile circumstances, corporate managements must think through the merger issues they are likely to face, establishing effective plans and alternatives. The material presented here focuses on fundamental topics managements need to address, emphasizing major acquisitions and divestitures and not product additions or line extensions.

Organization

The key organizational factor in the consummation of a successful merger is the role of the chief executive officer, who must be intimately involved throughout the acquisition and divestiture process. The CEO is the only one who can make the major merger decision. He is the key to setting an effective diversification strategy. He is the only one who can mobilize resources quickly to analyze a proposed deal. He bears the responsibility of presenting management's recommendation to the board. Typically, he functions as his company's best salesman. His presence is significant and flattering to any potential acquiree. In short, the CEO is vital to an expeditious and successful result. Without his direct involvement, the merger process is likely to falter.

Many organizational structures can be effective in implementing acquisition strategy. The proper structure obviously depends on the individuals involved and their "fit" within the organization. Because of the complexity and importance of implementing a diversification strategy, some companies have effectively used a committee consisting of the CEO, the CFO, the vice president of corporate planning, an outside director, and an executive with operational responsibility for an acquisition. In other cases, the chief financial officer is responsible for merger activity. Alternatively, a corporate development officer may report to the CEO. In any event, the CFO should be actively involved, since he will need to evaluate the impact of any action on the corporation's financial condition. The means of payment and issuance of securities in an acquisition can be the acquiring company's most important financing decision. The CFO must gauge his firm's ability to raise capital after the deal, as well as the likely short- and long-term impact on the company's stock price.

Organizational resources should be structured toward accomplishing strategic and tactical tasks efficiently. Major tasks involve defining objectives, devising merger strategy, searching for potential acquisitions, evaluating proposed acquisitions and divestitures, and implementing the merger. The organizational structure should be flexible enough to handle any particular situation sensibly. Different transactions have different needs, ranging from the full attention given an unsolicited takeover attempt to the divisional focus of a minor line-extension acquisition.

Strategy

Although setting strategy is perhaps the most difficult part of the merger process, it is nevertheless indispensable. The merger strategy must conform to an overall corporate plan. The goal is to enhance shareholders' wealth. Key questions seem simple; the answers rarely are. What are the company's strengths and weaknesses, both quantitatively and qualitatively? What factors have been essential to the company's success? What type of investment vehicle does management seek to offer to its shareholders? What are its overall commercial and financial goals? How can acquisitions or divestitures help meet these objectives? How can the company establish a competitive edge? All these issues must be subjected to a rigorous evaluation of their feasibility. The most sophisticated merger plans on paper are worthless if they cannot be operationally or financially implemented. It is the merger strategist's function to ensure that plans are realistic.

Corporate financial objectives are crucial to a sound merger strategy. Decisions must be made about the desired rate of return on investment, growth prospects, and degree of financial risk. The level of risk, measured by debt ratings, and the company's willingness to issue common stock can either free or restrain merger activity. Above all, the strategist must separate the short-term financial impact of a merger from its long-term effect.

Solutions that emerge from planning sessions may be as diverse as particular situations demand. Managements can variously decide to be inactive, sell or merge the entire company, or—as is more normal—sell or buy businesses. Sometimes the strategy can lead to a complete transformation of the business that is accomplished by carefully timed steps of major acquisitions and divestitures.

Planning to Implement the Merger Strategy

Premerger planning can position a company for quick and decisive action. This often spells the difference between success and failure in the acquisition arena. Premerger preparation is even more important in responding to an unsolicited takeover.

This second phase begins where the strategy-planning process leaves off. The extent of such planning varies greatly among companies, depending primarily on the importance of merger activity in the overall corporate profile. Efforts are made to pinpoint and understand likely acquisition candidates in selected industries. Management consultants can assist in developing a base of knowledge in a relevant area. In addition, investment bankers can help determine whether a company is, or would be, available for acquisition; this requires an intimate knowledge of the potential acquiree.

The objectives of premerger planning are (1) to determine the most desirable acquisitions and ascertain the probability of a transaction, and (2) to establish familiarity with likely targets to facilitate a transaction should a candidate come on the market.

One of the most important decisions involved in acquisitions is how aggressive the initial approach should be. The spectrum ranges from a casual "feeler" to an outright unsolicited tender offer bypassing the board of directors. An intermediate step is a written offer subject to acceptance by the board of directors. Each circumstance is different and requires an appropriately analyzed technique. Careful consideration with experienced financial and legal advisers is often advisable. Going directly to shareholders has both advantages and drawbacks. Often, it is the only way to "create" the opportunity for acquisition. A known willingness to go direct puts more bite into initial friendly conversations. But direct approaches do carry some risk. Knowledge of the acquiree is often incomplete, raising the possibility of an unsuitable acquisition. The target company's management is likely to be alienated during the process, leaving wounds that are difficult to heal. In most cases, the first unsolicited direct approach is rebuffed and another higher bidder is found. An unsuccessful attempt can be costly unless some profit is realized from the purchase of the target company's shares. Finally, a reputation for "unfriendly" takeover activity can inhibit "friendly" conversations with potential acquirees. The decision to go directly to shareholders is complex. It is important to consider the implications of the decision for the company's overall merger strategy.

Divestiture planning is much simpler. The strategic phase of planning identifies the businesses that should be targeted for sale. The company's own strategists tend to know the business well. Reliable outside advice can be obtained on the probable realizable value and the likely impact on stock price of the sale and subsequent investment of the proceeds. However, companies often err in their approach to a divestiture, waiting until the business has bottomed rather than implementing a strategic plan. The sale price in these cases is usually not what it could have been had management acted earlier or waited until the business turned around.

Evaluating the Acquisition

Once a proposed acquisition emerges as doable, the value of the target to the purchaser needs to be determined. The discounted cash flow valuation method has broad appeal in academic circles and among sophisticated financial officers. Critical factors in the model include the purchaser's discount rate (after adjustment for risk), projected cash flows of the acquiree (after taking synergistic effects into account), and a terminal value. However, uncertainties surrounding these factors, particularly regarding cash flows of an acquisition not intimately known by the acquirer, suggest that the model is *at best* a guide to the determination of value. Other considerations weigh heavily in the valuation process, such as the possibility of acquisitions in the same or similar markets, the strategic need to enter the business, the comparative cost of *de novo* entry into the business, and alternative uses of financial and managerial resources.

In the current merger environment, dealings with acquisition targets are likely to take place in a crowded arena. This makes necessary an assessment of competitors' possible prices. The task involves (1) an understanding of the company, its industry, and its competitors; (2) financial analysis of the target, including identifying "hidden values" and "breakup values"; (3) comparison with acquisitions of similar businesses; (4) analysis of likely competitive purchasers and their financial capability; and (5) an analysis of the combination including topics such as tax and accounting effects and common stock-market reaction. The merger market, like all markets, is heavily influenced by supply and demand. Certain "hot" properties command premium prices, while other businesses have little appeal to public companies and tend to sell at lower prices.

The assessment of other purchasers' likely prices often reveals whether pursuing a given acquisition makes sense. If management's price is substantially below that of its rivals, reduced possibility of consummation could make the effort to acquire not worthwhile. If management's pricing is competitive, insight into the "going level" will help form the basis of a negotiating strategy.

Structuring the Transaction

Structuring a merger transaction is a complex affair. Three separate and compelling sets of requirements must be satisfied: those of the seller, the buyer, and the transaction itself. The securities to be issued are rarely new inventions. After cash, choices include variations of long-term debt; convertible debt or stock; and preferred stock, common stock, and warrants.

The seller's needs are typically related to price, tax considerations (that is, tax-free or taxable; deferred or payable immediately), and the terms of securities (particularly in a tax-free transaction). Securities in a taxable transaction are really cash equivalents, as long as they are designed to be marketable and the two sides agree on market value.

The buyer's needs are mostly related to the impact of the deal on its stock price and its ability to raise capital. Key practical concerns are the amount of earnings-per-share dilution, the time to earnings-per-share breakeven, the impact on debt rating, and the amount of goodwill incurred. Although some companies proceed by hard-and-fast rules (such as not accepting more than 10 percent earnings dilution or a sub-A senior debt rating), the buyer's needs are best examined on a case-by-case basis.

For example, if the earnings-per-share dilution exceeds 10 percent initially but dilution is expected to disappear after two years, it is possible that the characteristics of the new combined company will command a higher price-earnings ratio than in the past. What is relevant is not the earnings dilution but the effect on the stock price. Additionally, some companies decline to incur substantial amounts of goodwill. Yet, goodwill is troublesome only if it hurts either the debt rating or the stock price; in most instances, it will not. Furthermore, if a company believes that a transaction will take it to a BBB rating but that it could reestablish an A rating within a reasonable time, an assessment of the benefit of the acquisition relative to the risk of this period of non-A rating is in order. The amount of capital to be raised in the near term can have a significant impact on this issue.

The needs of the deal dictate the structure of the transaction in a competitive environment. The faster the deal can be consummated, the less likely it is that an interloper will appear. A number of techniques can help assure the completion of a transaction. Invariably, these involve buying stock up front for cash or locking up control of the company in one way or another.

In short, practical considerations prevail in structuring the transaction. Meeting the above three sets of needs is crucial. Key questions—What will happen to the stock price? What is the value of the securities? What is the effect on the company's ability to raise capital? How vulnerable is the transaction to an interloper? —must be answered, or at least addressed. Analysis should cover the short-, intermediate-, and long-term effects.

Afterword

While this article has covered the key strategic merger issues, a number of topics that require the special attention of the CFO have not been discussed. These range from negotiating strategy—a critical phase of the merger process—to dealing with government agencies in the areas of securities, tax, and antitrust regulations.

Dealing in the merger marketplace is not a scientific undertaking. An understanding of the economics of the acquired company, the quality of its management, its competitive position, and its business outlook is crucial. Primary emphasis should be placed on doing as much detailed business analysis as possible; after the acquisition, it's too late. In the final analysis, managements must make tough decisions using their experience, insight, and intuition.

□ *Geoffrey T. Boisi and Kenneth D. Brody*

CAPITAL EXPENDITURES AND RETURN ON INVESTMENT

Capital expenditures involve current investments for which benefits are expected to be received in the future, usually over a period of years. Investments are made in fixed assets, such as plant and equipment, as well as in other projects having a long-term impact on a corporation. Investment decisions of this type are the key to the success or failure of an individual firm, because their results last for years and have marked effects on the general direction, competitive edge, stability, growth, and profitability of an enterprise. Thus it may be concluded that a firm's ability to effectively manage capital expenditure programs will to a large extent determine its future success.

Requirements of a Capital Expenditure Program

To develop a sound capital expenditure program, management must consider the objectives of the firm, the many facts of long-range planning, and immediate operating plans. The program must be sufficiently detailed to ensure intelligent decisions, yet it must not burden line personnel and thus become an obstacle to creative thinking and routine work.

Authors on the subject list many different requirements and components of an effective capital expenditure program. Each attempts to tackle the problem from a slightly different angle. However, there seems to be a common trend in the various approaches, a trend that links four major areas to be considered in a comprehensive program:

- Effective channels of communication must be established. They must permit plans for profitable investment opportunities to flow to top management so that they can be included in the long-range plans for the firm.

- A process of review, selection, and approval must be developed to evaluate a project, rank it against other projects, and authorize expenditures to be made. These functions must be consistent with the long-term objectives of the firm.

- Effective control over authorized expenditures must be instituted in order to ensure that the facility conforms to specifications and that the outlays do not exceed the amount authorized.

- A post-audit review and appraisal that will compare actual performance with estimated performance must be developed. A sound program of post-audit can do much to make earnings cash flow more conscientious and realistic.

Developing Communication

In a large decentralized organization, the initiating force for most capital expenditures will come not from the central management staff but from the widespread operating units of the company. It is a difficult task to clear the channels of communication between the various general office staff activities so they all work toward a common goal. To accomplish this between the various operating units is an even greater task, demanding more than mere lip service. A climate must be developed that will expand the scope of the managers of the operating units. Where their horizons are limited to their own operations, they must be broadened to the horizons of the firm. These people not only need to understand the overall objectives of the firm; they must take an active part in deciding the means by which these objectives are to be attained.

The primary role the management of the operating units will play in a capital expenditure program is one of maintaining a monitoring station that seeks out possible investments and gathers data for subsequent evaluation. In seeking out possible areas for investment, the only restriction should be that the investments satisfy a present or future customer need at a satisfactory profit to the firm.

In the monitoring process management must not receive only signals that indicate equipment investment potential. It must be tuned in to all wavelengths—product design and modification, new methods of distribution, techniques of financing, location of markets and operating units, and optimization of inventory balances. In essence, the operating units become the first line of defense against present and future competitors. The monitoring stations send back signals about the enemy's strength and weakness as well as the company's own vulnerability.

In gathering data for the subsequent analysis of the investment, operating management will be reinforcing what have been the weakest links in the capital expenditure chain of most firms. Basically, the analysis of a major capital expenditure necessitates two distinct steps: gathering relevant data on the investment, and rational analysis of these data. The data-gathering process, in turn, is geared to answering two basic questions. The first question asks the amount and timing of the expenditure. The second seeks to learn the amount and timing of revenues or cost savings to be achieved.

No analysis of a capital expenditure can be better than the available and developed data on which the analysis is based. No technique for the measurement of an investment's worth, regardless of its sophistication, can improve upon faulty data. Hence, sufficient effort should be directed at developing reliable estimates of cash flows.

Evaluation and Selection

The evaluation process is the analytical function that has gained much prominence in the past years. Business literature is laden with books and articles purporting to describe effective methods of evaluating capital expenditures. Evaluation should be based on cash-flow estimates on an after-tax basis, not on the income statement. Techniques of analysis range from the simple payback method to the complicated versions of the discounted cash flow method.

Management must recognize that there is no single method that is best in every situation. There are many acceptable methods to suit different situations. Some have less precision than others but give advantages that, too often, go unrecognized. When a company reviews its existing investment procedures or when new procedures are being established, consideration should be given to the pros and cons of several acceptable techniques. Whichever system is used, it must provide a sound basis for evaluating an investment and comparing its desirability with that of others. This is a critical requirement that must not be compromised.

Once a review process has been established, the selection and approval functions fall in place. The selection should be based on some acceptance criteria or relative ranking of the proposals. However, there are some exceptions to this rule. Some proposals—for example, office modernization, painting, or air conditioning—do not have quantifiable benefits or returns. These are expenditures made to maintain a standard of performance that the firm sets for itself. These projects should be checked for reasonableness and not be subjected to the same standard as others.

Approval is given to a project either on its own merit when a firm can expect to have enough capital to fund all proposed projects that are desirable, or on the basis of its relative ranking with respect to other projects when the firm is under capital rationing. Even an individual project selection calls for comparing the mutually exclusive alternatives for doing the same job. For example, the alternatives might be to purchase one large, high-capacity piece of equipment located in one producing point, or to purchase several smaller units and distribute them in several locales. The question to be resolved is, which alternative is the most profitable use of capital? It is also important to recognize whether a project is contingent on other projects. In evaluating a contingent project, characteristics of the project on which it depends must also be considered.

In practice, screening of capital expenditure proposals occurs at several levels of authority, from line managers to the board of directors, depending on the size, importance, and sensitivity of the proposals. However, it is a good idea to have some kind of centralized control on all significant capital expenditures. This is necessary to avoid duplicate efforts and suboptimum use of corporate capital.

Controlling Authorized Expenditures

The amount of control established on capital projects will be a function of the philosophy of management, the magnitude of the expenditure, and the duration of the project. While most firms have cost-accounting and budgetary control systems for items of expense, very few have an effective reporting system for capital expenditures. Often, after a project has been approved, management seems to lose interest until the completion of the project. This is the wrong time for interest to wane; during the period of construction or installation of the project, much light will be shed on the reliability of data furnished in the proposal.

Progress reports on the outlay of funds on a project should be available at regular intervals. The department head, the budget director, and (if available) the capital budget committee should compare actual expenditures with those called for in the original proposal. As the work is approaching completion, it will be possible to determine whether additional expenditures are required on the project. If expenditures above the authorized amount are required, the request should be accompanied by an explanation describing the cause of the overrun. The final report on the project will provide the first formal review of the validity of the original proposal.

Post-audit and Review

Capital expenditure management must not stop when a project is complete and operating. After the project has been in operation for a reasonable time, it will be desirable to determine whether it is performing in accordance with the forecast. This step is an attempt to maintain the integrity of the forecasts of profitability and to provide experience that can be used as a base for improving the reliability of future estimates. The original justification data will provide the yardstick for the measurement.

Since the early life of an investment is most important, it is advisable that the post-audit be performed after the first year. On projects with long lives, an audit may be performed several times—after the first, fifth, and tenth years, for example. In such cases, it may be necessary to adjust the results for price and labor-rate changes not contemplated in the forecast.

Since no one bats 1,000, there will be projects that do not achieve the desired results. In these cases, the audit function must seek remedies through either change or abandonment. The pressures of pride and sentiment, coupled with the forces of inertia, will produce many reasons for tying up capital funds in an investment that does not produce a satisfactory return. Vigilance and cold-blooded analysis in the post-audit activity will assist in keeping these noneconomic justifications to a minimum.

Methods of Evaluating Capital Expenditures

Many different methods are in use for the evaluation of capital expenditures. They vary in complexity and thoroughness; however, they share a common objective of providing a quantitative measure of desirability of a capital project.

Payback Method

One of the simplest and most commonplace methods of evaluating a capital project is the payback method. The payback period is the number of years required to recover the original cash outlay of an investment. If, for example, a project requires $50,000 initial investment followed by net cash inflows of $10,000 in the first and second years, $15,000 in the third year, $20,000 in the fourth and fifth years, and $15,000 in the sixth year, the payback period is $3\frac{3}{4}$ years, since the total inflow in the first three years is $35,000 and the remaining $15,000 of the initial investment is recovered in $15,000/20,000 = \frac{3}{4}$ of a year in the fourth year. If the payback period of a project is shorter than a predetermined cutoff value, the project is accepted; otherwise, it is rejected.

The advantages of the payback method are its simplicity and ready appeal. It is, however, not a valid method of measuring profitability, since it does not take into account cash flows beyond the payback period or consider timing of cash flows during the period. This method, nevertheless, gives a rough indication of a project's risk. Usually, the shorter the payback, the less risky the project. It is useful to consider payback period as a second criterion in conjunction with some profitability measure, particularly for firms with potential cash-flow problems.

Present-Value Method

The present-value method is a discounted cash-flow method that explicitly considers the time value of money, that is, the fact that a dollar earned today is more valuable than a dollar earned a year from now. Net present value (NPV) of a stream of cash flows is computed by first discounting future cash flows by appropriate factors and then algebraically adding all the discounted flows. For the previous example, assuming a discount rate of 15 percent and that the cash flows occur at the end of the period, the NPV of the investment is

$$\$-50,000 + 10,000/1.15 + 10,000/(1.15)^2 + 15,000/(1.15)^3$$
$$+ 20,000/(1.15)^4 + 20,000/(1.15)^5 + 15,000/(1.15)^6 = \$3,983$$

Standard convention is to give a negative sign to an outflow and a positive sign to an inflow. Under the present-value method, a project is accepted if its NPV is greater than zero; otherwise it is rejected. The rationale is that the sum of cash inflows must exceed the sum of cash outflows, after discounting, for a project to be selected.

The advantage of this method is its soundness in handling both the magnitude and the timing of cash flows. This method, however, assumes that the intermediate cash inflows are reinvested at the discount rate. The most difficult aspect of this method is to arrive at a meaningful discount rate. Usually, when a firm is not under capital rationing, the discount rate used is the corporate cost of capital. The latter consists of costs of both debt and equity capital and is a function of three factors: (1) pure time preference, arising from most people's desire to use a dollar or the goods it can purchase for an additional year; (2) expected inflation rate in the economy over a period of time, required to offset the diminishing purchasing power of a dollar with time; and (3) a risk premium specific to a firm, arising from both the risk inherent in the operation of the business (business risk) and the risk associated with the use of leverage funds (financial risk). This "building block" approach to discount rate is very useful in understanding and properly applying the present-value method in project evaluation. Actual measurement of cost of capital will be discussed separately.

It is now obvious that if the discount rate in an NPV analysis implicitly contains an expected inflation rate, all cash flows before discounting must be expressed in future-year or nominal dollars. On the other hand, to use a discount rate without an implicit inflation factor, cash flows before discounting must be in constant base-year dollars. If future-year dollars are to be considered, it is important to use the inflation rate applicable to a specific project and even different items of the project while estimating cash flows. If a project is deemed more risky than the overall corporate activities, an additional premium may be added to the discount rate to offset the risk.

The NPV measure, although properly indicating the desirability of a capital project, does not rank it with respect to other competing projects. It may be incorrect to conclude that a $1,000 project with $400 NPV ranks higher than a $100 project with $60 NPV simply because the former has a greater NPV. This is not a real problem if the firm is not under capital rationing, because, under nonrationing, any project with a positive NPV should be accepted and there is no need for ranking. For comparing mutually exclusive alternatives, incremental analyses would suffice.

Ranking of projects, however, is essential when there is not enough capital to fund all desirable projects. Although NPV itself is not a means of ranking projects, the present-value concept can be extended to rank projects on the basis of some kind of "rate of return." One such extension would be the NPV/investment ratio, or the profitability index. The problem with this index is the ambiguity of the denominator. If investment implies initial cash outlay, then this ratio would overestimate profitability for most practical projects, since investment in a project usually occurs over a period of years, perhaps punctuated by cash inflows, not just at the beginning. To alleviate this problem, we can introduce the concept of modified profitability index, which is defined as the ratio of NPV to the minimum of the net present values through each year of the project's life (since this minimum is almost always negative, its absolute value should be considered). The latter is the amount one has to have in the bank at the beginning of a project in order to meet all the funds required by it. Another simplified concept is the benefit/cost (B/C) ratio, which is defined as the ratio of the NPV of all inflows to the NPV of all outflows. These concepts are illustrated by means of the following example:

−$20,000	+$5,000	+$7,000	−$18,000	+$25,000	+$25,000
Year 0	Year 1	Year 2	Year 3	Year 4	Year 5

Assuming a 15 percent discount rate, the NPV of the above stream is $4,529 (all cash flows are assumed to occur at the end of the periods indicated.) Therefore, the underlying project should be accepted on its own merit, provided that the firm is not under capital rationing. To rank the project, its profitability index can be computed as 4,529/20,000 = 22.6 percent. Is $20,000 the investment in the project? Clearly, the answer is no, because there is an additional net outflow of $18,000 in the third year. Should we then combine the two outflows, in the present-value sense, to determine the investment? The answer is again no, because part of the $18,000 outflow will be paid for by the inflows in years 1 and 2, generated by the project itself. A rational way to determine the investment in the project is to calculate the NPV through each year of the project's life and select the minimum one.

$$\text{NPV through year } 0 = -\$20,000$$
$$\text{NPV through year } 1 = -\$20,000 + \$5,000/1.15 = -\$15,652$$
$$\text{NPV through year } 2 = -\$15,652 + \$7,000/(1.15)^2 = -\$10,359$$
$$\text{NPV through year } 3 = -\$10,359 - \$18,000/(1.15)^3 = -\$22,194$$
$$\text{NPV through year } 4 = -\$22,194 + \$25,000/(1.15)^4 = -\$7,900$$
$$\text{NPV through year } 5 = -\$7,900 \ \ + \$25,000/(1.15)^5 = +\$4,529$$

Investment in the project is $22,194; unless this amount is available for the project at the beginning, its cash-flow requirements cannot be met without borrowing capital from other sources. Thus the modified profitability index is 4,529/22,194 = 20.4 percent. To determine the benefit/cost ratio, the NPV of all inflows is calculated to be $36,364 and the NPV of all outflows to be $31,835, so that the ratio is 1.14 or 114 percent. It should be recognized that the benefit/cost ratio must be greater than 1.0 for a project to be considered for selection, whereas the modified profitability index needs only to be greater than zero.

In this context, it is possible to extend the definition of payback period. If NPV through each year of a project's life is plotted against year, the point where the graph intersects the year axis indicates the modified payback period, because this is the time when NPV switches from negative to positive. If the graph intersects the year axis more than once, then the point farthest from the beginning of the project should be used.

Internal-Rate-of-Return Method

This method is also a discounted cash flow method. It not only indicates the desirability of a project but also ranks it with respect to others. Internal rate of return (IRR) is defined as the discount rate that renders the NPV of a stream of cash flows equal to zero. It is the single most widely used measure for project evaluation. For the cash-flow stream in the preceding example, IRR, denoted by r, is determined by solving the following equation:

$$0 = -20,000 + \frac{5,000}{(1 + r)} + \frac{7,000}{(1 + r)^2} - \frac{18,000}{(1 + r)^3} + \frac{25,000}{(1 + r)^4} + \frac{25,000}{(1 + r)^5}$$

The solution is $r = 0.211$. Thus the IRR of the cash flow is 21.1 percent. IRR is not a measure of compound return on the initial outlay over the life of a project; it is a simple return on the amount that remains "internally invested" in a project. IRR is a characteristic internal to a project and, unlike NPV, does not depend on the discount rate or the cost of capital. However, for project selection, the computed IRR is compared with a predetermined required rate of return, or hurdle rate, which is usually the cost of corporate capital. If the IRR is greater than the hurdle rate, the project is selected; otherwise it is rejected. IRR also is a criterion for ranking projects.

Advantages of IRR are obvious: It is independent of the discount rate, it is a measure of rate of return that is easy to comprehend, and it serves as a vehicle for ranking. Disadvantages of IRR are subtle but serious. For IRR to be interpreted as a compound rate of return on the initial investment over the life of a project, it must be assumed that the intermediate cash inflows are reinvested at the IRR rate. But, clearly, that is absurd, because it implies that cash inflows from a 50 percent IRR project can be reinvested elsewhere at a 50 percent rate, whereas inflows from a 20 percent IRR project can be reinvested only at a 20 percent rate under an identical environment. This implicit reinvestment assumption is, however, not necessary if IRR is interpreted as a simple rate of return on the amount that remains invested in a project. IRR, being a solution of an equation, may not exist, and there may be more than one IRR for a given cash flow. It is possible that none of the multiple IRR values indicates any meaningful rate of return for the project. The situation is worst when there exists an unambiguous IRR value for a cash-flow stream and it is completely meaningless in relation to the project under consideration. Consider the following simple example:

−$1,000	+$4,000	−$4,000
Year 0	Year 1	Year 2

IRR of this cash flow is 100 percent, which is greater than any conceivable hurdle rate; hence the project should be selected according to the traditional logic. But it can be verified that the NPV of this project is negative for any discount rate (except at 100 percent it is zero, by definition); in particular, it is −$547 at the 15 percent rate. If a firm cannot make a profit, in the absolute sense, by investing funds costing only 15 percent, what is the relevance of 100 percent IRR for the project? The answer lies in the reinvestment assumption. If the intermediate inflow of $4,000 cannot be reinvested elsewhere at a 100 percent rate, the project is unprofitable. This example is only one from a large class of investment projects whose treatment is beyond the scope of this discussion. Fortunately, however, very few real projects seem to show such irregularities. Nevertheless, an astute analyst should be aware of the potential pitfalls.

There are other methods available in the literature. Most of them are based on accounting information rather than on cash flow; hence their application in capital expenditure decisions is severely limited. Of all the methods described, NPV is the soundest method. If NPV and IRR criteria lead to conflicting decisions, in most situations one should decide in favor of NPV. Since NPV by itself is not a ranking vehicle, modified profitability index may be used for ranking. Even though IRR is a very popular method, it is possible to eliminate or reduce its use without hurting capital expenditure management.

Cost of Capital

In the preceding discussion of discounted cash flow techniques, reference was made to the cost of capital as a discount rate for present-value computations. The "building block" approach to discount rate discussed earlier provides clear understanding of the concept, but the actual measurement of cost of capital, taking into account various sources of funds to finance investments, remains to be discussed.

A popular approach to measuring cost of capital is the weighted-average method. In this method, the cost of each component, such as long-term and short-term debt and preferred and common stock, is measured individually and then a weighted average cost is computed by giving a weight to each component equal to its proportion in the existing or future corporate capital structure.

Cost of long-term debt. The cost of long-term debt capital is essentially the current rate for long-term securities for any specific firm. This is only complicated by discount or premium factors that may prevail. The effective rate of interest for an outstanding issue can be determined by comparing the current market price for this security with the remaining application. For example, the effective rate of interest on a bond outstanding can be found by determining the rate of interest that equates the market price and the present value of the amount due at maturity, plus the present value of the interest payments.

Cost of short-term debt. The cost of short-term debt is similar to that of long-term debt, inasmuch as an interest cost applies. However, there are short-term liabilities that do not have explicit interest charges. These, of course, are the various taxes payable, wages payable, and at any given time the normal trade payables for a firm. Attempts can be made at quantifying the cost of maintaining and enlarging upon this source of funds. One would have to quantify, in the case of short-term trade payables, the discount lost, as well as any carrying charges that may be assessed, if these liabilities are extended.

Cost of preferred stock. The cost of preferred stock depends on the stated dividend. Although it is not a contractual obligation on the part of management, for most practical purposes it may be considered as a debt. This cost may be measured by the ratio of stated annual dividend to the net proceeds from a preferred issue.

Cost of common stock. The cost of common-stock capital is a function of the return expected by its owners. Although it is very difficult to estimate shareowners' expectations, the following methods are available to approximate it:

Comparable earnings. The basic notion in this method is that the required return on equity should be commensurate with that of other enterprises having comparable risk, and that this return may be used as a proxy for expected return for the determination of cost of capital. Shortcomings of this approach are obvious. Not only is it difficult to identify firms having comparable risks, it is also not proper to use their historical return on equity as the future expectation. Moreover, dissimilarities of accounting practices may lead to comparing apples to oranges.

Discounted cash flow method. In this method, cost of equity is defined as the discount rate that equates the NPV of the projected dividend stream over an indefinitely long period of time to the current market price of a stock. In its simplest form, cost of equity equals current dividend yield plus expected growth rate of dividends. Dividend yield is the ratio of dividends per share to the market price of a share. Clearly, the most difficult task is the estimation of future growth. A popular method is to use historical growth rate or some subjective variant of it. Performance of similar stocks may be used to check reasonableness of the result.

Capital-asset-pricing model. The CAP model attempts to estimate equity cost in a market context. It regresses actual return on equity for the firm, less the risk-free rate in each period, against the return from a market, less the risk-free rate. The regression coefficient is the widely known "beta," whose value indicates how risky a stock is relative to the market. Once beta is determined, average market return and average risk-free rate (expected values, if available) can be used to compute the cost of equity capital.

Of the three methods, discounted cash flow is the single most useful method of computing cost of equity capital. The other methods may be used to compare the results.

Effect of income taxes. Income taxes affect the calculations in measuring cost of capital because cost of equity capital is a distribution of income and, therefore, not deductible, while the cost of debt capital carries with it deductible interest charges.

Capital Rationing

Project selection on individual merit is a valid approach as long as a firm can expect to raise enough capital to fund all proposed projects that are profitable. Under such nonrationing of capital, the most widely used criterion for selecting a project is that its NPV (with the cost of corporate capital as the discount rate) is greater than zero or its IRR exceeds a predetermined hurdle rate, usually the cost of capital. If there is a conflict between NPV and IRR criteria, additional case-specific analysis should be performed; in most cases, the decision will be in favor of the NPV criterion.

Evaluation and selection procedures are quite different when capital rationing is effective. Under capital rationing, a firm must forgo, by definition, one or more of its profitable projects. This restriction necessitates ranking all projects on the basis of some consistent criterion and selecting them, beginning with the highest rank, until the capital fund is exhausted. Of course, mandatory projects must be funded first, and other nonquantifiable projects must be evaluated on a different standard. IRR may be used, although not satisfactorily, to rank projects. NPV cannot be used, but an NPV-related criterion, such as modified profitability index, may be used. The problem, however, lies with the discount rate for present-value computations. Traditional cost of capital can no longer be used as the discount rate. The concept of opportunity cost must be invoked.

Suppose a firm's overall cost of capital is 15 percent, but, due to unavailability of funds, it can approve only projects with a return of at least 28 percent. There are ten other projects with returns between 17 percent and 25 percent. All these projects would have been selected if there were no fund limitation. Because of the limitation, the best opportunity the company is forgoing is the 25 percent project. This is the "opportunity cost" to the firm in this context. Thus, in capital-budgeting decision making, 15 percent cost of capital is not relevant; what is relevant is the 25 percent opportunity cost of capital. But there would be an inconsistency if the present values used in the ranking criteria were computed using a 15 percent discount rate.

On the other hand, it is not possible to know the opportunity cost before ranking is done, so 25 percent could not possibly have been used as the discount rate in the first place. The problem is solved through an iterative procedure as follows: start with a reasonable discount rate, perhaps the cost of capital, rank all projects, and determine the opportunity cost. In the second cycle, use this opportunity cost as the discount rate, rerank all projects (relative ranking of projects will, in general, change), and determine the new opportunity cost. Continue the process through a few cycles until the opportunity costs in two successive cycles are about the same. The final ranking so derived can be readily used for project selection under capital rationing.

Although such a ranking method is a viable approach, it produces a nonoptimum result in the sense that it does not maximize shareowners' wealth, measured in terms of the sum of NPVs of all selected projects. Furthermore, it is difficult to reflect interdependencies of projects and their multiperiod behavior in a ranking method. The latter point perhaps needs some explanation. In reality, a budget constraint exists over a period of years and most capital projects require expenditures in more than one year. On the other hand, projects that are already initiated generate intermediate cash inflows, which would relax budget constraints otherwise prevailing. In addition, it is possible to postpone certain capital projects to respond to tight budgets in the early years and/or to make room for more profitable projects. These complicated timing characteristics of cash flows cannot be properly reflected in a ranking method. All these issues of capital budgeting can be satisfactorily addressed by the techniques of mathematical programming, which are beyond the scope of this discussion.

There is a school that does not subscribe to the capital-rationing concept. It maintains that setting a limit on capital expenditure is artificial; a firm can, in principle, raise a virtually unlimited amount of capital, albeit at an increasingly higher cost. Therefore, capital projects should be approved until the marginal return falls below the marginal cost of capital.

The major drawback of any method that handles capital rationing is that it requires all projects to be proposed and analyzed at the beginning of the planning process, whereas in real life project proposal and evaluation is almost always a process that occurs throughout the year. It may be advantageous to adopt a selection scheme based on frequent revisions.

Risk Analysis

Management of capital expenditures, whether under capital rationing or not, involves risk analysis. Risk in this context implies the variability of return, which arises primarily from the lack of certainty of cash-flow estimates. While there is controversy over how risk should be quantified, most people tend to favor a statistical definition, such as variance, standard deviation, or standard error of return. In order to compute a statistical risk measure of a project, it is necessary to estimate various possible values of each cash flow and their corresponding chances or probabilities. Once the complete spectrum of values of the cash-flow stream is established, analytical methods of statistics can be applied to compute both the expected return of the project and its risk. A more viable alternative is the simulation technique.

Once a project's risk is estimated, its selection may be decided in one of several ways. The simplest approach is to classify it as a low-risk, moderate-risk, or high-risk project, and add a corresponding risk premium (subjectively decided) to the discount factor to compute present-value-related measures. If the project qualifies on the basis of the newly computed measure, it should be approved. Another approach is to determine, statistically or by simulation, the likelihood of a project's becoming unprofitable (that is, showing a negative NPV or an IRR below hurdle rate); if that probability is below a threshold value (subjectively decided), the project should be accepted. A third approach is to use the "certain equivalent" concept. Using "utility theory," it is possible to construct a fictitious project with a "certain" return that is equivalent, in the sense of preference, to a risky project whose return is subject to variability. The "certain" return of the fictitious project is the certain equivalent of risky return of the original project. Obviously, the development of certain equivalent is a function of the risk preference of a firm. Finally, risk behavior of projects can also be handled within the context of mathematical programming.

Central Considerations

In attempting to establish a capital expenditure program, management must be totally aware of the questions that such a program seeks to answer. Frequently management's attention is absorbed by *how* a thing is being accomplished, instead of by the critical issue—*what* is being accomplished.

Although there are no canned programs worth their cost, there are some critical areas that must be considered by an effective program. Briefly described, these areas are:

1. A climate in which innovation flourishes must be developed.
2. There must be an acceptable method of evaluating proposals. (The key word here is "acceptable.") Make sure that the method is no more complex than is warranted by the proposal.
3. Expenditures on the project must be controlled and periodically reviewed.
4. Scorekeeping must be conducted through a planned post-audit program. It should be geared to encourage the collection of sound data at the proposal stage and to exert pressure on management to achieve the planned results.

The future success of a firm is being decided today, either by the thoughtful actions of its executives, or by its competitors because of the lack of such thoughtful action. A carefully developed capital expenditure program leads a firm a long way toward future success. The lack of such a program makes future success virtually impossible.

□ *Asok K. Chaudhuri* and *Paul R. Goodwin*
(and Kenneth A. Baker, the original author of this now substantially revised section)

FINANCING CORPORATE REQUIREMENTS

The purpose of external financing is to meet corporate cash needs in excess of the amount provided by internal generation. Since cash needs form the basis of the financing decision, no financing should be undertaken without a forecast of the sources and application of funds. This forecast should extend several years into the future; the first year is divided into at least monthly intervals, and later years' progress from a quarterly to an annual basis. Such a forecast permits the development of a coherent program for meeting long- and short-term cash needs in a way that will not jeopardize corporate solvency but will retain the flexibility necessary to meet unanticipated financing requirements in the future. The forecast will also indicate whether the particular financing should be long-term or short-term.

Short-Term Financing

The need for short-term financing can best be identified by looking at the duration of the need for the assets to be financed. If the need for the assets is temporary, the financing should be in short-term form. For example, a short-term bank loan would be appropriate in meeting seasonal working-capital needs, since the buildup of inventories and accounts receivable will be temporary. Long-lived assets should not be financed with short-term funds, because of the risk of being unable to obtain future refinancing at an acceptable cost.

Some short-term financing is spontaneous. That is, it is available through normal business practice or operation of the law without any particular effort on the part of the company. Trade credit, payroll, and tax accruals are examples of spontaneous financing. Negotiated sources of short-term financing, on the other hand, are principally bank loans and commercial paper.

Trade Credit

Trade credit arises through the purchase of materials from suppliers. If a company buys $10,000 worth of material on a 30-day open account, the vendor has in effect lent it $10,000 for 30 days. If the company buys more material, the financing will be automatically increased, subject to any credit limits imposed by the vendor. Credit terms will vary according to trade practice in the seller's industry and the credit worthiness of the buyer. While open account is the normal form of trade credit, the trade acceptance or some other form of promissory note is frequently employed in international trade. Although trade credit is usually inexpensive, the failure to take offered cash discounts—or the acceptance of penalty or financing charges for stretched-out terms—can represent very costly financing.

Bank Loans

There are three basic types of short-term commercial bank loans: casual, secured, and line-of-credit. Casual loans are made without prior negotiation and based on the general credit of the company. If the bank is uncertain of the credit, it may request that the loan be secured by pledge of specific corporate assets or endorsed by one of its officers or another company. Loans are also made against a previously negotiated line of credit in which the bank expresses its willingness to lend the company any amount up to a certain maximum at any time during a specific period—usually a year—provided that the company's financial condition remains substantially unchanged.

Banks charge their best customers a prime rate on loans—generally, a standard rate throughout the banking industry at any given time. Less desirable credits will be charged progressively higher rates of interest. In addition, bank loans usually require that compensating balances equal to 10 to 20 percent or more of the loan or line of credit be kept on deposit with the bank, thus increasing the effective rate of interest on the portion of the loan available to the company. However, to the extent that the company must maintain cash balances to meet checks and for other purposes, even without the loan, the compensating balance may represent little or no incremental cost. As an alternative, a company may pay fees to a bank rather than keep balances for the line of credit. If a company desires more assurance that the funds will be available, it might enter into a revolving credit agreement with a bank or banks. In this case, the company will be required to pay a commitment fee.

U.S. companies are becoming more frequent borrowers of short-term funds from foreign banks. Such borrowings generally require fees rather than balances. The loans can be established so that the U.S. company will not be required to withhold income taxes on the interest paid. Typically, more documentation is required in establishing such lines of credit. Also, there is not as much flexibility in the repayment of the loans. The borrowing rate is normally established on the basis of an amount over LIBOR (London Interbank Offered Rate) if the loans are established in the European market. If the borrowings are established in the Far East, the interest rate may be determined as a spread over SIBOR (Singapore Interbank Offered Rate) or HIBOR (Hong Kong Interbank Offered Rate). Such borrowings of dollars in foreign markets can at times be more advantageous than borrowing from banks in the United States. The Eurodollar market has grown to huge proportions, particularly since 1973, when the OPEC cartel began increasing prices at a dramatic rate.

Commercial Paper

Commercial paper represents the promissory notes of corporations. These notes are usually sold to investors through commercial-paper dealers, although some very large companies place their paper directly with financial institutions and other corporations that have a short-term cash surplus. The notes are negotiable and represent a highly liquid investment for the holders. For the issuers, commercial paper represents a quick, convenient, and flexible means of raising varying amounts of cash, usually at a cost below the prime rate on bank borrowings. Several independent agencies rate commercial paper. The better the rating, the lower the cost of funds to the issuing company.

Because ensured negotiability is essential to the value of the note, only large, highly credit-worthy firms are normally able to issue paper in the commercial market. Even for such a firm, any indication of a change in credit status can quickly dry up the market for its paper. Therefore, to assure negotiability, companies are required to back up their commercial paper dealings with lines of credit at commercial banks. Maturities on commercial paper normally range from one to 270 days.

Intermediate-Term Financing

Intermediate-term financing is generally long-term financing in a short-term form. As with short-term financing, the duration of the need for the asset financed is the clue. If the asset (or its replacement) will be permanently required, its financing represents long-term capital. That is to say, either the present financing arrangement must be continued indefinitely or some form of long-term capital must be substituted for it. In either event, the same dollar amount is part of the corporation's required permanent capital.

Bank Term Loans

Term loans are generally made by domestic and foreign commercial banks for periods of one to five years, although in rare instances maturities of up to ten years are granted. Rates depend on the availability of funds by the banks and the amount of competition among banks and whether the loans are secured or unsecured. Companies sometimes use bank loans for construction or other major spending programs to bridge the period until attractive permanent financing can be arranged. Borrowing under a term-loan agreement can be made periodically as required by spending, avoiding the need to invest the proceeds of permanent financing for the short term until needed. Frequently, companies will negotiate a revolving credit with a bank or a group of banks, under which the bank agrees to loan up to a stated maximum amount during the next few years. A commitment fee of about one-eighth to one-half of one percent is normally charged on the unused portion of the maximum credit, in addition to an agreed-upon interest rate, fixed or floating, on actual borrowings.

Accounts-Receivable Financing

Accounts-receivable financing involves the pledging of a company's accounts receivable, either with or without recourse, to a finance or factoring firm. If the finance company has recourse to the selling company in the event its customers do not pay, the financing process is called commercial financing. If it has no recourse, the process is called factoring. In either case, the sale of the receivables will be prearranged, and the finance or factoring company reserves the right to reject a certain portion or certain individual accounts offered by the selling company. Today, the bulk of accounts-receivable financing is in the form of commercial financing. Receivables financing has been the traditional source of funds for smaller firms unable to raise working capital in other ways or unable to support an internal credit function. Pledging receivables, often the bulk of a company's liquid assets, limits the ability to take on other financing, particularly of a short-term nature. The cost of receivables financing reflects handling costs, the cost of the funds provided, and the cost of whatever credit function is assumed by the finance company, and will tend to exceed term-loan costs. On the other hand, it is an extremely flexible source of secured borrowings.

Inventory Financing

Like receivables financing, inventory financing is essentially a secured, revolving term loan. Generally, the security is administered under a field warehousing arrangement whereby inventory is released from a bonded warehouse as payments are received against advances by the bank or other financial institution. It is generally important in seasonal industries such as food processing.

Project Financing

Project financing can be defined as a transaction in which the lender is satisfied to look principally to the cash flow and earnings generated by a project as the source of debt-service payments and to the project's assets as sufficient collateral for the loan. Borrowers generally want a stand-alone type of loan, while the lenders often want a credit link to the company involved with the borrowing. In establishing the credit worthiness of the project, the important criteria include the following: (1) the operation depends on proven technology; (2) if as part of a multiplant project, some parts of the operation can demonstrate the ability to work separately from others that may have downtime or be unable to produce at designed levels; (3) the project has a reliable supply of raw materials; (4) management has the expertise to operate the plant successfully; and (5) earnings and cash flow indicate that the project has economic strength. Such financing can also be arranged when there is more than one company sponsoring the project.

Installment and Lease Financing

Manufacturers of capital goods will often permit buyers to pay on the installment plan. Typically, a down payment of 10 to 30 percent of the price is required, and the balance is to be paid monthly over five years or less. The cost of such financing varies. A high cost might be expected, but some manufacturers occasionally use financing as a promotion device, charging barely enough to cover their own direct costs. The manufacturer will generally "discount" the receivable to a finance company or bank.

Long-term leases may be considered a form of installment financing. In fact, many "leases" are treated as installment sales for tax purposes. In a true lease, the lessee receives use of the asset without acquiring any ownership interest in the property during or after the lease period, except under a generally separate, arms-length transaction. The lease term must be shorter than the useful life of the property leased. In addition to its use in acquiring new assets, leasing is also used as a means of raising cash on presently owned property by means of a sale and leaseback.

The attractiveness of leasing as a means of financing corporate requirements is a source of much debate. Logically, interposing the lessor as a middleman between the lessee and the ultimate source of the financing should add to the cost. Tax considerations often cloud the picture, however. In general, leasing does seem to expand the amount of credit available to a company. The cost may or may not be higher than that of traditional sources of borrowing. A question remains as to whether the company, as a matter of policy, should seek to borrow up to this expanded total. Also, the amount of leasing may affect a company's debt ratings.

There are generally two types of leases. One is an operating lease, in which the user of the property never has an intention of having any aspects of ownership. An example would be leasing an automobile for a day or a week. The second type is a financing lease, in which the user assumes many aspects of ownership. Such a user is responsible for keeping the lessor whole, including an agreed-upon rate of return. At the end of the lease period, the lessee generally has the right to acquire the property at its fair market value at that time. Current income tax law can affect the structure of the lease agreement.

A leveraged lease is a form of the financing lease for project financing. The owner puts up the required equity funds and thereby receives the income-tax benefits, which include the interest deduction, the investment tax credit, and the accelerated-depreciation deduction. The amount needed in excess of the equity is obtained by the issuance of a specially created ownership trust or partnership. The debt financing is done without recourse to the equity investors and is secured by an interest in the project assets and an assignment of the lease. The user of the property leases it from the party that invests the equity. The tax benefits are usually shared with the lessee, even though the tax benefits are more valuable to the lessor. Since such a transaction is typically done for tax purposes, it is important that the project is properly established to satisfy all tax-code requirements.

Government Financing

Federal, state, and local governments have become increasingly involved in business financing as a means of promoting growth in the local tax base, or employment, or for other social goals. Industrial-revenue bonds issued by a state or locality have been a popular means of providing low-cost indirect financing to businesses. The transaction may take the form of a lease in which the user is given an option to purchase the project assets at a nominal price at the end of the lease. An alternative to the lease is to set up an installment-sale agreement. Another type of transaction is a loan agreement in which the government issues the bonds and loans the proceeds to the user.

Tax-exempt industrial-development bonds may be issued in unlimited amounts for such things as convention or trade show facilities, mass commuting facilities and vehicles, sewage or waste disposal facilities, certain facilities for furnishing electricity, gas, and water, and air or water pollution control facilities.

A second type of industrial-development bond is issued under the small-issue exemption. Whether the issuer has authority to issue the bonds and whether the bonds meet all the federal income-tax requirements to be tax exempt are determined by a study of all the factors, which are often complex. There are two separate limits on the dollar amount of the bonds. The first is that an issue of bonds may not exceed $1 million in the face amount, including those already outstanding in the same incorporated municipality in which the facility is located or in the same county if it is not located in any such municipality. The second limit increases the amount of bonds to $10 million. However, this higher limit must be reduced by capital expenditures incurred within a six-year period beginning three years prior to the date of issue of the bonds for facilities located in the same incorporated municipality or in the same county if not in an incorporated municipality. Additional incentives are provided for locating industrial facilities in distressed urban areas if the facilities qualify for an Urban Development Action grant. In such cases, the effect is to allow up to $10 million tax-exempt financing for a project that costs up to $20 million.

Long-Term Financing

Long-term finance is concerned with the provision of the company's permanent capital base. Long-term financing decisions should reflect a soundly conceived financial strategy, whose goal should be to retain the ability to raise capital for both planned and emergency needs, while maintaining the highest intrinsic value possible for the company's common stock. Three major factors must be considered in arriving at this goal: the optimum capital structure, the appropriate dividend policy, and the firm's cost of capital. "Capital structure" means the balance between debt and equity funds in the company's total long-term capitalization. An insufficient amount of debt may make it difficult for the company to earn a reasonable return on its common stock. Conversely, an excessive amount can make subsequent financing difficult or impossible and, most important, may substantially increase the common-equity return that must be earned to compensate for the added risk. Generally, the amount a company may safely borrow is a function of the basic risk of its business: the type of business, the age and size of the company, the stability of its earnings, management ability, and so forth. Thus a public utility may range up to 60 percent debt in total long-term capital, while a well-established industrial firm will normally stay under 30 percent to maintain a comparable quality for its debt and equity securities. Dividend policy will influence the need for capital from external sources but can also affect the cost of capital. The cost of capital, in turn, will reflect the company's decisions on capital structure and dividend policy and will determine whether additional capital can be economically employed.

In addition to considering the overall strategic elements, specific financing alternatives should be evaluated in the light of seven tactical considerations: (1) *source* (private placement versus public sale of securities); (2) *amount* (how much capital to raise now in view of present and prospective needs); (3) *timing* (the condition of the debt and/or equity markets now and in the future); (4) *type* (whether debt, equity, or incentive financing is preferable at the time); (5) *cost* (both the out-of-pocket cost of the security and its impact on the required rate of earnings or cost of capital); (6) *control* (both the direct control of voting securities and the hamstringing that may be present in indenture covenants); (7) *risk* (the risk that may be added to the business by the financing, and the risk of obtaining subsequent financing when required). These tactical issues interact with one another to suggest the nature of the financing that should be undertaken at any given time.

Debt Financing

Properly understood, debt financing is limited to the issue of straight debt—that is, securities without attached equity participation. Other types of so-called debt are really incentive financing. Debt financing provides a true leverage on earnings in exchange for a guaranteed return to the debt holder, whereas in combination debt/equity securities the leverage may be totally offset by future dilution. Long-term debt financing has become difficult for less than major firms to obtain, as the pace of inflation has seriously eroded the value of fixed-income securites. Some commentators view this situation as a temporary phenomenon and suggest that the widely advertised death of debt financing is highly premature in announcement, although the historical rate structure may be substantially revised. One such change may be an overall cut in the length of the maturity date. Another requirement more frequently being asked for by borrowers is an annual sinking fund, which also reduces the average life of the debt.

A type of debt financing that is now being sold by financially strong companies is debt at a price below par, with a stated coupon below the current market rate. The ultimate in this type of financing is zero coupon debt. This means that all the "interest" and principal will be paid at maturity. Such debt is usually sold with a maturity of ten years or less, particularly if the zero coupon debt is offered. These securities have been sold successfully in both the domestic and Eurodollar markets. Buyers of these securities have tended to accept less than the full current market yield, because the likelihood of the security being refunded is almost nil, and the yield on a part or all of the reinvestment income is locked in.

The usual route to debt financing is through an underwriting firm. The precise terms of a public offering and its cost to the company are usually determined through negotiation between the issuing firm and its underwriter. As an alternative to dealing directly with one or more lead underwriters, a company may decide to sell its securities on a competitive-bid basis. In this case, the company contacts a number of underwriters, which in turn establish separate groups for bidding for the securities. The company sets forth the basis and terms for submitting bids. At an assigned time, established by the company, the bidders submit sealed bids to the company. The general rule is that the bid that will provide the company with the lowest-cost funds is declared the winner and the bonds are sold to that group. However, usually the company reserves the right to reject all bids if the cost of money is determined to be too high by even the best bidder. Public debt offerings are usually limited to issues of $10 million or more and generally require a quality rating of Baa or better. Generally, if a public offering is to be made, a registration statement must be filed with the Securities and Exchange Commission. There are many forms available to a borrower, and the choice of forms often follows the credit worthiness of the company. Private placements of debt are also frequently handled through an underwriter acting as agent, who will place portions of the issue with several insurance companies, pension funds, or financial institutions. Private placements are occasionally handled directly with such investors. Generally, a debenture of somewhat lower quality can be placed privately. The cost of debentures will vary according to their quality; lower-quality issues carry higher interest. The indenture covenants of lower-quality issues may also entail a "cost" to the issuer in terms of reduced financial flexibility in the future.

In addition to debentures, which are unsecured general credit obligations of the issuer, mortgages can be used to raise long-term debt. The usual mortgage provides funds to build or acquire new real estate for the company. Occasionally, however, a firm with poor credit standing may be asked to secure its other long-term borrowings by a pledge of owned property.

Hedging with Interest-Rate Futures

Generally, interest-rate future contracts are used by banks, mortgage banks, pension funds, and others as a way to insulate themselves from fluctuating interest rates. When concerned about a change in rates, either up or down, financial futures can provide a hedge against loss. This can also be used in financing to ensure that the net cost of a security sold at some future date will be approximately the same as the current rate. This can be accomplished by selling interest futures. In the meantime, if rates go up, the higher cost will be offset by the gain realized in closing out the interest-rate future. If rates decline prior to the sale of securities, the lower interest rate will be offset by the loss realized on the interest-rate future.

Equity Financing

There are three basic forms of equity financing: common stock, preferred stock, and convertible preferred stock. As with debt securities, equity issues may be placed privately or sold on the public market. Private placements are usually made to investment funds or wealthy individuals, as banks and insurance companies are generally unable to invest in equities for their own account. These placements are frequently under an investment letter restricting the resale of the stock. Public sale, on the other hand, requires that the stock be registered with the SEC and/or various state securities commissions. Both public and private sales are normally handled through underwriting firms.

Common-stock financing. Additional money to share the risks of the business with the present owners is brought in by common-stock financing. If the new investors buy in at a price per share above the book value per share of the existing shareholders, the present shareholders will have their investment leveraged by the new shareholders, since the investment of the incremental amount will accrue to benefit both. The sale of common stock will expand or reestablish the company's borrowing base, and the common stock may be easier to sell than debt, particularly for new companies with poor credit standing. On the other hand, sale of common stock involves potential dilution of earnings and control, normally carries a higher underwriting cost, and requires a higher return than bonds or preferred stock.

Preferred stock. Commercial and industrial firms, other than utility companies, rarely employ preferred stock in financing because of the volatility of their earnings. Preferred dividends represent an after-tax leverage on the common stock, which amplifies the swings in common-stock earnings to an extent that has proved unacceptable in most cases. The sale of preferred does add to the company's borrowing base, however, and a small amount may prove an acceptable financing route when the capital structure is heavily leveraged with debt yet common-stock prices are temporarily depressed.

Convertible preferred stock. This form of financing has recently become popular in acquisitions. Since the stock is convertible into common yet carries the fixed dividend of a straight preferred, it permits structuring an acquisition deal with dimensions attractive to both buyer and seller. The seller receives a guaranteed minimum return and a chance to participate in the future growth of the business. The buyer may reduce dilution by being able to issue fewer common shares in conversion than would be required in a straight exchange of common stock, because the preferred status of the stock when issued may cause it to be valued at a premium above its conversion value. Other benefits may also accrue to the buyer: for example, lower voting power for the selling shareholders in the combined enterprise, or maintenance of existing dividend policy for the common stock.

Incentive Financing

Many types of incentive financing have been devised, or resurrected from the 1920s, in recent years. Basically, however, all involve the use of debentures, convertible into some form of equity or debentures with warrants to purchase equity attached. The objectives of such financing are to obtain capital that would otherwise be unavailable, to sell common stock at a price above current market, or to lower the cost of debt. The popularity of such securities has been enhanced by the recent rapid pace of inflation, which has seriously eroded the value of fixed-income securities.

To the investor uncertain about the future pace of inflation, incentive securities can be an attractive hedge, providing a guaranteed return in case of a slowdown while permitting participation in inflationary expansion if that occurs. For the issuing company, however, incentive financing can be an expensive source of capital in the long run. For example, the sale of a convertible debenture does result in a lower interest rate. A convertible debenture will generally not be called for redemption unless it is in "the money," that is, unless the market price of the common stock exceeds the conversion price of the debentures. The cost of this discount on the then current market value is likely to vastly outweigh the fractional interest-rate saving over straight debt, even on a present-value basis. In other words, the sale of debt now, followed by sale of common stock in the future, may result in cheaper overall financing. If the debentures do not convert, the company has both debt and an overhang on the common stock, which may impede future financings. On the other hand, if the company's stock is temporarily depressed and debt is unavailable, a convertible debenture can be a useful safety-valve source of needed funds.

Debentures with warrants can also provide an initially lower interest cost. Furthermore, if the debenture can be redeemed for part of the exercise price of the warrants, a large part of the debt may be expunged through an exchange of paper without corporate cash outlay. The warrants, however, may represent a serious future dilution of the common stock and may impede future common-stock financing. Like the convertible, the debenture with warrants is there if needed. To plan for its use as part of a regular financing program, however, may prove costly to the holder of common stock in the long run.

□ *Joseph M. Quigley* (*and Harry A. Lund, the original author of this now substantially revised section*)

CASH MANAGEMENT AND BANK RELATIONS

In the past ten years, corporate executives have learned how to make the asset side of the balance sheet strengthen overall corporate performance. Sophisticated cash-control techniques have enabled financial managers to support expanded sales levels and provide additional income to the company while maintaining fixed or declining cash balances. This has been done without significant expansion of increasingly expensive nonworking assets.

The pages that follow review the factors that have led to the dramatic surge in the use of cash management. They explore the delicate balances that affect bank and corporate relationships. They also provide a review of the cash-management techniques most often used, and place current trends in the field of cash management into perspective.

Objectives of Cash Management

The role and major contribution of cash management have expanded rapidly during the past ten years. In many corporations, formalization of the cash-management function has only recently evolved, often as a result of the senior corporate executive's direct involvement. The significant rise in the cost of capital to support existing operations and expansion policies has stimulated this evolution. And the mushrooming expansion of professional associations in cash management during the past several years testifies to its importance.

The primary objectives of cash-management programs include providing funds for transactional needs; developing and implementing programs to generate investment income; providing for overall corporate liquidity, including credit and noncredit needs; centralizing management of bank relations; monitoring bank compensation; and providing information sources for corporate business needs.

Senior executives have long recognized that the overriding objective of the cash management function is to provide for day-to-day funding needs. The corporation's ability to meet current transactional requirements and obligations as they come due is essential to its economic vitality. To this extent, the daily responsibility of cash management is to match receipts and available cash so that they are at least equal to current corporate funding requirements. Without this basic solvency, the corporation's viability is seriously impaired. It is the cash manager's responsibility to assure that day-to-day transactional needs are being fulfilled.

A central objective of the corporate executive is to reduce the level of nonworking assets required for business operation. This objective can be accomplished by reducing the cash and near-cash asset base within the company, while supporting existing levels of business and providing for increased investment income through sagacious development of investment programs. Accurate daily cash-flow forecasts and the implementation of daily investment programs support this objective. These investment programs include purchase of short-term and intermediate-term securities as well as loan paydowns of corporate debt. In this way, senior executives can reduce the overall cost of capital.

The overall cost of funds relates directly to the number of banking relationships required. Expanded business requirements during the last decade have forced a significant increase in the number of bank relationships. Managing these relationships and assuring fair compensation are other major objectives of the cash-management function.

Corporate liquidity, as defined by senior corporate executives, extends beyond the provision for transactional needs and now includes monitoring of current and future requirements for corporate credit. This means continual review of the current patterns of corporate receipts and disbursements and merging known future requirements in areas of corporate expansion. Corporate executives now require expanded planning that integrates corporate credit needs with those transactional requirements that represent key aspects of cash management.

The cash-management banking relationship also provides business with valuable information sources: credit checks, consolidated information on industry trends, and possible support in mergers and acquisitions, as well as in private placements. The trend toward management by objectives and the increased focus on tangible results underscore the importance of reliable information sources.

The key contribution of cash management to firms of all sizes is the significant reduction in working capital required to conduct business. This is a critical consideration for the small company as well as the large conglomerate. Corporate executives of firms of all sizes have become involved in cash management because of the significant returns made available through the application of a few simple techniques.

Cash-Management Techniques

Corporate leaders in cash management have been primarily responsible for developing and implementing innovative approaches. The interchange of ideas and concepts between corporations and the sharing of ideas among banks and other corporate customers have helped proliferate various techniques of cash management. The degree of applicability that one cash-management technique has in a given firm may vary considerably, depending on the corporation's approach to its business affairs. For example, a corporation that believes in providing autonomy for field operations will be disinclined to centralize the accounts-payable function, in the belief that field operations should be treated as autonomous profit centers. This is one example of how the overall corporate philosophy has a direct impact on cash-management programs.

The cash-management services offered by most banks today fall into five major areas: collection services, concentration-system design, funds mobilization, disbursement services, and audit control services.

Collection services accelerate receipts to the corporation through the use of services such as lockbox, preauthorized checks, and concentration banking. Corporations centralize their funds in a number of cash pools throughout their cash-management systems. Using other concentration techniques such as depository transfer checks, these minor pools of funds are concentrated into major money-center markets to facilitate balance management and investment strategies.

Concentration-system design refers to the analysis of specific collection points within the cash-management system, an analysis that identifies the optimum number of concentration points and the desired blend of regional and local banks required to provide credit and noncredit services to the corporation. Additionally, concentration-system design includes analysis of money-center banks or concentration banks and the role they will play in the cash-management program.

Funds mobilization, which is movement of money to optimize its use, is an integral element of daily cash management. Several methods are available to fulfill the need for same-day movement (Fedwire Service, for example). Others that cost less may take a longer time, such as depository transfer checks.

Disbursement services increase the disbursement control of the cash-management function. Services such as zero-balance accounts and remote or controlled disbursing are examples of techniques that help estimate the dollars of clearances on a daily basis.

Audit control services assist the cash manager in monitoring corporate activity. Examples include the use of account reconcilement services and forecasting and management information services.

Collection Services

The cash manager's primary strategy is to accelerate the receipt and deposit of receipts to reduce the outstanding float in the receivables process. The specific services most often used include lockbox services, preauthorized checks, and preauthorized debits.

Lockbox services. The oldest of the cash-management techniques is lockboxing. The RCA Corporation initiated this service shortly after the close of World War II in cooperation with a major New York bank and a major Chicago bank. The objective of the lockbox service is to provide a mail intercept point to reduce the mail float that occurs when the payer places a receipt or payment into the mail stream. Figure 2-17 is a graphic illustration of a lockbox processing system. The system is initiated when a customer places a payment in the mail. Instead of being directed toward the payee corporation, the payment is directed to a post office box and picked up on a predetermined schedule by the lockbox bank. In this manner, any internal processing cost by the corporation is eliminated and checks received are deposited faster for credit to the corporation's account. An additional benefit of lockboxing is to provide multiple lockbox locations so that nationwide payments may be directed to the nearest lockbox location rather than sent long distances. The location of the post office is very important because it affects the total mail time.

When a check is deposited, the company is sent detailed information such as customer name, account number, and amount paid. On the basis of this information, the corporation will update its accounts-receivable files. Used efficiently, this approach can provide significant additional earnings to the corporation. Periodic analysis of lockbox locations is an important consideration for achieving optimum results.

Because the payer profile changes over time, and because payers will sometimes misdirect mail receipts by sending them to a headquarters location rather than the receiving lockbox bank, periodic analysis may indicate a required shift in various lockbox locations. Banks provide lockbox-analysis services that review lockbox locations and determine actual mail times between given points in the United States. The service compares these to benchmark mail times provided by

Figure 2-17. Overview of lockbox-system processing.

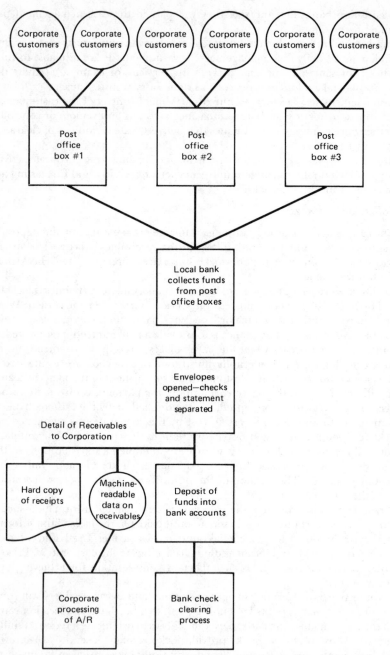

Reprinted by permission from *Contemporary Cash Management: Principles, Practices, Perspectives* by Paul J. Beehler, New York: John Wiley & Sons, 1978.

an independent research corporation, such as Phoenix-Hecht. The mail-time studies are used to determine the optimum locations of lockboxes throughout the country.

Preauthorized checks. Preauthorized checks (PACs) are signatureless demands for payment. PACs accelerate the collection of funds by eliminating mail float and internal processing float to the corporation. Most often, PACs are limited to fixed-payment amounts. Historically, retail customers have been reluctant to make preauthorized-check payments for variable amounts. The most common type of applications using PACs today are monthly and periodic insurance payments. Figure 2-18 illustrates the flow of a typical PAC system.

As shown in this flowchart, a customer signs an authorization agreement with the corporate headquarters and provides the bank with an indemnification agreement that states that the bank may honor signatureless checks presented against the customer's account for a specific company. Following this initiation process, the corporation will generate a file of information containing the drawee bank account number for individuals authorizing withdrawal and the specific account numbers within the banks. Following a periodic billing routine, the corporation will usually provide the bank with a machine-readable file so that the bank may create preauthorized checks on special bank-provided equipment in order to print check MICR line information. Following check production, banks will most often deposit the checks directly for the credit of the corporation's account. The checks then clear the banking system, using the normal Federal Reserve or direct-send clearing programs back to the drawee bank. The corporation

Figure 2-18. Preauthorized-check system.

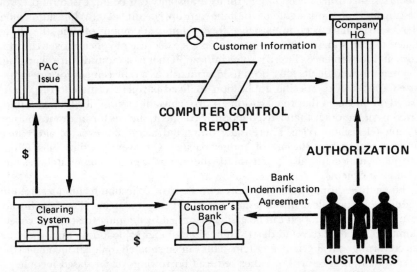

Reprinted by permission from *Contemporary Cash Management: Principles, Practices, Perspectives* by Paul J. Beehler, New York: John Wiley & Sons, 1978.

benefits from using PACs because checks can be printed prior to the date of deposit and also because the bank prints the check. Therefore, mail time is eliminated. Additionally, PACs save time and reduce collection float because the bank directly deposits the checks for clearance. Often, a corporation will offer the payer an incentive for subscribing to this type of service. For example, an insurance company may offer a 5 percent premium reduction to customers using PACs. The company's rationale is that over time fewer late payments will be made and fewer customers lost because of inadvertent lack of payment.

Specific advantages accruing to a company using a PAC system include reduction of collection float through the elimination of mail and in-house processing time; reduced billing costs because customers using a PAC system need not receive a periodic bill; improved cash-flow-forecasting ability; and reduction of follow-up expenses for collection and bad debts.

Preauthorized debits. Preauthorized debiting of accounts (PAD) is a data processing system in which a customer account can be automatically charged for funds due, without the generation of a paper-based document such as a check. Preauthorized debit items are sometimes referred to as paperless or checkless items. The most common use for preauthorized payments has traditionally been in a credit environment for payroll deposits. However, there seems to be a growing trend toward other applications.

The objective is to provide an automatic and recurring payment mechanism without the generation of physical documents. The individual's authorization procedure is essentially the same as for preauthorized checks. Preauthorized checks can be viewed as an evolutionary bridge between a paper-based preauthorization system and an electronic preauthorization system. For preauthorized debit systems using a value date, funds availability can be increased by preprocessing and warehousing items until the appropriate due date. While automated debit entries have been in existence for a significant amount of time, they have failed to gain widespread customer acceptance because of concern over control, cost, and convenience. There is some indication that basic attitudes are changing.

Preauthorized debits have been used primarily as a replacement for preauthorized checks, with specific application to fixed-payment transactions. This is based on the belief that retail customers are reluctant to subscribe to a preauthorized payment other than a fixed monthly payment, such as for insurance bills or a cable-television service. There is a growing indication, however, of alternative approaches, such as the use of budget payments to average utility bills. Given adequate notice (usually seven days), the system can accommodate variable-amount payments.

These three primary services represent the basic collection techniques used to reduce collection float in domestic cash-management systems. The benefits accruing to the corporation can be easily quantified by defining the current collection level per float day and determining the number of float days that would be saved through an alternative system. This can be equated to dollar income to the corporation, in the form of either reduced borrowings or increased income investments.

Mobilizing Funds

The evaluation of collection patterns is an important consideration. This evaluation determines how funds should be physically moved to concentration points (regional concentration banks or corporate lead banks) in order to use the funds for investment or loan paydown. The major techniques for funds movement include wire transfers and depository transfer checks.

Wire transfer service. The purpose of wire transfer services is to move and make available funds on the same day to a receiving party. The primary advantage of using wire transfer services is that funds may be moved from one location to another and made available to the company in the concentration location on the same day for investment or paydown of loans. The use of wire transfer services has increased dramatically in the past several years. For example, one West Coast bank turns over its entire asset base every three days, as measured by the dollar volume of wire transfers effected through its wire transfer department.

The major reasons for increased utilization include (1) increased value of funds and decreased breakeven points for wire transfer services, (2) improved management of bank target balances, and (3) increased need to cover transactional requirements.

Because of high interest rates for borrowing of funds and as return on investment of funds, corporate cash managers have been evaluating wire transfers in terms of economic breakeven points, which have lowered dramatically over the past several years. For example, recently a Midwestern company evaluating its cash-management program determined that one day's use of available funds could be gained by transferring funds from local depositories (where a high percentage of cash and immediately available items were deposited) to the concentration bank for immediate investment and loan paydown. Given the one-day improvement in availability, a cost of $5 per wire for the transferred amounts, and an interest rate of approximately 9.5 percent, the company determined that the breakeven point for transferring funds was approximately $19,000. Using this rationale, many companies are evaluating their potential use of wire transfer services. Over the last several years, wire transfer services offered by banks have grown more than 30 percent per year.

Establishing and maintaining target balances to cover credit and noncredit services have become an important consideration in the cash-management programs developed. Wire transfers help cash managers keep minimum excess balances at local depository banks or regional concentration loctions.

Transactional needs of doing business often require the movement of funds regardless of the amount involved. Noneconomic consideration such as due dates and prepayment terms may dictate use of wire transfer capabilities regardless of breakeven amounts.

This transactional need was underscored for many California savings and loan associations during 1978. Offering a new telephone transfer service required an immediate or same-day transfer promise to their customer base, resulting in an increased use of wire transfer services. The average amount of the transfers made was between $50 and $250, dramatically lower than the breakeven point calculated previously. Wire services were initially developed to handle high-dollar/low-volume transfers, but the increasingly diversified use of wire transfer services is changing the original development philosophy.

Essentially, two wire transfer systems are used to move funds: the Federal Reserve Wire Transfer System and the BankWire Transfer System.

The Federal Reserve offers its wire transfer system to banks for transfers that exceed a specified dollar amount. Originally, the Federal Reserve made the transfer system available to improve the efficiency of the payment system within the United States. Other facilities existed for communication purposes, and wire transfers were piggybacked upon the existing system for a very low marginal cost. The Federal Reserve has not charged explicitly for this service.* This position is likely to change as the Federal Reserve feels the impact of unbundling its service package. Pricing for individual services will produce a more favorable competitive position for the BankWire system. The settlement procedure using a Federal Reserve wire system is that the banks sending the wire and receiving the wire settle their accounts by an actual transfer of funds, using Federal Reserve accounts at the close of business each day.

The BankWire system is a privately owned wire communication system developed and implemented by participating banks. Historically, the BankWire system has charged for its services and been at a competitive disadvantage. Banks use the BankWire system because it efficiently links the banks (approximately 250) into a network and allows them flexibility for settlement through the use of correspondent accounts. The basic difference between the BankWire and Federal Reserve wire systems is the settlement procedures. The Federal Reserve Wire Transfer System results in the same-day settlement in Federal Reserve accounts, which is equivalent to the actual movement of funds between banks. Under the BankWire system, transfers are made by debits and credits to correspondent bank accounts, with appropriate credit being given to the receiving party.

Regardless of the type of service used, the net result to the cash manager is same-day availability of funds at the receiving location.

Depository transfer checks. The most commonly used alternative to wire transfer services is the depository transfer check (DTC). Depository transfer checks are unsigned checks drawn against the bank of deposit with the purpose of concentrating funds. A primary advantage over wire transfers is that they are significantly less expensive, costing in the neighborhood of 17¢ to 30¢ per check produced. Most often, depository-transfer-check systems are developed in concert with an automated deposit-reporting service. The purpose of the depository transfer check is to match the collection time of the depository check with the collection time of local items deposited at local deposit banks. Figure 2-19 illustrates the flow of information in a typical depository-transfer-check system. The flow of information originates at the location of a company making a periodic deposit to the local deposit bank. At the time of deposit, the location manager

---

* Explicit pricing for wire transfers by the Federal Reserve is estimated at approximately $3 per wire.

Figure 2-19. Typical concentration-network processing using depository transfer checks.

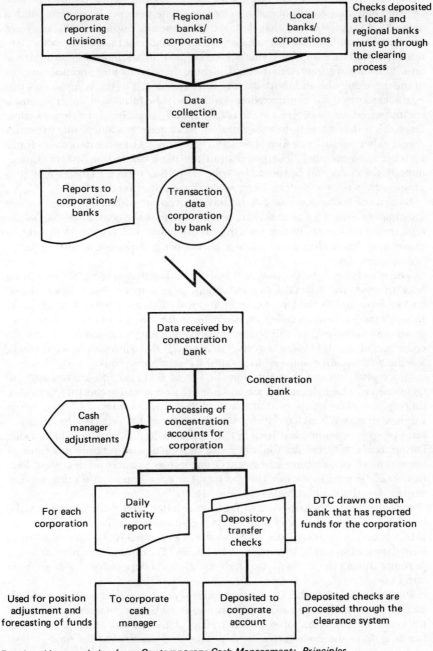

Reprinted by permission from *Contemporary Cash Management: Principles, Practices, Perspectives* by Paul J. Beehler, New York: John Wiley & Sons, 1978.

calls a toll-free number and reports the dollar amount deposited for that day. Deposits generally consist of cash and local check items drawn by residents of that area. At close of business that day, a transmission of information takes place within the communication service (for example, National Data Corporation, Automatic Data Processing, or General Electric) used to assemble deposit information. The data transmitted to the bank include the location identification number of the reporting unit and the dollar amount deposited. The receiving bank—that is, the bank used for concentration—will match the location number against a computerized file to determine the transit routing number of the deposit bank. Once this is determined, the concentration bank generates a depository transfer check, either manually or with automated equipment. Once the depository transfer check is generated, it is placed into the bank's collection stream. Consequently, the check may be routed for collection either through a direct-send program or through the Federal Reserve check collection system.

By close of business on the deposit day, a corporate cash manager may access information through a time-sharing terminal against the centralized files of the data collection center. In this way, the cash manager can receive an update on dollar amounts of depository transfer checks being deposited to his company's account that day.

The idea behind the depository transfer check is that as the DTC is clearing back through the normal check collection process to the local deposit bank, checks deposited by the local manager also will be clearing the collection system through the local bank's collection mechanism. Because there is a two-day maximum availability on checks deposited, most cash managers would expect that the collection of the DTC would very closely match the collection of local funds, leaving a minimum residue of funds at the local deposit bank.

Major problems can arise through the use of DTCs when local deposits are comprised of a high degree of cash and immediately available check deposits. Additionally, if checks deposited at the local level require a two-day clearance of funds by the local bank, and if the depository transfer check, because of direct-send programs, would clear back to the local bank in only one day, the drawing corporation could find itself in a negative collective balance position because of the mismatch of collection schedules. Often, excess balances on deposit at local banks can be used to compensate the local bank for deposit and other services provided to the local business representative.

An extension of the paper-based DTC is the automated clearing house (ACH) depository transfer check. This new service guarantees one-day availability on all DTCs processed through the ACH service. Consequently, balance buildup at local depositories can be minimized. The ACH/DTC application will grow in importance during the 1980s as float reduction at local depositories becomes more important.

Depository transfer checks or wire transfer services need not be used on a daily basis. The corporate cash manager can use a cost/benefit analysis to determine the optimum configuration for mobilization of these funds. For example, depending upon the dollar amounts deposited and the number of days of float saved, it may be more economical to use wire transfer services twice per week than to use daily depository transfer checks.

Disbursement Techniques

Acceleration of cash collections and the design of efficient concentration systems are two aspects in the architecture of a cash-management program. Also, disbursement control techniques can optimize disbursement float and therefore reduce the overall asset base required for the company to perform day-to-day business.

The objective of disbursement control techniques is to extend the clearing time or the settlement time of checks issued by the company in payment for obligations. Of primary importance to the effective development of disbursement control techniques is the corporate philosophy regarding the centralization of payments. Centralization of payables enables the cash manager to centrally control disbursements made and to track their clearances accurately. Centralization also allows a cash manager to take the optimum time, from an economic viewpoint, in settlement of obligations. This can be accomplished by evaluating purchasing terms or industry-established standards, and disbursing only as required to optimize the financial benefit to the company. Early disbursements can be as wasteful and uneconomical for a company as incurring late-payment charges for missed discount deadlines. For example, by paying an invoice amount of $25,000 in 15 days, rather than taking the full 60 days, the company loses potential investment income of approximately $184.93, assuming the funds can be invested at approximately 9 percent. Conversely, the delayed payments can also be costly because of discounts lost. An example of this occurs if a company buys goods on terms of 1/10 net 30, but does not pay within the stated discount period. By delaying payment beyond the ten-day discount period, the company does in effect pay 18 percent per annum for funds used for the additional 20 days. Through centralized accounts-payable files, the corporation can better track and implement the corporate philosophy. The centralization of payables has to be weighed against the company's desire to provide autonomy to geographically located units and to operate them on a profit-center basis. Some techniques may establish an acceptable degree of autonomy for field operating units and of centralization for the cash-management department. Specific disbursement services most often used in cash-management programs include zero-balance accounts, payable-through drafts, and controlled disbursements.

Zero-balance accounts. Zero-balance accounts (ZBAs) are bank-established disbursement accounts that contain no imprest or dollar balances. Checks may be written against these accounts and presented for payment to the bank on the understanding (1) that the bank will automatically transfer sufficient dollars to cover daily payments from a funding account, or (2) the bank will be funded in immediately available funds by the corporation, using a wire transfer. Figure 2-20 is an overview of zero-balance-account services. The purpose of the service is to allow autonomy of various corporate locations to disburse checks to local suppliers for purchases while maintaining cash-management control over clearances of funds.

Figure 2-20. Zero-balance disbursement flow.

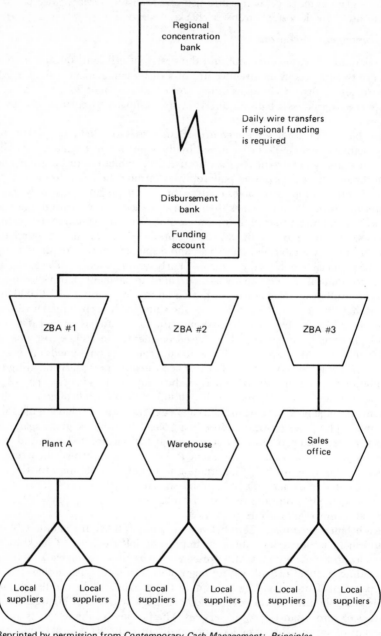

Zero-balance accounts require attention from a bank's viewpoint because of the potential one-day delay in the collection of funds at some banks, if dollar amounts presented are not funded on the same day. Most often, zero-balance accounts are funded through wire transfer by notifying the company of dollar amounts required on a given day. This approach is used extensively for smaller country banks that receive only one cash letter daily from the Federal Reserve, so that the bank may notify the company before close of business of the total dollar amounts required for clearance that day. For larger banks, where more than one cash letter is received per day, a system of debiting a funding account is more common, and a true collected balance overdraft position will not occur. Some major banks now offer same-day disbursement clearance information if accounts used allow identification to a separate branch or use a separate bank transit routing number established for that purpose. Zero-balance accounts are useful in cash-management programs because cash balances can be reduced to levels required to cover all daily transactions. Typically, small or nonexistent imprest balances are required for this service. Furthermore, banks may be paid in either fees or compensating balances. Major benefits derived from the zero-balance accounting include (1) centralized cash-management control over disbursement of funds; (2) decentralized autonomy of disbursements to the field; (3) reduced or eliminated imprest accounts and attending balances at local disbursing banks; and (4) possible extension of disbursement float through the issuance of disbursements by local plant or warehouse units located in remote country areas, thereby increasing the available cash pool for investment.

Cash managers also benefit from ZBAs because of the reduced number of accounts they need to control and monitor while still maintaining field autonomy.

Payable-through drafts. A payable-through draft (PTD) is a promise to pay issued by the corporation or the issuer of the draft. Drafts differ from checks in that they are drawn not against the bank but on the issuer, that is, the company, and the promise to pay is issued by the company. The bank acts only as an agent in the collection of the draft and the clearing and presentment of the drafts for final payment to the company. PTDs were developed, many years ago, to avoid a government tax on use of checks. Since then, their use has diminished greatly. They are often treated like checks by the banking system. To the cash manager, the benefit of using PTDs is that 24 hours are provided to refuse payment of the draft from the time it is received. Because of the volume of PTDs presented each day to the corporate cash manager, it is often impractical to physically examine each draft prior to payment. As a result, PTDs are most often treated exactly as checks by the bank and the company, although the bank's legal obligation is significantly different. Companies using PTDs are those which need to provide immediate disbursement control to many field agents and for which prior reporting of dollar amounts drawn is impractical.

For example, insurance adjusters often make disbursements with PTDs directly to recipients in the field. While this practice is widespread, often the recipient does not realize that the banks take no responsibility for the final payment of the draft. Consequently, the banks will maintain no stop-payment files or special instruction records. To cover the bank for disbursement float and account service, companies are often required to maintain an average day's clearances on balance with the bank as collected funds. Should the bank not require this, it will find, upon examination, that it is in effect making a one-day loan to the company for the dollar amount of PTDs presented.

Remote- and controlled-disbursement techniques. The use of remote disbursement has surged during the last five years, primarily because of the increased value of funds. The objective of remote disbursing is to lengthen the time for a check to clear the banking system and be presented to the drawee bank for settlement. The longer it takes a check to clear from the time it is written and mailed to the time it is finally delivered for presentment, the greater the dollar days of float available to the cash manager. These disbursement dollars, which are contingent liabilities, can then be used for investment or to reduce the working-capital base of the corporation. Although the Federal Reserve has tried to quantify the dollars of remote-disbursement float, it has been unable to do so to date. However, the dollar amount is significant enough to affect the overall money supply within the country. There are two approaches to remote disbursement: crisscross disbursement patterns and remote country disbursing.

Crisscross patterns of remote disbursing occur when a company establishes a disbursement policy in which checks written for payment of services on one location in the United States are drawn against a bank that is physically located on the opposite side of the country. For example, a manufacturing firm could open checking accounts on a major San Francisco bank and a major New York bank. For a customer settling accounts in New York, it would be the company's policy to issue checks drawn against the San Francisco bank. Similarly, for settlements made in California, checks would be drawn against the New York bank. The check deposited by a retail customer in New York, drawn against a California bank, would typically have a hold put against the account on use of the funds for approximately ten business days. The rationale is that the bank needs to ensure that the check will be presented to the California bank and that it will not result in uncollected funds and become a returned item. Depending upon the number of banks involved, the New York bank might feel that ten business days is a reasonable time to assure that the item has been collected. As a result, the depositor does not have use of his funds for ten business days.

As described earlier, the maximum number of days for presentment in the clearing system is two days using the Federal Reserve clearing system. Returned items, however, must be returned within 48 hours. If more than one bank is involved in the return process, each bank in the stream of returned items has 48 hours within which to return the item. For corporations depositing checks in New York, drawn against California locations, most banks (because of the deposit relationship) will honor the deposit and make funds available to the company within their stipulated availability schedule. Any returned items would routinely be handled and automatically debited back to the corporation's account. Most banks are reluctant to treat retail customers in the same manner because of the proclivity of retail customers to draw down balances or their ability to change banks in a short period of time. Although checks deposited through the Federal

Reserve are given two-day funds availability, it may actually take the Federal Reserve more than two days to collect the checks.

Disbursing checks from remotely located country banks is often referred to as true remote disbursing. The objective of this practice is to increase information on daily presentments and to generate a significant amount of Federal Reserve float. Because remotely located banks receive only one check presentment per day from the Federal Reserve for check clearance, and because the airline schedules and transportation schedules are not efficient for these locations, it often takes the Federal Reserve longer than its committed two-day time to actually collect the checks. Take, for example, a company issuing a check drawn on a distant point, say, a North Carolina bank from San Francisco, and mailing it to a recipient in Chicago. The company may find that it has mail time as a significant factor in its float, in addition to the amount of time it takes the check to clear back to North Carolina: four or five days instead of the two days that the Federal Reserve commits to make those funds good to the recipient in Chicago. Additionally, when remote locations are used for disbursement, because only one cash letter is received daily, these banks often can total debits for the corporation's account that night and, before close of business, contact the company so that these amounts may be funded daily through a wire transfer. Using a zero-balance-account remote-disbursement facility, many corporations are able to disburse funds against the bank without maintaining any collected balances and to pay with fees for services rendered. Sites used in remote disbursing include North Carolina, Montana, and areas within Texas, to name a few.

The Federal Reserve Board has recently become very concerned with the impact of remote disbursing on the recipient, on the money supply, and on the financial viability of the banks involved. The Federal Reserve is increasing pressure against banks involved in this practice. This represents an area of increasing controversy in the cash-management community.

Controlled disbursement services differ from remote disbursement in that their primary objective and intent is to offer early-morning same-day reporting on disbursement dollars clearing the corporation's account that day. This permits significantly improved daily cash management. Controlled disbursement services are offered by a number of large money-center banks, making it unnecessary to use a remote country bank to obtain same-day clearance information.

Many firms indicate that the primary benefit in using disbursement services is the control aspect of management where funding of daily clearances is possible on a same-day basis from the corporate cash pool. More banks are now offering controlled disbursement services that satisfy the control needs of cash managers without increasing Federal Reserve float. Such services expand the banks' disbursement business and at the same time lessen the chance of restrictions being mandated by the Federal Reserve Board because of expanded use of remote locations.

Audit Control Techniques

Cash managers are placing greater emphasis on audit control techniques as a criterion for bank selection. These services have assumed greater importance for

controlling cash-management expenses and increasing the level of services provided by the cash-management area. The specific services most often evaluated
include cash-management information services, account reconcilement services,
data transmission services, and business services.

Cash-management information services. Corporations and banks have become increasingly involved and interested in cash-management information services. From the bank's perspective, the objective of designing and implementing
these services is to attract and hold a corporation to the concentration or lead
banking relationship by providing essential management information consolidated on a nationwide basis. From the corporation's perspective, the use of these
services is increasing as an alternative to in-house systems. They are often economically justified because of deposit-reporting services and easier access to wire
transfer services.

Figure 2-21 illustrates the services included in cash-management information
services offered by banks today. These fall into three generic categories: (1) deposit-reporting services, (2) balance-reporting services, and (3) investment and
control services. These automated services are either developed by banks specifically for their customer base or subscribed to by banks and modified in response
to market needs, and then offered to their customer base. Third-party time-sharing vendors are most often used to provide these services. Specific companies involved in this area include Automated Data Processing, National Data Corporation, General Electric, and Interactive Data Corporation. Through the use of
established nationwide networks, cash-management information services are offered at lower cost per item than possible if the corporation were to develop its
own service. For this reason, they are becoming increasingly competitive and
available in the corporate marketplace and are being used for a greater variety of
applications.

Within deposit-reporting services, there is also an element of management-in-
formation reporting that allows the corporation to report deposits made at local
locations as described under depository transfer checks as well as to report other
information, such as gallons of gasoline pumped, units of inventory sold in a
given day, or other management information that can be used in inventory replenishment programs. Balance-reporting services link the bank and the corporation in order to provide the corporation with daily listings of the collected
and available balances. Under this direct bank communication link, the bank may
also provide detailed debit and credit information on specific accounts. An extension of this service is a multibank balance-reporting application. This enables a
number of the corporation's banks to report daily the same information, which
can be consolidated and manipulated according to the corporation's requirements to produce reports available in the corporate treasurer's office through a
time-sharing terminal.

The last major category is investment and advisory services. These services take
on several forms and provide investment information, including current rate
structure, investment alternatives, and forecasting modules for collection and
disbursements. The applications within this area are widespread and vary significantly by bank. Past demand for these additional services has been limited, be-

Figure 2-21. Cash-management information services.

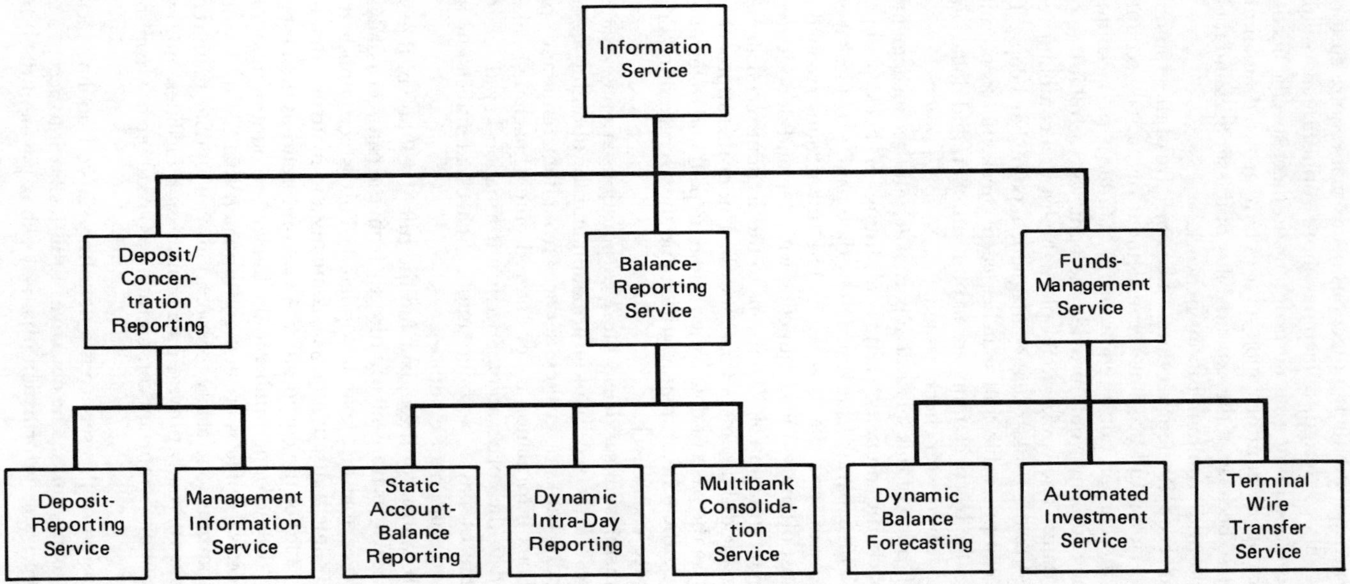

cause each corporation has indigenous needs that require customized programming and service design. Sometimes more sophisticated companies will have already developed time-sharing programs to meet specific needs in this area.

Cash-management information services have grown dramatically and will continue to do so because of the expandability of the services and their ability to provide a nationwide communications network.

Account reconcilement services.   The objective of these automated services is to provide either full account reconcilement or partial account reconcilement based on the corporation's requirements. Under a full account reconcilement service, the company would provide the bank with a full listing of checks issued and their dates. The banks would place the list in a computerized file. Data are transmitted to the bank by either magnetic tape or hard copy. The bank maintains this computer file and matches each check the corporation has written against this file by check number, account number, and dollar amount to match up checks cleared with checks issued.

A modification of this service is a partial account reconcilement service. Under this approach, the company receives only listings of checks paid periodically from the bank. This separate listing, sorted by date paid, provides an easy method for the company to reconcile its account. The full account reconcilement service is the one most often used in conjunction with demand deposit accounts for check disbursement and control. Extensions to the account reconcilement service now include a static disbursement float module. Under this approach, banks can profile checks on the basis of date issued and date paid and determine, by dollar size of the check, the time of month written and the average number of days of float generated for each check.

Data transmission services.   More corporations are now using data transmission services for the receipt of information and for updating accounts-receivable files. Basically, banks offer these services from their remittance-processing area, where lockbox information is key-entered onto a machine-readable device and transmitted to the corporation. Specific information keyed for transmission includes name of payer, account number, check identification number, dollar amount paid, and invoice number.

Through capture of these data and the full MICR line of the check, the company can receive its transmission directly from the bank on a daily basis so that its accounts-receivable files may be updated. This is accomplished by taking the check MICR line transmitted to the company and matching that number against a computer file for the corporation. A cross-reference is then established linking the transit ABA account number to the internal account number of the payer. An accounts-receivable file is created and updated that night. Through the use of this data transmission facility, corporations can update their receivables daily. Not all banks currently provide data transmission facilities. However, this area is becoming a more important consideration as credit terms are more closely monitored.

An extension of this service is a data transmission pooling facility now being offered by many banks. The objective of this facility is to accept a transmission of accounts-receivable information (that is, lockbox payment data) from a number of different banks acting as collection points within the corporate cash-management system. This facility consolidates the accounts-receivable information onto one data transmission file and sends that directly to the corporation on a daily basis. This data transmission pooling service is becoming more important as corporations limit their bank interfaces.

Business services. Cash managers sometimes evaluate the availability of business services offered by the bank. These business services represent a service bureau type of data processing facility, often offered at economical rates. This usually happens because the bank takes a marginal cost for data processing facilities and can provide programs for fixed business services. These services tend to appeal more to companies in the $5 million to $10 million annual-sales range than to the larger corporations. Often, corporations have indigenous processing requirements that can be satisfied only by the development and implementation of in-house systems. For firms with more standardized requirements, the services offered by banks include payroll services, accounts-receivable services, accounts-payable services, and inventory services.

For companies without special considerations, the standardized package is offered with options available that may meet the company's processing requirements and reduce internal processing costs. The payment for these services will be managed out of the cash-management area, because most often, compensating balances are used for payment of these kinds of services. The degree of sophistication offered by the service would become a selection criterion. Because of the reduced cost of hardware through mini- and microcomputers, many businesses are developing their own business-services package. Consequently, use of purchased business services will diminish over time.

Careful evaluation and development of the cash-management program and clear establishment of an overall philosophy of a concentration system are important. Specific evaluation of cash-management techniques and services offered by various banks is an essential step in bank selection, because quality of service and options offered by banks vary significantly.

Bank Selection Criteria

The ability of the bank to provide required services and its philosophy regarding cash management have a major impact on the corporation's ability to manage its cash. For any large corporation, the total number of banks used will vary significantly, depending upon the corporate philosophy of centralization versus decentralization. Regardless of the number of banks used, most corporations find that a few banks play key roles in cash-management programs.

Often, a large number of banks will be used because of numerous depositing locations within a company. For example, McDonald's chain of nationwide stores requires many local banks to receive and process receipts. Generally, in this type of system, a few large banks concentrate the funds in regional locations. The services required at the money-center bank generally differ significantly from those needed at the local deposit bank. Corporate activity is most often centralized in money-center banks rather than local deposit banks. Consequently, the ability of the money-center bank to provide not only cash-management service but also credit facilities assumes major importance.

Before completion of a bank selection program, the corporation must evaluate its internal financial requirements. This evaluation includes not only the credit and noncredit domestic business activity but also identification of international services that may be needed to conduct business, such as currency trading and international wire transfers. Internal evaluations and the development of criteria for bank evaluation are critical if an ongoing and profitable bank relationship is to develop. The major factors to be considered in this evaluation process include:

- Essential financial stability of the bank.
- Credit facilities available from the bank. These should be defined in terms of both the size of the line of credit that the bank can legally make available to the corporation and the bank's attitude toward the corporation and its marketplace.
- The bank's posture regarding credit-service and non-credit-service pricing.
- Quality of the bank's correspondent banking networks, both domestic and international.
- The bank's philosophy regarding cash-management programs, and its proven ability to develop and improve services key to the corporation and its cash-management program.
- Specific bank service evaluation in relation to corporate operations and its cash-management program.
- Personal contacts and references provided by the bank.   □ *Paul J. Beehler*

ACCOUNTS RECEIVABLE: CREDIT COLLECTIONS

The importance of the mercantile credit manager has increased substantially in recent years. This trend has been especially evident since the late 1970s, when the cost of funds rose into double-digit proportions on a continuing basis, thus increasing dramatically the cost of a company's investment in receivables. This increased importance of proper receivables management has, in turn, led to greater top-management involvement in the credit function. The fact is that senior managers of many companies now recognize that a credit department, although operating within a specialized area, does not need to be considered simply nonproductive overhead. A competent and professional credit department should now be viewed as being able to contribute, often substantially, to overall company profits.

Current Receivables Trends

From the mid-1950s through the early 1970s, trade receivables increased more sharply than sales for manufacturers and wholesalers. This rise was reflected in both increased days sales outstanding and a higher proportion of total corporate assets being tied up in slow-turning receivables. Although the level of receivables both as a percentage of assets and as related to sales has slowed down recently, their absolute level has continued to rise.

This most recent increase in receivables has been caused by the recent severe slowing in economic growth, which has increased competition in the business environment and forced many suppliers to give in to customer requests for special or deferred payment terms. Adding to the strain arising from a stagnating economy have been the effects of record-high interest rates. These rates have deterred many companies from borrowing through normal commercial financial institutions, because of either the high cost of the funds or their occasional unavailability.

Many credit professionals view the rate of business bankruptcies as also mirroring the higher level and deteriorating quality of outstanding mercantile trade receivables. In this respect, the amount of business bankruptcy filings has continued to escalate both in the number of failures and in total dollar liabilities of companies entering into bankruptcy proceedings. This trend has become especially pronounced since enactment of the Bankruptcy Reform Act of 1978, which went into effect in the fall of 1979. This trend toward greater debtor use of court protection is documented by the fact that in 1980 corporate bankruptcies increased 55 percent over 1979.

Function of the Credit Manager

The credit manager's responsibility rests solely in the cultivation and control of the marginal account, which—depending upon his company's policies—may vary from 5 percent of total sales to 50 percent or more. "Marginals" can be defined as "accounts deficient in character, capacity, or capital—or all three." They are frequently slow in payment of obligations and universally represent a higher-than-average degree of risk.

Increasingly, credit is being recognized as an adjunct of sales; it has cast off the negative image of "the watchdog of the treasury." An unwarranted acceptance of all customer orders without restriction will lead to excessive bad-debt losses; an unduly harsh selective process will result in loss of sales. A dilatory collection follow-up system will result in ballooning receivables; stern and unrelenting payment pressure on customers will negate sales efforts. Today's credit manager must be imaginative and creative in striking the proper balance in these areas to achieve maximum profit return for his company consistent with its own financial ability to nurture the marginal client.

Value of Information

Errors in credit decisions, both positive and negative, more often result from lack of ingenuity in obtaining data than from faulty interpretation of data. For virtually every unresolved question there is a source that can provide the answer, and the credit manager's expertise should include instinctive knowledge of where to turn for each fact, as well as the ability to probe every source adroitly until the full story unfolds. Information should not be developed merely for its own sake, nor should investigative expense be incurred for superfluous facts. No major decision, however, need be made in a void in today's information explosion.

Aside from nominal orders, on which published ratings will suffice, or cases in which costs for the development of even minimum data are prohibitive, the normal starting point in the evaluation of customer credit acceptability is the review of a Dun & Bradstreet report. In many cases, adequate material to obtain the proper conclusion will appear in the report, and the credit manager need go no further. Should doubt persist, however, many avenues remain to be explored, including banks, credit interchange (a service of the National Association of Credit Management), specialized industry reporting services (typified by the *Blue Book* or *Red Book* ratings, reports for packers and shippers of perishable fruits and vegetables, and the United Beverage Bureau, which covers carbonated-beverage bottlers), references, industry credit group discussions (both local and national), salespeople's comments, personal visits to the customer's plant, and financial statements submitted directly.

Evaluation of Risk and Credit Control

Where reliable financial statements are available, the credit manager, in making a credit decision, should give preponderant weight to the story those statements disclose. Some managers rely on cash-flow analysis or various budgets and projections. Others place their faith in the interpretation of key financial ratios and their trends in determining the financial stability of their marginal accounts. If problems exist, they will inevitably result from distortion in one or more of the six ratios that measure profit on sales, inventory turnover, the collection rate of receivables, the investment in fixed assets relative to net worth, the existence of either overtrading or undertrading on invested capital, or the unwarranted diversion of funds into such areas as financial support of a subsidiary or loans to officers. Should any account stray too far from industry average in these key factors, the effect will be manifest in working-capital deficiency or a burdensome debt structure. The credit manager capable of interpreting a customer's financial statements properly will have little difficulty in predicting the payment pattern and the degree of overall risk present.

Where financial data are unattainable, the principal elements of customer appraisal are—in order of importance—the payment record, any evident trend, bank comment defining balances, loan experience and collateral requirements, the age of the business and its growth potential, the experience and background of the principals, and personal appraisals of salespeople or others acquainted with the company.

Making the Credit Decision

Much effort has been spent in recent years trying to identify and measure the most important factors, both financial and nonfinancial, that force classification of an account as being marginal as far as credit goes. The objective has been to assign correct weights to these factors so that automatic credit clearances or denials can be given to all orders. Considerable progress has been made in this field, and many corporations have now succeeded in labeling their accounts and classifying them by degree of risk, thus enabling the majority of orders to be approved automatically. The fact remains, however, that no universal formula has been derived to totally automate the credit-granting function. Determining proper amounts of credit to be extended to marginal accounts remains an art in which considerable judgment and subjective decision making are still needed.

Risk Reduction and Payment Enforcement

When it is determined that a purchaser represents an unacceptably high credit risk, it is common to request that shipments be made on a COD or CWO basis. The use of sight draft shipments, whereby payment is received prior to release of merchandise held by a third party, is another popular approach. Sometimes, however, in a competitive market such stringent approaches are not feasible, and the imaginative credit manager must find other ways to work out credit arrangements for these marginal potential customers. Tools such as enforceable personal guarantees from responsible guarantors, subordination of other indebtedness to the creditor's claim, obtaining a security interest in specific assets of the potential customer, or the use of irrevocable standby bank letters of credit may be used to maximize sales while minimizing exposure to bad debts.

Controls

Countless systems can be devised to control dollar exposure levels for individual accounts. As mentioned previously, a corporation that is successful in categorizing its customers according to risk categories will be able to more easily devise appropriate credit control techniques. Regardless of the type of procedure initiated, the goal of any control system should be to permit the practice of credit management by exception, whereby a majority of orders are entered with a minimum of clerical effort and the efforts of the professional credit manager are concentrated on minimizing true high-risk exposures.

Making Marginal Accounts More Profitable

An approach that has gained considerable momentum over the past several years is to add a service charge on past-due invoices. Typically, this is imposed on an account that pays beyond standard selling terms; the amount of the service charge customarily runs from 1 percent to 1.5 percent per month on past-due balances. A common method for determining the amount of a service charge is to base the charge on the current prime interest rate. Regardless of what formula is used to invoke a service charge, it has become increasingly important in recent years to make sure that the sometimes stringent usury statutes of various states are not violated and do not conflict with a firm's service-charge policies. The service charge is not usually intended to be a revenue producer in itself but is used as a tool to reduce days sales outstanding by discouraging customer delinquency.

Another effective means to discourage customer delinquency is for the credit manager to provide financial and other management counsel to the customer to aid the account in surmounting any temporary difficulties. Efforts by the credit manager to develop personal rapport with the customer may also provide opportunities to capitalize on goodwill and to educate the client regarding the seller's payment expectancy. Finally, proper enforcement of selling terms, including cash discount charge-backs, can also be vital in improving receivables turnover, thus building company profitability.

Collection Procedures

The key to successful collections is the information developed on the account at the time the credit decision was made. Knowing the account—the degree of risk present, its payment patterns, even the personality quirks of the principals— will dictate the approach best suited to bring results. Two added essentials for collection success are (1) the timeliness as well as regularity of follow-up and (2) the negotiating skills of the credit manager in getting fast results yet still keeping the customer "working on the same side of the street." Erratic, widely spaced contact will encourage customer disregard for terms and abuse of them. Alienation of the account will lead to resistance, argument, and probably loss of sales or loss of the balance owed.

The medium used will vary according to the evaluation of the account. Options include letters, phone calls, statements, duplicate invoices, telegrams, and salespeople's efforts, as well as personal visits by the credit manager. Many credit managers prefer to be accompanied by members of their sales departments, if at all possible, when making customer visits, since this builds a better linkage with the sales function.

Extreme Collection Measures and Insolvency

If the credit manager has exhausted all practical collection avenues open to him without satisfactory results, or if he has reason to suspect impending financial failure, he should waste no further time in placing his claim for immediate handling with attorneys or a responsible private collection agency. Another option is to consider placing the account with an adjustment bureau of his local credit association. Subsequent payments, other than those made within the customary free-demand period offered by many commercial collection agencies, will be subject to fees based on a percentage of the account eventually collected.

Involvement in Bankruptcy Proceedings

The high rate of business failures caused by recent high interest rates, coupled with the passage of the Bankruptcy Reform Act of 1978, has had substantial ramifications for all firms extending mercantile credit. The new bankruptcy code contains many fundamental changes in areas important to the credit manager, such as creditors' rights, exemptions, and reorganizations. It has also made important changes within the area of preference payments, which can have the effect of ballooning credit exposure significantly once a bankruptcy action commences.

In short, it is now more necessary than ever for the professional credit manager to fully understand many of the areas of the new bankruptcy code and their potential implications on receivables in order to minimize both bad-debt expense and frozen accounts.

Reporting Results

As a rule, a monthly summary of receivables statistics is sent to top management. This summary shows each division's or plant's individual performance and the aggregate attainment for the company. Totals and percentages are refined to portray special-terms exposures, past-due balances according to age (30, 60, 90, or more days delinquent), and days sales outstanding. Comparative figures for the preceding month and the same month for the previous two years, along with a short explanatory comment from the credit manager, provide background material for detection of trends and for decision making.

Planning Receivables Collections

Tight money, with its increasingly high interest rates, has made management aware of the importance of planning cash requirements in advance. Cash management (or cash planning) has become a vital operation for companies of all sizes, from the largest corporations with their treasurers and money managers to the small family-owned businesses. Since accounts receivable represent a significant asset that can be converted into cash relatively easily, their timely collection is usually an integral part of any cash-management program. The continuing search for improvement in the flow of accounts-receivable collections can lead management from conventional cash forecasting to the use of outside financing.

Cash-Flow Method of Forecasting

The cash-flow method accumulates the expected receipts and disbursements for the period being forecast. When sales on credit are significant, analysis is necessary to determine the projected time when cash will be available from collections. The analysis should be prepared with the assistance of the sales and credit personnel. The method used for forecasting collections will vary and can best be determined by analysis of past experience with continuing reference to current actual results. As a minimum, however, where sales are made to different classes of customers—government, business, or individuals—it is advisable to keep separate sales records and analyze collections separately. The segregation of sales in this or a similar manner provides data that usually lead to more accurate collection estimates.

Borrowing Against or Selling Accounts Receivable

The use of accounts receivable to obtain funds is customarily divided into three areas: factoring, accounts-receivable financing, and industrial time sales and equipment financing. These methods of accelerating collections are costly because of the interest expense and fees. These related costs have contributed to the downgrading of this type of financing. However, if this is the only manner in which a company can obtain the necessary cash flow from its accounts receivable, the company cannot afford to overlook it, regardless of the cost. The cost of having funds provided is as much a part of doing business as the costs of raw materials, labor, plant, and machinery. A typical company using these financing methods might operate a business in which trade practices govern the accounts-receivable collection patterns at, for example, 90 days, whereas its raw-materials purchases must be paid within 30 days.

Before commenting on each of these three methods, it should be mentioned that in recent years another approach has sometimes been used by companies to accelerate cash flow from their receivables, namely, the setting up of a captive finance company. Under this arrangement, many of the parent's receivables are often downstreamed to the captive, which customarily adds to its receivables portfolio on the outside and operates as a commercial finance company, obtaining its own financing and operating independently of the parent. Many factors, such as the nature of the parent's product, the nature and term of the parent company's receivables to be downstreamed, the debt capacity of the parent, and the comparative cost of obtaining funds by the parent as compared to the captive must be carefully considered before this approach is used.

Factoring. Factoring is an arrangement under which the factor purchases the accounts receivable of his client without recourse to the client as to the credit risk involved as long as the credit has been approved by the factor. The purchase of the accounts is on a notification basis. All risks (such as fraud, returned merchandise, and similar conditions), other than the client customer's ability to pay, are borne by the factor's client.

The principal advantages of factoring receivables are that it protects the company against credit loss and relieves it of the time and expense of credit checking, bookkeeping, and collecting its accounts receivable. This type of financing, for which the factor charges a commission, is usually attractive to companies (1) selling to a limited number of customers where individual credit exposures are large, (2) selling to large numbers of customers where credit information is limited, (3) where there may exist significant bookkeeping or collection costs, or (4) where the client company may need greater borrowing ability than is available on an unsecured basis.

Payment is made by the factor to the company at maturity of the receivables purchased, unless the company has a need for working capital on a more timely basis. In these cases, the factor may make advances against the receivables sold to him and the company will pay interest, in addition to the commission, from the date of the advance to maturity.

Commercial financing (accounts-receivable financing). Under commercial financing the company does not "sell" its accounts receivable but instead enters into an arrangement with a bank or finance company to borrow against the security of the receivables, usually without notification to the borrowing company's customers and with full recourse to the company for credit risks. These borrowings usually range between 75 percent and 100 percent of the net receivables assigned. Unlike under factoring, all credit, collection, and bookkeeping services are handled by the company in its customary manner. The charge for this service is in the form of interest based on the average daily amount owed; and although a premium rate of interest is charged, this can be an efficient and economical method of borrowing.

Time sales and equipment financing. Financing through sales and equipment involves the sale of installment contracts covering the sales of equipment and machinery, usually with notification to the equipment purchaser. These contracts may be sold with full, limited, or no recourse to the company. The interest charge is added on to the contract or charged to the company on a discount basis. The main advantage of using this method is the quick realization of cash, together with reducing the bookkeeping and collection efforts.

□ **Richard H. Wiesner** (*and Donald E. Miller and John T. Shanahan, Jr., the original authors of this now substantially revised section*)

GENERAL ACCOUNTING AND FINANCIAL STATEMENTS

Any large accounting function is divided into various segments. The following eight segments are relatively standard separations of functions under the jurisdiction of the controller or chief accounting officer: (1) general or financial accounting, (2) cost accounting, (3) systems and procedures, (4) data processing, (5) internal auditing, (6) budgeting, (7) tax reporting, and (8) financial analysis. The key unit is general or financial accounting.

General Accounting

A clear understanding of the scope of responsibility of the general-accounting unit is necessary to provide a bridge to all the other various areas of accounting. In addition, a study of general accounting leads to comprehension of the basic tenets of a general accounting system, the concepts behind the system, the chart of accounts and how it defines the accounting system, and the philosophy behind the system indicating the trail for the development of accounting records, from source documents through the general ledger.

Definition and Function

The committee on terminology of the American Institute of Accountants (now the AICPA) proposed in 1941 that the term "accounting" be defined as "the art of recording, classifying, and summarizing in a significant manner and in terms of money, transactions and events which are, in part at least, of a financial character, and interpreting the results thereof."

Interestingly, many people raise the question of whether accounting is an art or a science, or has aspects of both. Many qualified writers feel that this question cannot be answered solely by definition. Those who do take a position tend to agree that accounting should be deemed an art and not a science.

Some believe that accounting basically can be broken down into three major fields: public accounting, government accounting, and management accounting. This discussion is not concerned with public accounting or government accounting. The general-accounting unit is the hub of the overall accounting function;

therefore, this unit is the base unit in a management accounting system. Accounting can be considered as having the primary function of facilitating the administration, control, and reporting of economic activity. Accounting can therefore be considered a service in that it records economic activities and reports a summary of the results of those activities to all interested parties.

Many people tend to think of accounting only in the sense of answering two basic questions: (1) What is the profit or loss resulting from particular operations for a specific period of time? (2) What is the financial position of a specific operation at a specific time? The general-purpose statements, the income statement, and the balance sheet provide the answers to these questions. They provide a base of measurement and, when compared with prior reports of a similar nature, indicate trends and point out areas where management action may be required.

In addition to preparing these general-purpose reports, accountants are frequently called upon to provide data for specific purposes, generally special-purpose reports. Sometimes these reports are in the form of analyses of and statistical data on information shown in the general-purpose statements. Frequently, they take data from the general-purpose reports and present them from different points of view to facilitate management decisions regarding the future course. Many additional reports are developed, supplying financial data designed to be useful to management, at all levels, in planning and administering a business operation (or personal assets, in the case of an individual). Wherever economic resources are employed, such reports are required.

On a broad basis, these reports can be categorized as (1) those useful in short-range and long-range planning, where it is important to consider all feasible alternatives in financial terms; (2) those useful in administering operations where it is important to evaluate deviations of current actual results from planned results; and (3) those necessary to report results of financial operations to people in an ownership, taxing, creditor, or other legal relationship. While other units in the overall accounting function may be involved, the source data in large part are initiated in the general-accounting unit.

It is widely recognized that accounting information is one of management's most useful tools. As businesses become more and more complex, the reliance on the accounting function increases. The chief accounting officer—whatever his title—is looked to increasingly to provide guidance, direction, control, and protection to senior management. Gantt once stated: "There is no moral right to decide, on a basis of opinion, that which can be determined as a matter of fact." Accounting must be able to provide the required facts, when they are needed, to enable executives to effectively evaluate past operations and to facilitate decision making. It should be apparent that the general-accounting function, at the hub of all accounting activity, assumes a tremendous responsibility to management.

Administration of the Accounting System

A primary function of the general-accounting unit is the continuing administration, maintenance, and control of the accounting records and the source documentation supporting those records. Accounting records generally comprise the following:

□ The general ledger indicating the accounts of significance to the business, the activity affecting each account in terms of money, and the money balances of the accounts that provide the information appearing in financial statements and reports.

□ Subsidiary ledgers that contain the detailed support for those general-ledger accounts which are routinely affected by a large volume of transactions (for example, accounts receivable, accounts payable, fixed assets, and so on).

□ Journals that contain details on individual transactions and events and the various accounts affected (for example, general journal, cash-receipts-and-disbursements journal, sales journal, purchase journal, payroll journal, and so on).

Source documentation represents the entire spectrum of paperwork providing the information on transactions and events that forms the basis for accounting entries—for example, invoices, purchase orders, vouchers, deposit slips, bank statements, time cards, W-4s, and so on.

Chart of Accounts

Important to a system of effective accounting administration is a sound chart of accounts. While the general-accounting unit should be responsible for the final form of the chart of accounts, other accounting units, such as cost accounting, systems and procedures, and internal auditing, should assist in its development. A chart of accounts is simply a listing of accounts, systematically arranged. It should record both account names and numbers. This chart can be expanded into a manual of accounts by adding descriptions of the use of each account, as well as an explanation of the general operation—or, if desired, the philosophy behind the account system.

A properly designed chart of accounts is an important part of effective internal control procedures. As such, it should be designed to reflect transactions by accountabilities and responsibilities to the extent possible. While this may be more easily done with balance-sheet accounts, income-and-expense accounts should also reflect responsibility for transactions by individual or position. Effective internal control requires that the chart of accounts and the accounting records clearly designate personal responsibility for all assets and transactions. It is, therefore, important that the organization structure be carefully articulated so that responsibility can be clearly identified with specific functions or positions.

Consider an example of a basic numbering system and two systems approaches to the development of a strong and effective chart of accounts.

Basic numbering system. The groupings in this system are as follows:

100–199:	Assets	
200–299:	Liabilities	} Balance Sheet
300–399:	Equity	
400–499:	Income	
500–599:	Expenses	} Income Statement
600–699:	Special and tax items	

Within each grouping, subsegments should be established as required. For example, under "Assets" six subsegments may be established:

100–129	Current assets
130–139	Investments
140–159	Fixed assets
160–169	Intangible assets
170–179	Deferred charges
180–199	Other assets

Systems approach. The numbers in the preceding tabulation are usually called either *primary* or *main* accounts in most numbering systems. In a systems approach, two basic charts of accounts with those numbers as the beginning point may be constructed:

Number of Digits	First System	Second System
		Location:
One		Area
Three		Office/Plant
Three	Primary	Main
Two	Secondary	Sub
Three	Tertiary	Item
Four		Detail

The use of three digits is illustrated in the basic numbering system previously shown.

Each system must be custom-designed to provide sufficient internal control. Here are two examples of numbers in charts of accounts developed with the use of the two illustrated systems concepts:

First System:	Primary	100	Cash
	Secondary	− 02	Payroll account
	Tertiary	− 234	Second National Bank of _____
Second System:	Location:		
	Area	1	Eastern United States
	Office/Plant	145	New Jersey Refinery
	Main	100	Cash
	Sub	− 02	Payroll account
	Item	− 234	Second National Bank of _____
	Detail	− 3456	Confidential-salaried

A flexible concept in the systems approach will permit the administration of all data in a consistent manner providing the necessary controls, including audit trails, so that each entry can be traced from the books of entry to its source.

Internal Control

In addition to its other functions, the general-accounting unit is responsible for ensuring that sufficient controls exist within the accounting system to minimize the occurrence of undetected errors or irregularites. One important feature of effective internal control is a clear assignment of responsibility and accountability to a specific person (or position) for the safeguarding of specified assets and correct processing of specified transactions. Another necessary control feature is that the various steps in processing any transaction through the accounting system are divided strategically between people or departments to the extent possible. For example, an employee who handles cash or checks received, on account, from customers should not also record that receipt in the accounting records. A foreman submitting payroll information for the preparation of payroll checks should not also distribute those payroll checks among employees. There are also numerous opportunities to achieve effective internal control by arranging for frequent checks and balances within the system. These might include policies for routine review and approval of check requests and journal entries, dual signatures on checks, and use of cash registers, check protectors, lock boxes, and so on.

Financial Reporting

The responsibility for all accounting reports and financial reports is usually assigned to the general-accounting unit under the direction of the controller or the chief accounting officer. Success in developing reports that fulfill their purpose depends upon (1) an appreciation of sound, fundamental principles of reporting and (2) an ability to understand management's philosophy and needs. Not only is it important to know the business, it is also necessary to understand the idiosyncracies of management. This means that the report authors must recognize specific ways in which management may want information presented if the reports are not standard in presentation format. Many instances of nonstandard reporting formats exist because management is not adequately accounting-trained or accounting-oriented. To avoid nonstandard reporting formats, the chief accounting officer should assist the appropriate members of management to better understand the purpose of the various reports submitted to them.

The following elements are important for effective financial reports: accuracy, appearance, brevity, clarity, completeness, intelligibility, necessity, readability, reliability, simplicity, and timeliness. From the point of view of the authority responsible for preparing and issuing financial reports, the following questions should be asked regarding each report prior to its issuance: What is the report intended to accomplish? What is the potential distribution for the report? When is the report required? Has all pertinent information been screened to ascertain the material facts? How can the material facts best be presented?

Financial Statements

A financial statement is any presentation of financial data derived from the accounting records. Financial statements may be classified as *primary* and *secondary*. The basic primary financial statements are the balance sheet, the income statement, the statement of retained earnings, and the statement of changes in financial position. Each of the primary statements is discussed in the following pages.

The function of secondary financial statements tends to be more limited in nature. Among these reports are the statement of cost of goods sold, the statement of selling and administrative expenses, the cash-flow report, the accounts-receivable report, the inventory analysis, the report of working capital, the capital expenditure report, and the fixed-asset report.

Balance Sheet

A balance sheet is a statement of financial position presented in terms of an entity's assets, liabilities, and equity as of the close of business on the date specified in the report. The AICPA, in its Research Bulletin No. 9, defines a balance sheet as

> A tabular statement or summary of balances (debit and credit) carried forward after an actual or constructive closing of books of account, kept by double-entry methods, according to the rules or principles of accounting. The items reflected on the two sides of the balance sheet are commonly called assets and liabilities, respectively.

Total assets should always equal the total of the liabilities plus equity (capital). Simply stated, this equation is: Assets equal liabilities plus equity ($A = L + E$). Because claims of creditors take precedence over those of owners/stockholders, this equation can be restated as: Assets minus liabilities equals equity ($A - L = E$). A balance sheet using the first equation is called "the account form of balance sheet," while one prepared using the second equation is called "the report form of balance sheet." Examples of each are shown in Figures 2-22 and 2-23. The account-form example is set up on a noncomparative basis, while the report-form example has been set up in a comparative format. Either form of balance sheet may use a comparative or noncomparative format.

The account groupings for balance sheets in commercial and industrial companies, as indicated by Regulation S-X of the SEC, are listed in the following paragraphs.

Assets and other debits. *Current assets* on the balance sheet include the following groupings: cash and cash items; marketable securities; notes receivable (trade); accounts receivable (trade); reserves for doubtful notes and accounts receivable (trade); inventories; other current assets; and total current assets.

Investments groupings on the balance sheet are securities of affiliates; indebtedness of affiliates—not current; other security investments; other investments; and total investments.

Figure 2-22. Account form of balance sheet.

ABC Company, Inc.
Balance Sheet
(000 omitted)

Assets

Current assets			
Cash		$ 250	
U.S. government securities at cost			
(market value: $380)		240	
Receivables (gross)	$2,000		
Less: Allowance for bad debts	80		
Receivables (net)		1,920	
Inventories		800	
Total			$3,210
Fixed assets			
Buildings	$3,800		
Machinery and tools	1,800		
		$5,600	
Less: Accrued depreciation		2,800	
			$2,800
Other assets			
Cash surrender value of life insurance			130
Deferred charges and prepaid expense			
Prepaid insurance			20
Total assets			$6,160

Liabilities

Current liabilities			
Accounts payable		$1,800	
Notes payable		190	
Accrued taxes		200	
Total			$2,190
Long-term liabilities			
5% 20-year debentures (due 1992)			600
Total liabilities			$2,790

Stockholders' Equity

Capital stock			
Common stock, no-par-value			
(authorized 1,000,000 shares,			
outstanding 580,000 shares)		$ 580	
Retained earnings		2,790	
Total stockholders' equity			$3,370
Total liabilities and stockholders' equity			$6,160

Figure 2-23. Report form of balance sheet.

ABC Company, Inc.
Balance Sheet
(000 omitted)

	December 31 1980	December 31 1979	Increase or (Decrease) Dollars	Increase or (Decrease) Percent
Net Assets in which Capital Is Invested				
Current assets				
Cash	$ 250	$ 135	$115	85.19
U.S. government securities at cost				
(market value: 12/31/80—$380	240			
12/31/79—$125)		55	185	336.36
Receivables (gross)	$2,000	$1,750	$250	14.29
Less: Allowance for bad debts	80	70	10	14.29
Receivables (net)	$1,920	$1,680	$240	14.29
Inventories	800	900	(100)	(11.11)
Total current assets	$3,210	$2,770	$440	15.88
Less: Current liabilities				
Accounts payable	$1,800	$1,435	$365	25.44
Notes payable	190	190	-0-	-0-
Accrued taxes	200	180	20	11.11
Total current liabilities	$2,190	$1,805	$385	21.33
Net current assets	$1,020	$ 965	$ 55	5.70
Add: Assets other than current				
Buildings	$3,800	$3,800	$ -0-	-0-
Machinery and tools	1,800	1,700	100	5.88
	$5,600	$5,500	$100	1.82
Less: Accrued depreciation	2,800	2,725	75	2.75
	$2,800	$2,775	$ 25	0.90
Cash surrender value of life insurance	130	120	10	8.33
Prepaid insurance	20	20	-0-	-0-
Total	$3,970	$3,880	$ 90	2.32
Less: Liabilities other than current				
5 percent 20-year debentures				
(due 1982)	600	800	(200)	(25.00)
Total net assets in which capital is invested	$3,370	$3,080	$290	9.42
Sources from which Capital Has Been Obtained				
Common stock, no-par-value (authorized 1,000,000 shares, outstanding 580,000 shares)	$ 580	$ 580	$ -0-	-0-
Net income employed in the business	2,790	2,500	290	11.60
Total capital invested	$3,370	$3,080	$290	9.42

Fixed assets are grouped as follows: property, plant, and equipment; reserves for depreciation, depletion, and amortization of property, plant, and equipment; and total fixed assets.

Intangible assets groupings are patents, trademarks, franchises, goodwill, and other; reserves for depreciation and amortization of intangible assets; and total intangible assets.

Deferred charges groupings include prepaid expenses and other deferred items; organizational expense; debt discount and expense; commissions and expense on capital shares; and total deferred charges.

Other assets (to be stated separately) are the total of amounts due from directors, officers, and principal holders of equity securities (other than affiliates); all special funds, including pension funds; and any other item (individually identified) in excess of 10 percent of the amount of all assets other than fixed and intangible.

Liabilities, capital stock, and other capital. *Current liabilities* on the balance sheet are grouped as follows: notes payable, accounts payable (trade), accrued liabilities, other current liabilities, and total current liabilities.

Deferred income is entered separately as warranted by amount or nature.

Long-term debt groupings include the following: bonds, mortgages, and similar debt; indebtedness to affiliates—not current; other long-term debt; and total long-term debt.

Other liabilities groupings also include commitments and contingent liabilities and total other liabilities.

Capital shares and surplus on the balance sheet are grouped as capital shares, surplus, and total capital shares and surplus.

Income Statement

The income statement is a statement of the results of operations for an organization—a summary of income or revenue and expenses. It can be prepared for each operating unit or can be a consolidated presentation for several or all units of a firm. It can be prepared to show the results for a specified period alone, to compare results with those of a prior period, or to compare results to a budgetary projection. Supplemental reports of a general operating nature could include a product profit and loss statement; a plant, office, or divisional profit and loss statement; and an analysis of general or selling expense.

The income statement can be a detailed listing of all related general-ledger accounts or may be summarized into the following general categories: (a) operating (or gross) revenue; (b) cost of sales; (c) gross profit—(a) minus (b); (d) general operating expense; (e) other income; (f) other deductions; and (g) net income (or net loss).

As with balance sheets, there are two basic approaches to an income-statement presentation. The format outlined in (a) through (g) is sometimes called the multiple-step or report form. Figure 2-24 is an example of this approach. The second approach, which has gained increasing popularity in recent years, is the one-step form shown in Figure 2-25.

Figure 2-24. Report form of income statement.

ABC Company, Inc. Income Statement (000 omitted)	
Net sales	$7,480
Cost of sales, including depreciation	4,500
Gross profit	$2,980
Selling, administrative, and general expense	1,800
Net operating income	$1,180
Provision for federal income taxes	600
Net income (or loss)	$ 580

Figure 2-25. Single-step form of income statement.

ABC Company, Inc. Statement of Net Income (000 omitted)	
Sales	$7,480
Costs:	
Cost of Sales	$3,500
Salaries/wages	2,400
Depreciation	400
Federal income taxes	600
	$6,900
Net income for year	$ 580
Income per common share	$ 2.00

Briefly summarized, the segments of Regulation S-X of the SEC on income statements for commercial and industrial companies are stated in the paragraphs that follow:

Operating (or gross) revenue is gross sales minus discounts, returns, and allowances. Sales to affiliated companies or organizations should be indicated separately if practicable.

Cost of goods sold is stated in accordance with the system of accounting followed.

Gross profit is operating revenues after deduction of cost of goods sold.

General operating expenses relating to affiliated companies or organizations are shown separately if practicable. Separate expenses are classified as operating expenses; other operating expenses; selling, general, and administrative expenses; provision for doubtful accounts; and other general expenses.

Other income includes dividends, interest on securities, profits on securities, miscellaneous other deductions, and total other deductions.

Other categories include the following items: net income or loss before provision for taxes on income; provision for income and excess-profits taxes; net income or loss; special items; and net income or loss and special items.

Statement of Retained Earnings

This statement is an analysis of activity in retained earnings. It reflects the beginning balance of unappropriated retained earnings, charges and credits to them during the period, and the ending balance. Charges and credits during a period can include any or all of the following: (1) the net increase (or decrease, in event of a loss) transferred from the income statement, (2) transfers to and from appropriated retained earnings, (3) dividends declared, (4) reductions from acquisitions made of the firm's own capital stock, and (5) material

Figure 2-26.   Statement of retained earnings.

Balance at January 1, 19— unappropriated		$ XXXXXXX
Transfer from amount previously appropriated for		
contingencies (no longer restricted)		XXXXXXX
		$ XXXXXXX
Deduct:		
Net loss for year	$ XXXXXXX	
Cash dividends declared on common		
stock at xx cents per share	XXXXXXX	XXXXXXX
Balance at December 31, 19—		$ XXXXXXX

nonoperating charges and credits made directly to retained earnings. The analysis of retained earnings may appear as a separate statement, as indicated in Figure 2-26, or as part of a combined statement of income and retained earnings. The latter is merely an extension of a standard income statement.

Statement of Changes in Financial Position

One financial statement of growing importance is the statement of changes in financial position. This statement, as shown in Figure 2-27, presents the following information: (1) the portion of total funds provided from operations, (2) funds provided from various outside sources, (3) the disposition of funds, including the proportion of funds applied for various uses, (4) the impact of funds flow on working capital, (5) an indication of the impact of funds flow upon the future liquidity and solvency of the firm, and (6) the ability to compare the financial strength of the firm with others in the industry.
□ *Thomas H. Voss* (and *William T. Thornhill, the original author of this now substantially revised section*)

COST ACCOUNTING AND ANALYSIS

The major objective of a cost accounting system is to identify, report, and interpret all costs incurred in producing a product, providing a service, and maintaining a business entity. Traditionally, the role of the cost accountant has been limited to simply identifying and reporting costs; however, recent economic trends require a much greater emphasis on the interpretation of historical cost data, the analysis of current costs, and the projection of future costs. In other words, the modern cost accountant has become an active member of the management decision-making team responsible for planning, coordinating, and controlling operations.

Cost accounting systems should not be designed to meet the needs of accounting alone. The major ingredients in most successful systems are the recognition of the many users of cost information and a strong effort to address each user's

Figure 2-27.   Statement of changes in financial position.

ABC Company, Inc.
Statement of Changes in Financial Position
Year ended December 31, 19___
(000 omitted)

Source of Funds

Net income	$ 300
Depreciation	75
Increase in deferred income tax	125
Other	50
Total from operations	$ 550
Proceeds from sale of common stock	580
	$1,130

Application of Funds

Additions to properties, plant, and equipment	$ 250
Payments on long-term debt	200
Dividends declared	100
Increase in noncurrent receivables	175
Other	105
	$ 830
Increase in working capital	$ 300
Cash	$115
U.S. government securities	100
Other marketable securities	85
	$300

---

individual needs. For example, the needs of the sales organization may be centered on product-line profitability in order to price effectively, while the operating organization may be more interested in the cost of running an individual operation. Furthermore, it is not enough to merely make cost information available to a large number of users. The cost accountant's responsibility is to ensure that this information is communicated in a clear, understandable manner.

Computer technology has enabled the cost accountant to provide a wealth of data at a reduced cost. As a result of these new capabilities, cost systems have grown much more sophisticated in recent years. However, this increase in sophistication must be balanced against any additional costs in terms of dollars and the possible confusion of major users. Management simply will not use a system that it does not understand.

The ideal cost system will provide timely and accurate information to management for use in controlling costs and planning the operation of the firm. A cost system must be tailored to the organization structure, size, production process, and any other unique characteristics of the firm. Generally, two broad approaches to cost accounting have evolved over the years: process cost accounting and job-order cost accounting. Each method may use actual costs or predetermined standard costs.

Cost systems may also be classified according to their treatment of fixed costs. Full or absorption costing charges all fixed costs to a product, while direct or variable costing charges only variable costs to a product.

Process Cost Accounting

The objective of the process cost accounting system is to assign total production costs to all products in process during the accounting period. In order to accomplish this objective, it is necessary to isolate the costs of raw materials, labor, and manufacturing overhead as they are incurred in each step in the production process. Accordingly, process costing requires the division of the total production process into separate and distinct accounting entities, commonly called *cost centers*. This emphasis on the cost center not only provides an easy means of isolating costs but also enhances management control through the assignment of responsibilities.

Process cost systems are commonly used when identical or nearly identical products are produced (as opposed to individually designed products), when products are mass-produced in a repetitive, continuous manner, or when products move through a series of production areas. These conditions are generally found in industries such as steel, food processing, chemicals, glass, cement, textiles, and petroleum. A conceptual picture of the information flow in such a system is shown in Figure 2-28.

The fundamental aspect of process cost accounting is the accumulation of cost by process (Department A, Department B, and so on) rather than by jobs. A unit cost of production is calculated for each process, and the total unit cost is the sum of the unit costs for all processes through which a product must move. Therefore, all products in finished goods shown in the figure include the direct ma-

Figure 2-28. Process cost accounting.

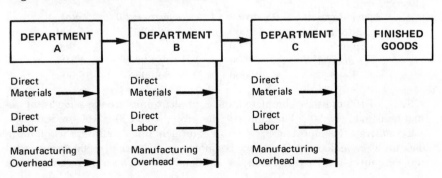

terial, direct labor, and overhead incurred in all three production departments. Such unit costs are simply calculated as follows:

$$\text{Unit cost of process} = \frac{\text{total cost of process}}{\text{units produced in process}}$$

The total cost of each process is not difficult to determine, since each cost element is readily identifiable by process. The only source of difficulty is arriving at the "units produced in process."

Equivalent Units

"Equivalent units" is a term used to indicate the number of completed units that might have been made with the amounts of material, labor, and overhead used in producing some finished and some partly finished units; for example, 100 units that are half-completed are equivalent to 50 completed units. In a given process run or batch in process, the equivalent units may be different for each element of cost. Assume, for example, that 1,000 gallons of paint were started in process and that 600 gallons were completed and 400 gallons are still in process. Assume, further, that the 400 gallons are three-fourths done as far as material is concerned, one-half done as far as labor is concerned, and one-half done as regards overhead. The equivalent units of material, labor, and overhead would be 900, 800, and 800, respectively.

In process costing, the three elements of cost may be charged to a common work-in-process account entitled "work in process," or each element of cost may be charged to a separate, appropriately titled account as "work in process—material," "work in process—labor," and "work in process—overhead." Of course, it follows that since the primary basis for collecting costs in a process system is a cost center or department, separate accounts should be established for each department—for example, "work in process—material: Department 1," "work in process—material: Department 2," and so forth.

For illustrative purposes, consider the following simplified case: A firm that produces a single product, X, through two departments has no beginning or ending inventories of work in process but incurred the following costs in producing 100 units:

Element of cost	Department 1	Department 2	Total
Material	$1,000	$3,000	$4,000
Labor	500	400	900
Overhead	500	600	1,100
Total	$2,000	$4,000	$6,000

Since all 100 units are completed, the equivalent units are the same as the actual units, namely, 100. The unit cost, therefore, is $6,000 ÷ 100, or $60.

To illustrate the importance and use of equivalent units, consider the following data for a single department. At the beginning of the period, 4,000 units in process were three-fourths completed; an additional 8,000 units were received in the department. During the period, 8,000 units were completed and transferred to finished goods, and 1,000 units were lost. The ending inventory of 3,000 units was one-third completed.

Cost Element	Beginning Inventory	Incurred During Period
Material	$ 2,400	$ 3,000
Labor	3,900	6,000
Overhead	3,900	6,000
Total	$10,200	$15,000

There are two generally recognized methods of valuing inventories in process cost accounting: the average method and the first in, first out (FIFO) method. In the rare case of no beginning inventory, the problem of which method to use would be unimportant because, without a beginning inventory, the calculations and the results would be the same by either method. Of course, it must be remembered that once a method has been selected, it must be used consistently in succeeding periods and that one period's ending inventory becomes the following period's beginning inventory.

In practice, one method would be selected and used consistently, but for illustrative purposes the previously mentioned production will be valued by both methods.

The Average Method

Under the average method, the units in the beginning inventory will be mingled with the units received during the period, and the costs in the beginning inventory will be added to the similar costs incurred during the period. The costs must be isolated by elements because, in most cases, the number of equivalent units may differ for one or more of the three cost elements. It follows that if only a total value is given for the beginning inventory, the average method cannot be used even though the FIFO method could be used.

		Average Equivalent Units		
		Actual Units	Stage of Completion	Equivalent Units
	Completed	8,000	1	8,000
	In process	3,000	⅓	1,000
	Total	11,000		9,000

Elements	Beginning Inventory	Added	Total	Equivalent Units	Unit Cost
Material	$ 2,400	$ 3,000	$ 5,400	9,000	$ .60
Labor	3,900	6,000	9,900	9,000	1.10
Overhead	3,900	6,000	9,900	9,000	1.10
Total	$10,200	$15,000	$25,200		$2.80

The value of the goods finished and transferred is (8,000 × 1 × $2.80) $22,400. The work in process is (3,000 × ⅓ × $2.80).

The FIFO Method

Under the FIFO method, the value of the beginning inventory is kept separate from the costs incurred during the period. Therefore, the equivalent units in the beginning inventory must be kept separate from the other equivalent units.

The 8,000 units completed during the period are composed of the 4,000 units in the beginning inventory and 4,000 other units. Since the 4,000 units in the beginning inventory were three-fourths complete, only 1,000 equivalent units had to be made during this period in order to transfer out 4,000 units. Thus the 8,000 completed units represent current production of only 5,000 units. The ending inventory is one-third completed, thus representing 1,000 equivalent units. Total equivalent units under FIFO are 6,000.

The equivalent units in the beginning inventory and their costs are excluded from the calculation of the current unit costs, which are calculated as follows:

Elements	Current Costs	Current Equivalent Units	Unit Costs
Material	$ 3,000	6,000	$ .50
Labor	6,000	6,000	1.00
Overhead	6,000	6,000	1.00
Total	$15,000		$2.50

The period's production would be valued as follows:

Beginning inventory	$10,200
Cost to complete (4,000 × ¼ × $2.50)	2,500
Total cost of beginning inventory	$12,700
Units started and finished	
(4,000 × 1 × $2.50)	10,000
Total cost of finished goods	$22,700
Work in process	
Material (3,000 × ⅓ × $ .50) $ 500	
Labor (3,000 × ⅓ × $1.00) 1,000	
Overhead (3,000 × ⅓ × $1.00) 1,000	
Total work in process	2,500
Total production costs	$25,200

Job-Order Cost Accounting

Job-order costing is a method of accumulating costs for each unit of production. This type of cost system is commonly found in industries such as ship-

Figure 2-29. Job-order cost sheet.

Customer: XYZ Corporation	**Job #:** 102
Product: Widgets	**Completion Date:**
Quantity: 10	**Shipment Date:** June 1, 19__

Department	Direct Material	Direct Labor	Direct Overhead	Total
1	500	1,000	1,000	
2	200	600	600	
3	—	300	300	
	700	1,900	1,900	4,500

building, construction, research, and heavy-equipment manufacturing, where continuous physical identification of a particular job or order is necessary. The major component of a job-order cost system is the job cost sheet, on which all costs are recorded. Each job undertaken is assigned a number and a job cost sheet. The job cost sheet will, in effect, follow the job through the production process. All costs associated with the job will be recorded on the cost sheet. Therefore, job-order costs are said to be specific as opposed to the average cost developed in process cost accounting.

The major difficulty encountered in job-order cost systems is the assignment of manufacturing overhead to individual products. Overhead costs are not directly transferable to the product; therefore, a method of assignment must be developed. Most assignments key on some measure of activity such as direct labor hours, direct labor costs, or machine-hours. From a management accounting perspective, a final job cost sheet can be extremely useful in comparing job cost estimates with actual job cost data in order to isolate problems in approved estimating techniques. The determination of selling prices and profitability per job are also closely linked to the analysis and estimating of actual cost per job.

Job-order costing is synonymous with job costing, job-lot costing, lot costing, batch costing, and specific-order costing. A job-order cost sheet should contain the information in Figure 2-29 as a minimum.

Standard-Cost Accounting

In actual cost accounting systems, cost control is accomplished by analyzing the trends in product costs. The two major weaknesses in such systems are the inability to isolate product costs fairly and the failure to indicate the organizational unit responsible. A standard-cost system will address these weaknesses by providing management with a predetermined estimate of what the costs should be. By comparing these standard costs with actual costs, management has a yardstick to evaluate performance.

Although standard-cost systems were initially designed to promote cost control, they also serve as valuable tools in meeting other management objectives such as planning and budgeting, the study of alternative methods of production, and the pricing of present and new products. In view of this, standards should be established with the most scientific and accurate method possible.

Several basic conditions are necessary for the successful operation of a standard-cost system:

- □ Operations must be standardized in order for accurate standard costs to be developed.
- □ A system of responsibility accounting must be in place.
- □ A well-developed communication and reporting system must be in operation.
- □ A group of qualified personnel with a variety of background must be assigned the responsibility for establishment and revision of standards.

To ensure a continuing commitment to the system, standards must be developed for each process through a joint effort between the person responsible for the process and the firm's industrial engineers, time-and-motion-study specialists, and representatives from the personnel and purchasing divisions.

When standard costs are being established, a question normally arises concerning how difficult the standards should be to achieve. One theory is that standards should represent nearly perfect performance. Such standards could be achieved only under perfect conditions. The major justification for such an approach is the need for a precise measure of efficiency. A more realistic approach is to set standards that are attainable with good performance. Such standards can realistically be used for cost analysis, inventory valuations, and pricing decisions. More important, obtainable standards are psychologically better than perfect standards, because perfect standards tend to discourage operating management.

Since the primary value of standard-cost accounting is to provide management with a model for use in planning, controlling, and evaluating operations, the system must be sufficiently flexible to adapt to new operating practices, purchase prices, and so on. Standards should be reviewed at least once a year, and if necessary, changes should be made. More frequent changes to the system may run the risk of destroying the value of the model as a planning and controlling device.

For standard-cost accounting purposes, a "variance" may be described as "a change or deviation from the established standard." The difference between a standard cost of a unit and its actual cost is the overall or net variance. Such an overall variance is relatively useless in fixing responsibility. To be useful, an overall variance must be broken down into its components. It is common practice to isolate two variances for material and labor. It should be pointed out here that in accounting presentations, when the terms "material" and "labor" are used, direct material or direct labor is implied unless otherwise indicated. In the case of overhead—because of the heterogeneous costs included in one account—a greater variety of analytical methods has been developed.

Material and Labor Variances

In the case of material, it is usual to isolate a price variance and a quantity variance. For illustrative purposes, consider a case in which 1,000 gallons of product A are purchased at an actual cost of $1.10 per gallon when the standard cost is $1 per gallon. Also, 800 gallons were actually used in producing commodity X in such a quantity that only 750 gallons of A should have been used at standard. The typical calculations and entries follow.

To record the liability at the actual amount and to charge the inventory with the standard price:

Price variance = (actual price − standard price) × actual quantity
Price variance = ($1.10 − $1.00) × 1,000 = $.10 × 1,000 = $100

Raw-material inventory	$1,000	
Materials-price variance	100	
Accounts payable		$1,100

To record the removal from inventory of the actual amount of raw materials used and to charge work in process with the standard amount:

Quantity variance = (actual quantity used − standard quantity)
                              × standard cost
Quantity variance = (800 − 750) × $1.00 = 50 × $1.00 = $50

Work in process	$750	
Materials-quantity variance	50	
Raw material in inventory		$800

The calculations of labor variances are quite similar to the ones for material, except that it is more appropriate here to refer to a rate variance rather than to price variance, and to a time or efficiency variance rather than to a quantity variance. Also, in the case of labor, both variances are calculated at the same time. For illustrative purposes, assume the following cost data: The actual labor cost was $133,250 for 41,000 hours; the standard rate was $3 per hour; and the standard time allowed for the amount of production for the period was 40,000 hours.

Rate variance = (actual rate − standard rate) × actual hours
Rate variance = ($3.25 − $3.00) × 41,000 = $.25 × 41,000 = $10,250

Efficiency variance = (actual hours worked − standard hours)
                                × standard rate
Efficiency variance = (41,000 − 40,000) × $3.00 = 1,000 × $3.00
                             = $3,000

Work in process	$120,000	
Labor-rate variance	10,250	
Labor-efficiency variance	3,000	
Payroll		$133,250

The purpose of computing rate variance and efficiency variance is to relieve the payroll account of the actual cost of labor and to charge work in process with the standard cost.

When management has an analysis by causes of the materials variances and the labor variances, responsibility can be fixed, and if the variances are significant, corrective steps can be taken through consultations with or instructions to those responsible. For example, the purchasing agent is responsible for materials prices; therefore, he is the one to check with if the prices are out of line. But if too great a quantity of material has been used, the foreman of the department in which the material was used should be checked with, since the foremen are responsible for the quantities of material used in their departments.

In the case of labor variances, the person or persons (usually, the personnel manager) responsible for setting wage rates and assigning employees to jobs should be consulted if there are significant differences between standard rates and actual rates. But if there are significant differences between the standard hours allowed for the work accomplished and the actual hours, the foreman of the department in which the variance occurred should be checked with.

Overhead Variances

In the case of material or labor, only one class of cost is involved, and in each case it is a direct as well as a variable cost; therefore, the variances are quite easily and objectively analyzed. However, in the case of overhead, a vast variety of different expenses is collected in one account. All of them are indirect, and they vary in type from variable through semivariable to fixed. Thus the analysis of overhead variances becomes more subjective and more complex than the analysis of material and labor variances.

A common two-variance method of analysis is illustrated on the basis of the following data:

Actual overhead	$42,000.00
Budgeted overhead for 10,000 units (normal)	$40,000.00
Budgeted overhead for 8,000 units	$36,000.00
Actual labor rate	$4.50
Standard labor rate	$4.00
Actual hours worked	11,000
Standard hours per unit of product	1
Units produced	9,500
Overhead rate—percentage of labor cost	100

The amount of overhead applied to production is standard hours worked per unit (one hour) × the standard hourly labor rate ($4) × overhead rate (100 percent) × the actual units produced (9,500), or $38,000.

The overall overhead variance is the difference between the actual costs incurred and the amount applied: $42,000 − $38,000, or $4,000. Since the actual cost is greater than the applied amount, the variance is said to be unfavorable. Also, the overhead is underapplied. It is this amount that must be analyzed, regardless of whether two or 22 variances are isolated. The actual costs and the applied amount have been established. To isolate two variances, only one more figure is needed: the budget at the standard-allowed level of operations. Since 9,500 units were produced, a budgeted cost for that level of production is needed. A budget cost of $40,000 for 10,000 units and a budget cost of $36,000 for 8,000 units are given. Therefore, by interpolation, a budget cost of $39,000 can be established for 9,500 units.

A controllable variance (sometimes referred to as a spending variance) can be calculated as follows:

Actual overhead costs	$42,000
Budget at standard allowed	39,000
Unfavorable controllable variance	$ 3,000

A volume variance (sometimes referred to as a capacity variance) can be calculated in the following manner:

Budget at standard allowed	$39,000
Applied overhead	38,000
Unfavorable volume variance	$ 1,000

The sum of the unfavorable controllable variance and the unfavorable volume variance is $4,000, the amount of the overall variance.

Before closing the discussion of standard costs, it is important to note that such a system lends itself to management by exception. Top management is not forced to deal with a large amount of detailed cost figures but can easily focus its attention on areas reporting large deviations from standard.

Direct Costing and Absorption Costing

Direct costing, also called marginal costing, is a method of cost accounting that assigns only variable manufacturing costs to the product. The theory behind this system is that fixed costs will be incurred whether or not a product is produced. Therefore, variable costs are the only true costs of production. In other words, fixed costs represent the cost of being in business, and variable costs represent the cost of doing business.

Direct costing includes only variable costs in work in process and finished-goods inventories. All fixed costs are treated as period expenses and accordingly written off in the period in which they are incurred.

Direct costing is especially helpful to management in decision making in cases of idle capacity and high fixed costs. It is also very useful in making decisions for the short run.

Inventory costs in a direct costing system are sharply different from inventory costs under absorption costing, which is also called conventional total or full costing. Under absorption costing, all production costs, both fixed and variable, are charged to production.

In stressing the marginal-income concept of direct costing, a distinction should be made between the terms "gross profit" and "gross margin," even though they are sometimes used interchangeably. Gross profit (used in absorption costing) is the result of subtracting the total cost (both fixed and variable) of goods sold from sales revenue. Gross margin (used in direct costing) is the result of subtracting the marginal costs (variable or controllable costs only) from sales revenue.

Under absorption costing, it is not necessary to separate the many factory overhead accounts into their fixed and variable components, since all factory overhead will be charged to inventories. However, under direct costing, every account that contains elements of fixed costs and variable costs must be separated so that the variable part may be charged to inventory and the fixed part charged to expense for the period.

The following assumed data are used to illustrate and compare inventory valuations by absorption costing and direct costing:

Direct material	$ 40,000
Direct labor	20,000
Variable factory overhead	20,000
Fixed factory overhead	20,000
Total costs	$100,000
Units produced	1,000
Units sold	750

	Direct Costing	Absorption Costing
Marginal (direct) cost	$80,000	$ 80,000
Fixed (period) costs		20,000
Charges to inventory	$80,000	$100,000
Less: cost of sales	60,000	75,000
Inventory	$20,000	$ 25,000

For further comparison, a comparative income statement for the XYZ Company is presented in Figure 2-30.

The cost of goods sold and the inventory are smaller by direct costing than by absorption costing because of the exclusion of period costs. Because of the separation of the period costs from variable costs in direct costing, as indicated in the preceding comparative statement, it is possible to establish a gross margin—or marginal contribution, as it is sometimes called—and a merchandising margin. These values are not available under absorption costing. Awareness of the importance of these figures for management decision making will come when the meaning and importance of marginal income are considered.

Marginal income is the excess of revenue over the additional cost of earning the revenue—that is, the excess of sales revenue over the variable cost of making the sales.

Figure 2-30. Comparative income statement.

XYZ Company
Comparative Income Statement
Year Ended December 31, 19—

	Absorption Costing	Direct Costing
Sales	$800,000	$800,000
Cost of goods sold		
Material	$200,000	$200,000
Labor	200,000	200,000
Variable factory overhead	200,000	200,000
Fixed factory overhead	200,000	
Total production costs	$800,000	$600,000
Less: Ending inventory	400,000	300,000
Total cost of goods sold	$400,000	$300,000
Gross profit	$400,000	
Gross margin		$500,000
Operating expenses		
Selling	$ 40,000	
Administrative	40,000	
Total operating expenses	$ 80,000	
Variable operating expenses		
Selling		$ 20,000
Administrative		20,000
Total variable operating expenses		$ 40,000
Merchandising margin		$460,000
Period costs		
Fixed factory overhead		$200,000
Fixed selling expenses		20,000
Fixed administrative expenses		20,000
Total period costs		240,000
Net operating profit	$320,000	$220,000

The direct-costing concept may be applied to either process cost systems or job-order systems and may be used either with or without standards.

When a plant has idle capacity or when prices are being depressed, management can use direct-costing methods to an advantage in determining the lowest possible price to accept for additional units of production.

When there is idle plant capacity, the fixed costs of the plant become sunk costs and therefore irrelevant to decisions in regard to the additional use of the plant. The only relevant costs are the additional costs of producing the additional units. However, the adverse effect that a special sale at a reduced price can have on regular sales must be considered. It is better for a facility to operate than not to operate if the revenue from operations is greater than the variable costs of operating, even when total costs (fixed and variable) are not recovered, because operating the facility under these circumstances reduces losses. In the long run, however, total costs must be recovered.

Direct costing is helpful to management in special pricing decisions for the short run. If management relies too much on direct costing for costing production, there is a danger that goods will be underpriced in the long run to the detriment of the firm.

Direct costing is very useful to management, but it is not generally accepted by the SEC, Internal Revenue Service (IRS), AICPA, or the American Accounting Association.

Cost Accounting for Defense Contracts

The Department of Defense (DOD) is the country's largest single customer, entering into contracts for goods and services amounting to $20 billion to $30 billion annually. Accounting for defense contracts has become a specialized area of accounting to both government accountants and industrial accountants.

Anyone who contemplates entering into a defense contract should become familiar with the special requirements and clauses of the various types of contracts awarded by the government. This may be done through consultation with experts in the area and careful study of the Defense Acquisition Regulations (DAR). Section XV is especially important. It is divided into six parts. Part 1 is introductory in nature, and in it the various types of contracts, as well as applicable cost principles and procedures, are discussed. In Part 2, cost-reimbursement-type supply and research contracts are treated, as well as special cost factors, definitions, and procedures applicable to these types of contracts. Part 3 deals with special problems, costs, cost factors, and special contract features occasioned by contracting with educational institutions. Part 4 deals with the cost and accounting problems and procedures, as well as special contract features applicable to construction contracts. Part 5 is concerned with cost and accounting problems peculiar to contracts for the construction of industrial facilities. In Part 6, the various types of fixed-price contracts are defined, and the use and application of Parts 2, 3, and 4 are further elaborated.

In addition, contractors must comply with the cost-accounting-standards clause and about 20 cost accounting standards (depending on applicability). Companies must certify that they are in compliance with the standards. Companies may be required to submit a disclosure statement, depending on the level of government business. The threshold is currently $10 million of "covered contracts" for a fiscal year. "Covered contracts" mean contracts requiring the submittal of a DD633 (cost and price proposal). The disclosure statement is a lengthy statement in which management must tell in considerable detail various facts about the company. It is suggested that companies considering participating in government contracts subscribe to Commerce Clearing House series for both DAR and cost accounting standards.

Types of Contracts

There are two basic types of government contracts: fixed-price and cost. Each of these classes can be further refined. Fixed-price types of contracts include (a) firm fixed-price, (b) fixed-price with escalation clause, (c) fixed-price with redetermination-of-price clause, (d) fixed-price incentive, (e) time and materials, and (f) labor hours.

Cost (reimbursement) types of contracts include (a) cost-plus-fixed-fee (CPFF), (b) cost-plus-incentive-fee (CPIF), (c) cost-sharing, and (d) cost.

Care should be exercised by the contractor, as well as by the contracting government officer, in the selection of the type of contract; risks and obligations assumed will depend in general on the type of contract signed. A contractor assumes the highest degree of risk with a firm fixed-price contract. Such a contract should be used only when the contractor has thorough knowledge of production costs and reason to believe that they will not change during the life of the contract. Such a contract should be of short duration. If the contract is to continue over a long period of time, the contractor should insist on another type of contract—perhaps one including an escalation clause or a redetermination-of-price clause. The escalation clause is especially appropriate in cases where it is likely that costs will increase during the life of the contract but the amount of increase cannot be reliably estimated.

A key point to consider is whether to include the *estimated* escalation as part of the contract cost. This approach allows the contractor to use the cost plus estimated escalation as a base to add general factory, selling, general and administrative, and profit amounts. If the escalation is determined after the fact, the government does not allow any change in the profit dollars; therefore, a lengthy contract during double-digit inflation will cause the profit percentage on the order to be watered down significantly.

Another point to bear in mind is whether to keep the estimated escalation "open-ended." It may be wise to include in the contract a provision that will allow you to recalculate the actual escalation and adjust upward or downward within 30 days of the completion of the contract. This feature protects both parties.

In cases where the contractor has not experienced a cost of production for the contracted item or a similar one, a cost-type contract would be much less risky.

Accounting for Defense Contracts

The government will not prescribe the accounting system to be used by the contractor. However, a contractor is expected to consistently follow generally accepted accounting principles and to maintain books, records, documents, and other evidence in sufficient detail to support all claims against the government. A major risk to the contractor in using an inadequate accounting system is the danger of loss because of the failure of a claim. A contracting office may disallow costs that are not supported by adequate evidence. Either job-order or process costing may be used, as appropriate to the type of production involved. Standard costs may be used, provided variances are adequately identified and charged to various products.

Since process accounting results in average costs for production, as opposed to the specific costs developed for each job under job-order accounting, job-order accounting may be preferred if it is suitable to the particular production system. Under normal circumstances, it would be easier for the government auditors to identify costs with specific contracts when job-order accounting is used than when process accounting is used.

In the event of termination of a fixed-price contract for the convenience of the government, cost data are needed to support each item of the contractor's claim for reimbursement of the cost incurred. Special tools and equipment—that is, items usable only on the contract terminated—are charged to the contract on a unit-of-production basis. Any cost of such special tools and equipment not charged to production by the time of termination of the contract is charged to the government, according to the termination clause. For example, if a specialized piece of equipment, of value only in the production of a certain item, is required for the efficient production of the contracted item, the contractor, in placing the bid, spreads the cost of that specialized equipment over all the units called for in the contract. Thus, if the contract had been terminated when only half completed, only one-half of the cost would have been charged to the contract. The balance of the cost of this equipment could be recovered under the termination clause if the claim is properly supported by evidence of the cost of the equipment.

Direct costs.   Any costs that can be specifically identified with a particular unit of production (contract) are direct costs. The physical association of the cost-creating item with the end product is not necessary.

Indirect costs.   Indirect costs are any costs resulting from common or joint activities and of such nature that they cannot practically be assigned to production (contract) as direct costs. Consistent treatment of costs for defense contracts and nongovernment work is essential. When a given type of cost is treated as direct for contract purposes and the applicable portion is charged directly to a contract, the balance of that cost should not be charged to a pool of indirect costs which are then charged indirectly to both government and nongovernment work. Hence, all such charges must be eliminated in the computation of the overhead rate to be used in applying overhead to a contract.

Allowable costs.   For costs to be allowable, they must meet four broad standards. They must be reasonable; they must be allocable; they must result from the application of generally accepted accounting principles; and they must comply with the terms of the contract.

Allocable costs.   An allocable cost is any cost that can be assigned or charged to a particular cost objective, job, contract, or process. A cost is allocable (in whole or in part) to a government contract if it is incurred especially for that contract or if it is necessary to the operation of the business.

Reasonable costs.   A cost is reasonable if (1) in type and amount it is necessary to the completion of the contract or for the performance of business; (2) it is not in excess of an amount that would have been arrived at as the result of a competitive "arm's-length" transaction; and (3) it is in compliance with the terms of the contract.

Costs generally allowed. Fourteen types of costs are generally allowed. They are as follows: (1) bonding; (2) compensation for personal services, except for limitation on executives' compensation and on wages that are discriminatory against the government, as compared with civilian work (some severance pay is allowed; under certain conditions, training costs are allowed); (3) depreciation, except for amounts improperly taken or taken on idle facilities (a reasonable use charge will be allowed on fully depreciated assets); (4) employee morale, health, welfare, and food-service and dormitory costs and credits, except for unreasonable amounts; (5) insurance and indemnification, except for certain limitations; (6) labor relations costs; (7) maintenance and repair costs; (8) manufacturing and production engineering costs; (9) materials costs; (10) patent and royalty costs; (11) plant protection costs; (12) precontract costs of activities necessary for securing the contract; (13) recruitment costs; and (14) rental cost, if not excessive (problems arise in sale and leaseback).

Costs generally disallowed. The types of costs that are generally disallowed are almost as numerous as the types allowed. They include (1) advertising, except for recruitment of help, the procurement of scarce items, and the disposal of surplus material and scrap resulting from a defense contract; (2) bad debts; (3) contributions and donations; (4) entertainment costs, unless in connection with professional or technical meetings; (5) excess facility costs, except for reasonable standby costs; (6) fines and penalties, except those resulting from compliance with specific contract provisions or written orders from a contracting officer; (7) interest and other financial costs; (8) losses on other contracts; (9) organization costs; (10) plant reconversion costs, except the cost of removing government property; and (11) profit or loss on disposition of plant, equipment, or other capital assets.

These lists of allowed and disallowed costs are not all-inclusive, and they lack detail. They are intended only to provide the reader with a general concept of which costs are allowable and which are not. For detailed information, DAR should be consulted.

A general comment: the government wants a "fair shake" when dealing with contractors, and a reasonable profit is allowed. The weighted guidelines allow for 10 percent to 12 percent before taxes (on a cost basis). If a contractor wants to do business with the government, the contractor should keep reasonably accurate records. Generally, the government requirements ask that contractors do what reasonably prudent businesspeople would do anyway.

Contracts in excess of $100,000 will require a pre-award audit by government auditors. To make the audits go smoothly, it is recommended that the contractors assign an individual of supervisory level to government contract work. The supporting detail necessary to prepare the cost and pricing proposal should be made available to the auditor. Copies of work papers for each element of cost should be assembled in an orderly manner. The auditor will be looking for verification of all major cost elements. The auditor wants to feel comfortable with the contract and feel that the government is getting that fair shake.

Contract Termination

All defense contracts in excess of $1,000 include a termination clause. A contract may be terminated for the convenience of the government or because of default by the contractor.

The government may terminate a contract for its convenience when the need for the product is reduced or ceases to exist, or when termination is in the best interest of the government. The default clause permits the government to terminate a contract in the event a contractor fails to perform according to the terms of the contract. In case of the termination of a cost-type contract for default, the contractor shall be reimbursed for his allowable costs and an appropriate portion of the total fee. The contractor will not be allowed the costs of preparing his settlement proposal. In case of default on a fixed-price contract, the contractor may be charged with the added cost incurred by the government for acquiring the items from another source, as well as liquidated damages, if provided for in the contract, or for actual damages in the absence of the provision for liquidated damages.

A termination for the convenience of the government may be either partial or complete. A termination is complete if the termination notice orders a complete work stoppage on the unperformed portion of the contract. A termination is partial if a stoppage of performance of only a part of the uncompleted portion of the contract is ordered. That part of the contract which has not been terminated is referred to as the continuing portion. Upon receipt of a termination notice, the contractor must immediately stop all work on the terminated portion. If the termination is complete, all work must be stopped at once. If it is a partial termination, the contractor is expected to complete the continuing portion of the contract.

A termination may be settled with or without cost to the government. In cases where a contractor has incurred very little or no cost on the terminated portion of the contract, the government may negotiate a settlement without cost to itself. In case of a termination, a contractor must file a termination claim with the contracting officer within a year from date of termination.

Terminated fixed-price contracts may be settled on an "inventory basis" or (with prior approval of the contracting officer) on a "total-cost basis." To establish the amount of the claim under the inventory basis, the contractor may include only costs allocable to the terminated portion of the contract. All items in the termination inventory must be listed at cost. To establish the gross termination claim, an allowance for profit is added to, or an allowance for loss is deducted from, the inventory value. The inventory basis for settlement is usually preferred, but under some circumstances the total-cost basis is more practical. The contracting officer may approve the total-cost basis under the following conditions: (1) when production has not started (only preproduction costs have been incurred); (2) when it is difficult or impossible to establish production cost per unit of product or when the contract does not specify unit prices.

When the total-cost basis is used, all costs incurred on the contract are itemized regardless of whether they apply to the completed or the terminated portion of the contract. To the total of the costs is added an allowance for profit, or an allowance for loss is deducted. The claims of subcontractors are added to the above sum or difference. From this amount are deducted the contract price of units accepted by the government, as well as all advance or progress payments. In case of a partial termination, a settlement proposal cannot be submitted on a total-cost basis until the continued portion of the contract is completed.

When a cost-reimbursement-type contract is terminated, the contractor may continue to voucher incurred costs for a period extending to the last day of the sixth month after the termination date. He may elect to discontinue vouchering costs at any time during the six-month period. After a contractor has vouchered all costs applicable to the particular contract (within the six-month period), he may file a substantiated claim for his fee. The claim for fees must be submitted within one year from termination date unless he has been granted an extension.

After a contractor has discontinued vouchering costs, either because of the expiration of the six-month period or because he elected to do so, he may present a settlement proposal. Such a proposal may not include any previously vouchered costs, any previously disallowed costs, or costs subject to a reclaim voucher.

□ *J. Lee Ledbetter* (*and W. Asquith Howe, the original author of this now substantially revised section*)

INVENTORY VALUATION AND CONTROL

The term "inventory" designates assets of a concern held for the purpose of sale, or conversion to products for sale, in the general course of business. For most concerns, investment in inventory is of significant size and has a substantial influence on total capital investment required.

Manufacturing companies inventory raw materials purchased for conversion or incorporation in a final product of the manufacturing process. The end products of one process, of course, may well be the raw materials of another. Retailing or distribution companies normally purchase finished or semifinished goods and offer them for sale at a markup over their costs.

Work in process is raw material in the process of conversion to finished goods. Included in its value are the raw materials, the labor applied, and a portion of the manufacturing costs that cannot be specifically identified with an individual product, that is, manufacturing overhead or burden. Examples of burden are indirect labor, supervision, maintenance, quality testing, utilities, depreciation, insurance, and property taxes.

Finished goods are the end products of manufacturing processes—the completed goods held for sale. These products may serve another company as raw materials or purchased parts or may be sold to a distributor or retailer as finished goods for sale to the ultimate customer.

Inventory Valuation and Performance Measurement

The value of inventory on hand must be determined periodically, along with the value of other assets, to enable a company to determine its cost of goods sold and to state its financial position. The basis used for inventory valuation has a significant effect on the costs and earnings reflected in the operating statements, and on the asset value shown on the balance sheet, which reflects its financial position. The basis for valuation also determines the allocation of costs between accounting periods. In essence, the higher the costs allocated to the final inventory, the lower the cost of goods sold and, therefore, the higher the profit for the period. Since the ending inventory of a period becomes the beginning inventory for the subsequent period, these higher inventory costs will increase the subsequent period's cost of goods sold, thus decreasing the profit reported for that period.

A variety of methods can be used to value inventory. Income-tax computation, accounting principles, ease of application, management reporting, and control considerations all influence the approach used. From a management point of view, the evaluation method that is selected should take advantage of benefits that may affect the operating statement but should also be easily used or converted to effective reporting for management evaluation and decision making.

The conventional accounting method for valuing inventories is known as "the lower of cost or market." This method does not allow profits to be earned in inventory, but does recognize losses when the realizable sales value minus distribution costs declines below the purchase and/or conversion cost of the inventory. In this manner, the company's inventory value on the balance sheet is fairly and conservatively represented.

Cost Determination

Typically, cost is used as the basis for inventory valuation, and reserves are applied to reflect lower realizable values. Other charges that reduce inventory value, such as physical deterioration and obsolescence, may also be covered by reserves, leaving only the physical units to be costed by regularly applied methods. IRS regulations (S 1.471-11) stipulate three general classes of costs for inclusion in or exclusion from inventory valuation. Costs includable in inventory are direct production costs (material and labor), acquisition value of semifinished or finished goods, and certain conversion costs incident to and necessary to production. These conversion costs include maintenance, utilities, occupancy expense, indirect labor/materials, and cost of quality. Costs not includable in inventory are marketing, advertising, selling and distribution expenses, interest, R&D expenses, pension, and other general administrative expenses. There is another category of costs whose inclusion in inventory is at the company's option depending on their treatment in the financial statements. Examples of costs in this category are taxes, employee benefits, rework, scrap, spoilage, insurance, depreciation, and production administrative expenses.

Accordingly, inventory costs generally consist of costs of purchased materials, conversion labor, and overhead. While material can generally be identified with the manufactured product on a per-unit basis, it is much more difficult to do this with conversion costs. Therefore, the principal methods of cost determination for financial-statement preparation begin with standard costs and/or average costs, which provide a basis for assigning conversion costs to the manufactured product. The development of standard or average unit costs allows the extension of physical units by these costs to determine the ending-inventory value, which, when subtracted from the beginning inventory plus materials purchases and conversion expenses for the period, equals the cost of goods sold for the period. Ending-inventory values, and correspondingly cost of goods sold, may be further adjusted by the use of FIFO (first in, first out), LIFO (last in, first out), or cost-of-specific-lot methods. For retail and distribution companies, which don't incur conversion costs, the gross-margin (retail) method is the commonly accepted valuation method.

Standard costs. A simply administered technique for determining inventory cost is provided by standard costs. To facilitate its use, standard costs representing the expected costs of purchase and conversion must be established for materials, labor, and other expenses directly related to each inventoried unit. Those manufacturing expenses (overhead or burden) not directly identified with a product or inventory item are usually assigned to each unit of production on a realistic basis. Thus supervision might be assigned on the basis of the labor hours required to make a product, and depreciation, insurance, and taxes might be assigned on the basis of the machine-hours required to make a product. Each company must take care to select the most reliable basis for cost assignment to ensure that the valuations are proper and that management has the most accurate facts available for pricing and product-profitability analysis. Inventory value is quickly determined by applying these standards to each unit of stock on hand.

Of course, when actual costs are not equal to the standards, variances result and must be recorded. If these variances are substantial, they are accumulated and reallocated to all the production of the period and the inventory on hand. If the variances are minor, they are generally taken as an expense as they occur. Standard costs are also used in management reporting for profit performance and control of operating costs. To remain accurate and effective, standard costs must be revised at least annually by correcting for changes in costs and methods; otherwise, the values derived lose validity either for valuing inventory or for controlling purchasing or operations.

Average cost. Many companies use an average unit cost to determine inventory value. Two methods are used for this purpose: an average calculated by dividing the total cost of beginning inventory and purchases by the total number of units represented; and a moving average, calculated after each new purchase is made. Where the time lapse between valuations is long or price changes are rapid, the two methods produce somewhat different results. It is important to note that the moving average requires the maintenance of perpetual records, while the weighted average may be computed periodically. In either case, the use of averaging tends to spread the effect of short-range price changes and level their effect on profit determination.

FIFO. The FIFO method assumes that the goods are sold in the order in which they were received or manufactured. With the use of FIFO it is not necessary to identify lots or physically segregate items in the order of purchase. Under this method the final inventory is priced by determining the costs of the most recent purchases or using the most recent standard costs. Generally, this is done by working back from the most recent invoices of units manufactured until the quantity on hand has been covered.

LIFO. The LIFO method assumes that the last goods received or manufactured were sold first. In a period of rising prices, this method reduces profits and postpones tax payments, because the highest-cost items are used to compute the cost of sales. Although the final inventory can be calculated by keeping perpetual inventory records and historical cost figures, this method is generally not used because of the clerical work required. Instead, a simpler dollar-value approach using price-index levels is employed. This method assumes that all items in inventory, or in a segment of inventory, are homogeneous. This assumption allows the use of price indices to convert the final inventory priced at current prices to the same inventory priced in terms of the base year (the year in which LIFO was adopted).

Generally, any company with the following characteristics should adopt the LIFO method if it desires to postpone the payment of taxes and thus receive an "interest-free" loan from the government: (1) inventories that are significant relative to its total assets (a manufacturer or distributor); (2) inventory costs that are increasing; (3) an effective tax rate that is not expected to increase significantly; and/or (4) inventory levels that are expected to remain stable or increase. Conversely, if inventory levels or unit costs are expected to decline or the tax rates increase, a company should not use the LIFO method because LIFO could increase rather than decrease the company's future tax liability.

Cost of specific lot. For the capital-goods industries and some other industries it is usually desirable to maintain the identity and actual costs of specific lots or items. This is done by recording the actual raw-materials purchase price and conversion costs for each lot or item in inventory. The application of this method is usually limited to inventories containing high-value, low-quantity items or to those situations where such records are practical or mandatory.

Gross-margin method. The gross-margin method of pricing inventory has been developed in the distribution and retailing industries to facilitate inventory valuation by having items in inventory priced at an adjusted selling price rather than cost. Since the actual cost of each item in inventory is difficult to trace, a ratio must be determined that relates the retail value of the ending inventory to the original cost. The basis for computing this ratio is an established average margin, or markup, to the cost to arrive at the selling price. Assuming that the goods in inventory are representative, in terms of their markup, of goods purchased during the recent operating period, their cost is easily determined by using the ratio to recompute the inventory value. Using this method, the ending-inventory value is determined by extending the physical units by their selling prices and then reducing the extended amount by the average markup percentage. As with other methods, cost of goods sold is calculated by subtracting the ending-inventory value from beginning inventory plus purchases. Of course, accurate records must be kept of markups over the initial markup, of markdowns, of variations among margins on various classes of goods, and of other alterations or changes, so that the value of the inventory is not distorted. This does provide an easily applied method for inventory valuation, while controlling the current profit margin and identifying the effect of shortages and losses. However, because it is an averaging method, changes in mix can affect the accuracy of the final inventory value. (See the discussion of the open-to-buy method for recent technology developments in the retail field.)

Selection of method. The size, age, and type of inventory must be considered in selecting the method used for valuation. The techniques chosen should provide for the requirements of financial and tax reporting as well as relate to the methods used by management for measuring its performance in inventory management and control. For consistency in financial reporting, it is mandatory that the method of inventory valuation remain constant. If at any time a change in method is made, the effect on the financial results must be clearly stated.

Asset Management

One of the prime responsibilities of managers at all levels is the optimum use of assets. The dollar value of inventory represents a major capital investment, ranging from 30 percent to 60 percent of a company's current assets. The investment made in inventory, therefore, is a significant portion of working capital. Investment in inventory should be carefully watched by management and is a key factor in determining asset-management performance. Recognizing that inventory reduction is one of the easiest methods of generating additional cash flow, managers should institute effective policies on inventory management and control to reduce the amount of inventory required to support the marketing forecast and meet the company's customer-service goals. Methods for accomplishing these objectives are discussed under "Inventory Management and Control."

Turnover. This is the most common measure of inventory utilization and the effectiveness of the company's planning and control activities. It is calculated as follows:

$$\text{Turnover} = \frac{\text{cost of goods sold}}{\text{average inventory value}}$$

The quotient represents the number of times the given amount of inventory is "used" during a period of measurement. To evaluate inventory management on the basis of past performance, actual cost of goods sold and average inventory balance are used for the turnover calculation. Alternatively, turnover can be calculated to determine the number of times existing inventory is expected to be absorbed in subsequent periods. Using this approach, current inventory balance is used in the denominator while future expected withdrawals from inventory (based on sales forecasts) represent cost of goods sold. In either case, the measure indicates the utilization or activity of the investment. Slow turnover may indicate poor use of the asset and greater exposure to obsolescence, damage, or shrinkage. Too rapid a turnover or low coverage, on the other hand, may indicate that stock is moving too quickly, thereby increasing the cost of ordering the materials handling. It could also indicate that raw-materials-price discounts, based upon volume, are not being realized or that the desired level of customer service is not being achieved.

Return on investment. ROI also measures the use of assets, including inventory. Simply stated, the calculation for ROI is

$$\text{ROI} = \frac{\text{profit}}{\text{sales (margin)}} \times \frac{\text{sales}}{\text{assets (turnover)}} = \frac{\text{profit}}{\text{assets}}$$

It can be seen that these calculations combine common management measures (turnover and return on sales) into one factor for evaluating the profitable use of inventory and other assets. Any reduction in the value of assets will increase both turnover and return on investment.

Profit Management

Another primary measure of management performance is profitability. Inventory policies and procedures have a strong influence on the ability of a company to achieve reasonable objectives in this area. Inventory investment directly affects sales and, ultimately, profit performance, since the ability to respond to an order for products or services relates in part to the availability of required parts or finished products. Because production facilities may not profitably be left idle and serious fluctuations in production create additional problems of training and maintaining an adequate labor force, manufacturing management generally attempts to build inventory during seasonally low sales periods. This provides stock for seasonally high demand periods and equalized month-to-month utilization of equipment and cost of labor. Thus a balance between customer service, efficient use of production facilities, and minimum inventory investment must be achieved as a part of effective profit and asset management.

Inventory losses represent another way in which inventory value and its control may affect company operating results, since such losses reduce profits. Several types of conditions account for most inventory losses. Obsolescence is caused by purchasing or producing products, in excess of the demand for use or sale, which are displaced by newer or more desirable goods. The obsolete goods must be disposed of at prices sometimes less than cost. The difference between the cost of the inventory and its disposal price is the loss caused by obsolescence. In addition, the investment in excessive inventory of these items generally precludes the purchase of other more desirable items, requires space for storage, and increases the effort required for taking physical inventory.

Inventory not used quickly, or stored in inadequate facilities, is exposed to damage or spoilage. A certain amount of such losses may be expected under any condition, but they can be held to a minimum by careful planning, handling, and facilities maintenance. The most effective control is the limitation of purchases and inventory to necessary quantities. Evaporation, chemical changes, date expiration, and spoilage must also be recognized as types of loss that may be best controlled through limiting the amount of inventory and the time the inventory is on hand.

Pilferage or theft is a special loss consideration, especially in certain industries where inventoried items are small or of high value and may be consumed by employees or easily disposed of without identification. In addition to the control of inventory areas, preventive measures include extra care to limit (1) opportunities for access to the inventory, (2) the number of people with access, and (3) the routes for removal of the most susceptible items.

In many states, the value of the inventory has yet another direct influence on profit performance, since it is the basis for certain personal property taxes on corporations. This consideration usually prompts managers to plan substantial reductions in materials and finished goods on hand immediately before the valuation date. The ability to accomplish this effectively, however, is dependent on good planning of production and sales requirements in order that the tax savings will not be offset by losses in sales and increased expenses.

The cost of carrying inventory (interest, warehouse, insurance, obsolescence, and so on) is usually in the range of 15 percent to 30 percent per year depending on interest rates, storage costs, and other factors. Therefore, any reduction in the amount of inventory required to support a given sales level can have a significant effect on the firm's profitability and also free capital for more productive uses.

Inventory Management and Control

The function of managing and controlling inventory starts and ends with planning. A method is required for planning, and *constant* replanning in order to consider the endless stream of changes that take place in sales forecasts and on the factory floor. The real world of inventory management and control is one of constant change. Within this environment, management must establish effective techniques for making good decisions and properly reporting company performance. Consideration must be given to customer service, return on investment, inventory turnover, and good manufacturing and vendor scheduling. In addition, controls must be in place to monitor obsolescence and excess supplies and, where appropriate, evaluate causes of shrinkage.

Initially management viewed the "planning of requirements" as the major inventory management and control function. In fact, this view helped popularize the reorder-point system of determining requirements. As broader definitions of inventory management and control have developed, along with expanded responsibilities, an alternative approach—material requirements planning (MRP) —has emerged. These two divergent approaches and the open-to-buy method used by retailing companies will be discussed.

Reorder-Point Method

This method concentrates on individual items as if there is no interrelationship with any other item. In this system, as the item is used and the quantity on hand falls below a preestablished reorder point, a replenishment order is triggered. This order, it is assumed, will be filled before a minimum safety stock is broken. This method is commonly referred to as a reorder-point method. Simplistically, a typical "two-bin system" on the shop floor or as used in a replenishment ware-

Figure 2-31. The reorder-point method.

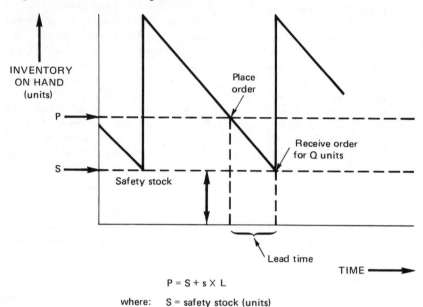

$$P = S + s \times L$$

where: S = safety stock (units)
        s = average daily sales (units)
        L = lead time (days)

house illustrates this approach. Spare parts or maintenance supply requirements in some companies are projected by this method. The major problem with this technique—basing actions on the past activity of individual items—is that it is not coordinated with potential future marketplace changes and thus projects only a haphazard relationship to the true requirement. Obsolescence is often excessive with this method.

Figure 2-31 graphically illustrates the application of the reorder-point method. This system is useful when the consumption of inventory is not related directly to marketing demand or the consumption of related material.

Material Requirements Planning (MRP)

Another method of determining inventory requirements uses a sales forecast and a bill of materials (showing item interrelationship) coupled with a routing file. Using this system, the sales forecast is "exploded" to determine the materials, labor, and machine-hours or factory time required to meet the forecast after the current production plans and available inventory are accounted for. The production forecast is usually for weekly periods and covers the next 3 to 12 months or can go farther into the future. It is usually updated on a weekly or biweekly basis, depending on the volatility of the sales demand. This method is commonly referred to as material requirements planning (MRP). Normally this method is associated with the use of a computer. Planning component requirements for an automobile assembly plant is a typical example of the use of this method. The basic problems of using MRP in a manufacturing and/or an inventory replenishment environment are the need for a high degree of discipline and for a total commitment to this technique by all the functions involved (manufacturing, marketing, and senior management). Effective users of this approach have demonstrated that favorable results can be obtained despite sales forecast inaccuracies. In fact, overcoming forecast inaccuracies may be one of the most important benefits of an effective MRP system.

In the evolution of improved inventory management techniques, one fact seems evident. Material requirements planning has established itself as the most important building block of all. In fact, since picking up many more users in the 1970s, MRP has revolutionized the field of inventory management and has obsoleted many of the traditional theories. This is not to say that we have not learned to selectively use a few of the time-tested techniques within the MRP environment, but no longer are they viewed as panaceas or stand-alone solutions. Two of the key techniques that have been retained are the ABC method and economic order quantity.

The ABC method. This approach is still being used to effectively identify high-dollar-value or high-usage inventory items so that priorities are in place to conserve management time and focus on the important items. In most companies the large number of items in inventory, both materials and finished goods, can create a burden in voluminous record maintenance and detailed physical counting. Although modern data processing capabilities have reduced these problems, the value of inventory can be greatly reduced by using an ABC inventory method. It is characteristic of most inventories that a relatively small number of items account for a high proportion of the value and activity. This method, also referred to as 80/20 analysis (from the fact that 20 percent of the items usually account for 80 percent of the value), selects items according to their contribution to sales, profit, or value of inventory. The following is a typical mix:

Class	Number of Items	Percentage of Items in Inventory	Percentage Contribution to Cost of Sales	Frequency of Receipts (Weeks)
A	156	7	51	Weekly
B	835	35	38	4–8 weeks
C	1,409	58	11	26–52 weeks
Total	2,400	100	100	

The few items identified as representing the largest contribution can be given tight control at reasonable cost. Items of lesser dollar importance may be controlled by less demanding or less expensive methods. For instance, A items may be limited to one week's stock, while C items may be allowed six months' stock.

Economic order quantity (EOQ). This technique can best be used to calculate general guidelines for quantity-buying decisions on low-dollar-value items, using either the reorder-point or the MRP system. Group analysis is necessary to maximize and control benefits. However, because this approach concentrates on individual items, it is being replaced by the more modern view of planning and controlling aggregate inventory, that is, blanket ordering with releases, capacity buying, and manufacturing (and/or buying) matched sets of items as required.

The economic-order-quantity method calculates the theoretical minimum annual cost for ordering and stocking an item. The EOQ computation takes into account the cost of placing an order, the annual sales rate, the unit cost, and the cost of carrying the inventory (interest, insurance, obsolescence, and so forth). The formula is illustrated in Figure 2-32, which also shows that, as the number of orders placed is reduced, the cost of ordering is reduced but the cost of holding (carrying) increases. The economic order quantity and frequency occurs where the sum of the two costs is the minimum. The cost of carrying inventory, it has been observed, usually ranges between 15 percent and 30 percent of the item's cost. Since the formula for calculating the EOQ uses the square root of the cost of carrying inventory, the EOQ is not very sensitive to this cost and the 15–30 percent range is usually considered adequate. Once determined for an item, the EOQ is not frequently changed except for changes in sales or use requirements.

In addition, some fundamentals that were not properly understood previously are now more clearly viewed by the practitioner. The most important example is

Figure 2-32. Economic order quantity.

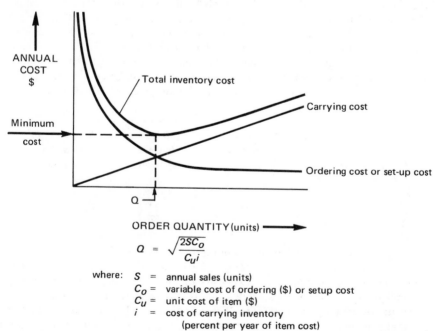

$$Q = \sqrt{\frac{2SC_o}{C_u i}}$$

where: S = annual sales (units)
C_o = variable cost of ordering ($) or setup cost
C_u = unit cost of item ($)
i = cost of carrying inventory
       (percent per year of item cost)

the difference that exists between capacity and priority, both in planning and control. In the inventory management area, each of these must be fully understood and dealt with separately. [See the comments under "MRP Elements," specifically, the discussions of capacity-requirements planning (for capacity) and dispatch list (for priority).] Confusion over this separation has caused many a headache in U.S. plants. The text *Production and Inventory Management in the Computer Age** dedicates 120 pages to this topic and details the emphasis and need for understanding this problem.

The computer. The function of planning requirements of material components could have started in early Roman days. Prior to assembly of a chariot for the great races of the period, the craftsman knew that he must have one axle, two wheels, the proper number of spokes, the body, one tongue, and so on to complete the job. This was not the plan of a mathematical genius, just a logical plan of a craftsman who had built chariots before. Today, the same principle is used in MRP, but with the complexities of our modern industries adding enormously to the task of coordinated planning. This is where the computer becomes a valuable tool—processing data at ever-increasing speeds with a correspondingly lowered unit cost. We are not making one chariot a month but 50,000 units per week or per day through many stages of manufacturing and through many distribution points. Also, each "chariot" has thousands of parts plus an almost unlimited number of colors and options. The computer can handle this data-manipulation task well but does not make the decisions that people still do best. The computer's job is to process, categorize, list, store, and do whatever else of a mundane nature needs to be done, on the basis of the logic and instructions given to it by the people involved.

Resource planning. As more companies have become effective users of MRP, their experience shows that the true power of this technique is far greater than initially imagined. Some companies have extended the original acronym (MRP—material requirements planning) to a newly broadened MRP II—manufacturing resources planning. This new acronym speaks to the many expanded uses of these techniques. MRP II can be used to better plan the various internal resources required from all disciplines and functions, including distribution planning, manufacturing, quality control, quality assurance testing, industrial engineering, product engineering, and so on. MRP II pulls together, in a vertical sense, all the disciplines required to manufacture and distribute a product.

A few companies, on the leading edge of this technology, have been successful in further broadening the MRP concepts into both the supply side and the demand side of the business. Work has been done with suppliers to better integrate their planning with those of the buying company—in effect, "closing the loop" on the complete cycle. This has brought the suppliers much more into the internal workings of their customers' plants. A freer sharing of information concerning *true* needs has benefited both the supplier and the manufacturer by leading to better priority planning and capacity control. Some assembly-type companies have carried this to the ultimate by having suppliers deliver the exact

* Oliver W. Wight, Boston, MA: Cahners Publishing Company, 1974.

amount of each day's production requirements on the day needed—thus avoiding carrying raw materials and the necessity for storage space. The Japanese refer to this as the "just in time" approach, or the Kanban method.

On the demand side, a domain which had heretofore been fairly confined to those in the sales and marketing functions, improved understanding through MRP has highlighted many areas of commonality between sales and other disciplines of the company. Selling more than the capacity of a manufacturing plant is a sure way to a customer-service disaster and should be viewed more broadly than merely as a "manufacturing capacity" problem. On the other hand, when inventories are increasing as a result of trying to maintain plant personnel levels, sales campaigns with proper timing can be effectively used to minimize *overall* costs. In effect, this is a conscious act of managing sales to bring them into better harmony with the realities of the business.

In addition, on the demand side, external dealings have begun with customers, similar to those that have occurred with suppliers, with corresponding success. If a customer has a workable MRP system already in place and has done his own forecasting and netted supply to demand, why redo what has already been done? Unfortunately, many companies forecast all demands, whether independent or dependent. With improved communications and cooperation between companies, potential growth in this area, with the resultant reductions in inventories and costs, seems almost unlimited at this time.

MRP elements. Several excellent texts* are available on MRP, and more are in process. The reader should avail himself of these, since doing justice to all facets of MRP is impossible in these few paragraphs. However, some of the fundamental supporting elements of the MRP concept will be discussed in the following paragraphs.

- Inventory accuracy (How much do we have?). No longer just an accounting responsibility, this is the starting point for every good MRP system. Determination of quantities on hand must be accurate and timely (probably daily). To improve accuracy, cycle counting is becoming very popular. Not only does it provide repetitive updated counts, but it also assists in locating the source of the error for timely correction and can eliminate the need for costly annual physical inventory counts as well as surprise inventory "shrinks."

- Bill-of-materials accuracy (What is the product made from?). This is the basis for an accurate material requirements "explosion" and must be kept up to date. Also, this is necessary for effective work-in-process cost development of products.

- Routing accuracy (Where is the product made?). Good routings are necessary to properly plan and control the work-in-process flow. In a sense, routings are the basis for network scheduling—that is, detailed requirements through each major production center by time period.

---

* Joseph A. Orlicky, *Material Requirements Planning.* New York: McGraw-Hill, 1975; George W. Plossl and Oliver W. Wight, *Production and Inventory Control—Principles and Techniques.* Englewood Cliffs, N.J.: Prentice-Hall, 1967; see also *Production and Inventory Management,* published quarterly by the American Production and Inventory Control Society, Inc., Washington, D.C., for current developments.

- Production plan (At what capacity should we produce?). This is the function with upper-management involvement—the production plan is the most important element of MRP II. The general direction of the total company effort (sales, manufacturing, distribution, purchasing, and so on) is planned at this point. All disciplines must be involved in setting, and agreeing to, the production plan, because they are responsible for seeing to its proper execution.
- Distribution-requirements planning (DRP) (Where, when, how much should we ship?). This area is applicable to distribution and/or retailing companies plus manufacturing companies that have distribution warehouses. Replenishments must be planned for each of the distribution locations to determine the proper demands on central shipping and/or the manufacturing facility. These replenishments are mathematically planned for every item by using the distribution center's appropriate share of the national forecast, safety stock, transit time, and economical shipping quantities. The plan must be updated frequently to ensure that valid replenishment needs are placed against central shipping.
- Master scheduling (What individual items do we really intend to produce?). It is said that this is where "what you would *like* to produce is converted to what you *can* produce." Its importance to a manufacturing plant can be likened to a steering wheel's importance to an automobile. You better have one that works! Planned orders, firm planned orders, and shop orders—these are three categories of (progressive) orders in a typical MRP system for which the master scheduler can use the computer to better control the plant planning. Established time horizons assist in this control to avoid "overnervousness" in the system. In total, the master schedule must equal the production plan.
- Capacity-requirements planning (How many hours are needed in this work center?). This provides the requirements for labor and equipment at all work centers in line with the needs of the master schedule. Overloading a key work center is a sure way to miss the master schedule, regardless of how good the intentions.
- Dispatch list (Which job should be done next in this work center?). This technique is used for *priority* control. This is not an expedite list, since it is within the plan and truly reflects the most important priority at the time. It is not unusual to produce a daily dispatch list to keep current with the ever-changing environment of a typical company.
- Input/output. This is a workflow tracking technique to monitor and control the volume of work through the various major work centers. Personnel requirements in the centers are reviewed at least weekly. Companies effectively using MRP find that this technique assists in properly solving the lion's share of the overtime problems and has been responsible for significant dollar savings without adversely affecting customer service.
- Capacity buying (Let's use MRP with our "outside factory"—our suppliers.). This item, by definition, means going outside the direct management jurisdiction of the manufacturing operation. Purchasing or planning provides the connecting link to suppliers in most organizations. These are items on the "buy side" of the make/buy equation. Had they been on the "make side," it would have been obvious that they would have been managed within the internal MRP system. There-

fore, the objective in this concept is to include the external items within MRP, regardless of supply source.

All these elements are important for MRP II but not necessarily all-inclusive. Future effective MRP work is expected to broaden the cooperation with all disciplines of the company, because MRP, by design, is the true simulator of the user's business. The future for MRP has never looked brighter. When those people responsible for making a system work can feel, see, and understand the workings of their business—and this is the case in an MRP environment—they will improve it. The statement that MRP is a journey, not a destination, has never been truer than today.

The Open-to-Buy Method

Retail businesses have used an open-to-buy inventory control system for many years. Simply stated, under this sytem a department buyer is limited to a specific amount of funds that may be committed to the total of inventory on hand and on order. This amount is related to the sales expected in the immediate future, usually a month or season. To calculate the open-to-buy amount, the allowable closing inventory for the month, at retail price, is added to sales planned for the month. The goods on hand (at retail) and open purchase orders (at retail) are subtracted from this total and adjusted for markup percentage to arrive at the funds available for purchases. Adjustments for markups and markdowns are made so that the available amount is not affected by these changes. The allowable closing-inventory value is usually related to the average inventory-turnover performance expected in the buyer's department and the sales expected in the succeeding month. It should be noted that this technique primarily affects budget control and does not identify the items that should be in stock or tell their number. Therefore, other procedures are sometimes used along with the open-to-buy method for the selection decisions.

Although the open-to-buy method is usually thought of in relation to retailing, it is also being applied in other fields. In one application, for example, a manufacturer may establish a limit for the number of units that may be planned for production, on the basis of the sales plan, the units in inventory, and the units already in process or planned for production. Similarly, the open-to-buy amount for the purchase of parts and materials can be related to the production plan and the dollars of materials on hand and already on order.

Some retail merchants have adapted EOQ methods to control the inventory of high-volume staple goods because the limitations of open-to-buy rules too often result in stock shortages in items of high demand. Rather than lose sales for this reason, managers are allowing EOQ purchases to override the open-to-buy restraints. This practice, however, does not relieve the buyer of responsibility to correct the "overbought" position by reducing inventory of slow-moving or overstocked items that are not controlled under the EOQ system.

The recent development of point-of-sale recorders has given retail stores the ability to track inventory movement by item or SKU (stock-keeping unit) and also compute the weeks of supply on hand on the basis of historical sales. This new technology will certainly lead to improved control and management of retail inventories, particularly in the major retail operations. This technology will also enable stores to determine the cost of goods sold on an individual-unit basis, which was not possible with the traditional open-to-buy method.

Physical Inventory

Regardless of the accuracy of perpetual inventory records and the care with which they are prepared, the unit stock records must be adjusted periodically after a physical count for confirmation of accuracy and balancing to the general ledger. Of course, if no perpetual records are kept, such a count is required to determine the number of units on hand at a specific date. Since no system is flawless, the count also serves to test the effectiveness of the control systems and identify weaknesses requiring improvement.

Many companies have switched to a cycle count system, that is, count $1/12$th of the inventory each month or $1/52$nd each week. This method will improve accuracy, pinpoint errors in the record-keeping systems quickly, avoid shrink "surprises," and avoid the expense and disruption of an annual physical inventory. Cycle counts can also be administered to concentrate on the high-value or high-movement items, with less frequent counts of the low-value, low-movement items —that is, they can use the ABC system mentioned previously.

Each company must establish written procedures for counting, recording, pricing, and summarizing physical inventory. The initial counts are usually re-checked—on a sample basis, at least—by different counters or clerks. These procedures are well documented in other publications and therefore are not covered here; however, certain problems recur in physical inventory counting and valuation and should be given careful management attention:

- *Units of measure.* To decribe an ounce of material as a pound, or a dozen as a gross, can seriously distort the inventory value. In many cases the units of measure used by the company that sells the material are not the same as those used by the company that purchases the material, so care must be taken to ensure that the valuation is based on a consistent unit of measure.

- *Liquid inventories.* Special measurement procedures should be defined for items of inventory that are not easily counted. Tank calibrations or similar methods may be appropriate. If meters or gauges are used, independent calibration prior to inventory should be performed.

- *Goods in transit.* Goods shipped F.O.B. and assigned to a common carrier must be included in inventory even if not received at the time of inventory. A careful record of shipments to customers where title passes at time of shipment must also be kept so that these goods are not included in inventory. Care must be taken to ensure "clean cutoffs" for the receiving and shipping functions as well as for the material moving through a manufacturing process.

- *Damaged goods.* Products or materials of questionable value should be segregated for special valuation.

- *Obsolete goods.* Items of excessive age or long inactivity should be segregated for special valuation. The month's supply on hand should be calculated for major items to be sure the stocks are not excessive.

- *Work in progress.* If good cost records are maintained, determination of the state of completion and value is not difficult. However, if cost records are not maintained, adequate procedures must be established for estimating the amount of cost contained in each item inventoried.

Summary

The policies and procedures related to inventory management require the attention of the firm's CEO. The key criteria for successful inventory management and control systems can be summarized as follows:

- The CEO and his subordinates must understand the concepts of the systems used and *be committed* to making them work effectively. The numbers must be timely and accurate, and the marketing, manufacturing, and distribution plans *integrated* so that ony one plan or forecast is used and then updated as often as necessary to effectively manage the company's business.
- The manufacturing/inventory planning systems must be soundly conceived and integrated with the financial and cost accounting systems. *It is essential that a single data flow serve all systems.*
- Accountability and responsibility for inventory levels, shrinkage, obsolescence, as well as accurate and timely record keeping must be clearly assigned to specific management functions within the company. Computer-based systems must be updated on a daily basis for the key items manufactured, used, or purchased.
- Responsibility for sales and product forecasts, procurement, and the maintenance of product data records (bills of materials and cost standards) must be clearly defined and accepted by the various members of management.
- Management, from top to bottom, and particularly the lower level, must be *trained* in the use of the systems and the need for the *disciplines* required (timeliness and accuracy) to make the systems effective.

Effective manufacturing, inventory, and control systems can help the company reduce its working-capital requirements and manufacturing costs while improving customer service. The responsibility for having and using effective systems clearly lies with the CEO of the company.

☐ **Lester E. Hammar, John Yoder,** and **C. Dow Caldwell** (*and Robert P. Gibbons and Charles F. Stamm, the original authors of this now substantially revised section*)

FEDERAL INCOME TAX RESPONSIBILITIES

Management's role in federal income-tax matters is both defensive and offensive. Defensively, the corportion must be protected against unnecessarily heavy impact of the tax law and against disallowances on the tax return because of failure of substantiation or inability to comply meticulously with tax regulations. Offensively, management may substantially achieve the subsidizing of necessary or desirable expenditures by having the costs treated as valid tax deductions. With the federal income-tax rate at nearly 50 percent for corporations, the government will pay almost half the costs of expenditures tailored to the conditions set forth in the Internal Revenue Code (IRC), that is to say, of deductible items.

Often, that subsidy of nearly 50 percent is on a collision course with management's prerogatives in running the corporation. For example, the IRS cannot tell a corporation how much an officer's salary can be. But the IRS can and does tell the corporation how much of the salary is deductible. This is that part of the salary which is deemed *reasonable*. And to the extent that the subsidy is not allowed, the expenditure probably will be too costly. Its after-tax cost will be nearly doubled.

Management's Limitations

Management must recognize the limitations of its own ability to make decisions: that is, decisions that will be afforded tax cognizance by the IRS. These limitations cover many areas, such as what is ordinary and necessary; how much should be paid in dividends if the accumulated-earnings tax is to be avoided; what intercompany price or fee structure may be used without the IRS being able to make a reallocation of income or expenses; and whether the cost of a repair is currently deductible or must be spread over the remaining useful life of the asset being repaired. Management may think that it can discontinue its qualified pension or deferred profit-sharing plan at will; for if the company devised a plan and paid for it, the company also may drop it. Technically, the company *may* do so. But if this is done without the prior approval of the commissioner of internal revenue and the secretary of commerce, the tax consequences will be expensive—disqualification of the tax deduction for all years not yet closed by the statute of limitations.

Management's Options

Management's role in tax matters, however, is more than the defensive one of seeing that what appears on the tax return is not subject to disallowances or reallocations. In many areas, management may make valid and acceptable decisions as to a course of action with definite tax-savings potential. Among these areas are capital structure, depreciation methods, inventory methods, compensation arrangements, tax-free reorganizations, involuntary divestitures, use of affiliates as indicated by economic reality, and abnormal obsolescence.

Capital Structure

Management may choose any original capital structure for its corporation, provided the structure claimed is the same as the one actually used, apparent debt or equity relationships are bona fide, and the structure conforms to IRS regulatory specifications. Since virtually all forms of interest are deductible and dividends are not, a capital structure that makes use of debentures or other bonds results in lower taxable income and therefore is subject to close IRS scrutiny as to whether the debt instruments are actually disguised equity. This is also quite relevant in determining whether, upon corporate insolvency, stockholder advances to the company will be treated as bad debts (deductible) or as equity (capital loss).

If the necessary tests are met, a corporation's capital structure may be reshuffled as a tax-free recapitalization.

The corporation may make preferential tax treatment available to the purchasers of its securities by careful choice of the language, book treatment, and tax treatment of the certificates issued. For example, holders of bonds that really are bonds may have them redeemed on a capital basis, whereas stock that is redeemed by a corporation at a time when there are earnings and profits will result in dividends unless it can be shown that the redemption meets one of the "safe harbors" provided by the IRC, such as a redemption to pay death taxes, the complete elimination of a shareholder, or a partial liquidation.

Depreciation Methods

New or used assets with determinable useful lives, placed in service after December 31, 1980, may be written off under the accelerated cost recovery system or the straight-line method. The accelerated cost recovery system provides for asset-class lives of three years, five years, ten years, and fifteen years, and accelerated rates of write-off with provision for automatic change to straight line at a time to maximize the deduction. Assets placed in service prior to December 31, 1980, with determinable useful lives, may be written off under any consistent method that correlates adjusted cost and remaining useful life, such as straight line or unit of production. In the case of such assets that are acquired new and that have a useful life of three years or more, an accelerated method may be elected. Or, if the taxpayer can keep proper records to show that its replacement policy will provide for the retirement of assets at the end of their use cycle, the generally far more liberal guidelines established by the IRS for specific industries may be used. Depreciation on the tax return is not necessarily the same as depreciation on the books. The former is what the IRS is expected to allow, while the latter is what management believes is the proper figure.

Inventory Methods

The taxpayer may choose any consistent inventory method, provided that it conforms to the best accounting practice in the industry and clearly reflects income. Thus there is a choice, which is not confined to the most common methods —cost, market, or lower of cost or market.

During an inflationary period or at any time when the replacement costs of inventory exceed original cost, the LIFO method will reduce taxable income by charging out goods at current prices rather than at the lower costs of the past. But the IRS will permit the use of LIFO only if the taxpayer agrees to use this method on all financial statements, reports to stockholders, credit reports, and the like (with the exception of foreign subsidiaries).

Compensation Agreements

In straight salary arrangements, management should not be concerned solely with the possible loss of part of the tax deduction because of unreasonableness.

To a high-bracket executive or other employee, higher compensation means higher marginal rates, and thus salary increases or large bonuses may not be too valuable to him in spite of the 50 percent maximum rate of tax. But management has available a variety of other compensation arrangements with preferential tax treatment to the recipients: incentive stock options, employee stock-purchase plans, deferred-compensation techniques, qualified pension and/or profit-sharing plans, group insurance procedures, and various fringe benefits.

Tax-Free Reorganizations

Ordinarily, if there is a disposition (including an exchange) of property, gain will be taxable to the extent that the value of what is received exceeds the adjusted cost of the property surrendered. But if the exchange can meet the rigid requirements of the IRC, the transaction may be effected on a tax-free basis. This may include such situations as a statutory merger or consolidation; the acquisition by one corporation, solely for voting stock, of stock of another corporation; the acquisition by a corporation, solely for voting stock, of substantially all the properties of another corporation; the transfer of assets to a controlled corporation for stock; a recapitalization; or a mere change in form or place of organization. Spin-offs and insolvency reorganizations are among the types of reorganization that receive tax-free treatment. If management is not satisfied with the tax treatment of a reorganization, or with its carryover of basis, losses, and other characteristics, it can take steps to prevent the transaction from qualifying as a tax-free reorganization.

Involuntary Divestitures

Ordinarily, a corporation may choose the time of a sale or other disposition of property so that it will take place when it is most advantageous to the corporation's tax situation. But this is not always possible. In the case of an involuntary conversion (destruction, theft, seizure, requisition, or condemnation of property), gain is not recognized to the extent that the proceeds from the insurance company or government agency involved are invested in replacement property within two years of the close of the taxable year in which the property was converted involuntarily.

Gain or loss is not recognized if securities are disposed of in pursuance of an SEC order and the necessary conditions are observed. A taxpayer may elect to have the rules relating to involuntary conversions apply where property is disposed of under a Federal Communications Commission (FCC) order.

Timing of Transactions

Management may control the taxable year in which a transaction is reported for federal income-tax purposes by such devices as the installment method of reporting, use of deferred-sales techniques, or adoption of the long-term-contract method.

Expenses may be related to income by the use of percentage leases or contingent compensation arrangements.

An accrual-basis corporation has a choice as to the year of deduction in the case of charitable contributions that are authorized in one taxable year but are paid within the first 75 days of the following taxable year.

Write-offs

Management has considerable discretion in the taxable year to be used for write-offs for abnormal obsolescence, abandonment, or demolition, provided the necessary paper documentation can be developed.

Other techniques. Other tax alternatives available to management almost defy count. Among the more popular are the sale and leaseback, the gift and lease-back, and the lease of property with option to purchase.

Business Growth

Management generally regards the growth of the business as a natural process if not a compelling objective. It should be recognized that growth brings tax problems.

If earnings are retained to finance expansion or for other purposes, there is a possible accumulated-earnings tax problem, the risk of which will vary depending on the special circumstances and the type of corporation involved. The mere fact that the corporation intended to expand will not necessarily avoid tax; something must have been done about it, and there must be proof that management took this into account when dividends were considered.

If a corporation acquires another company that happens to have a net operating loss or any other tax credit or allowance that would have been unavailable except for the acquisition, the IRS is authorized to disregard the carryover or other tax advantages of the acquisition unless the taxpayer can prove that the avoidance or evasion of taxes was not a principal purpose of the acquisition.

A corporation may consider entering upon another type of activity or even a different form of the business in which it is engaged. All expenses for the purpose of determining whether it is advisable to enter upon this other business that are incurred prior to the time of entering that business are not deductible for tax purposes. Thus market surveys, feasibility studies, and even such routine expenditures as salaries and travel expenses may be amortized as start-up costs. Start-up costs incurred before July 29, 1980, are disallowed as *prebusines expenses* if, at the time of their incurrence, the corporation was not engaged in that field of endeavor.

The Tax Department in the Large Corporation

The large corporation's internal tax function typically performs its role under the general supervision of the chief financial officer. However, it can operate successfully as a division of the general counsel's office and frequently is located there, with indirect ties along functional lines to corporate finance, controller, treasurer, accounting, and data processing. In a few instances, the role of the tax department is recognized as sufficiently distinct from the finance and legal areas to warrant its reporting directly to the CEO.

Essentially, the internal tax function requires a certain independence from all the disciplines with which it interacts, in somewhat the same fashion as the federal government system recognizes the independent-agency status of IRS from the Department of the Treasury, through which it nominally reports. The reason for this independence is clear when one considers that various government taxing jurisdictions (primarily IRS) share the profits of the large corporate business enterprise to the extent of approximately 50 percent (and sometimes more) in a way that is not unlike the profit interest any equal (but inactive) partner in a business would command, but with the very important difference that this partner, to a great extent, makes and alters the "partnership" rules unilaterally. What's more, the government "partner" can penalize its business partner severely for not playing by the rules *as it interprets them.*

Given the existence of this equal profit-sharing partnership with the collective taxing jurisdictions in which a company conducts business, it is obvious that the skill or expertise of the company's tax department is the only factor that can maintain harmony between the two sides while keeping the government partner's share as small as possible to preserve the company's primary right to enjoy maximum current and accumulated earnings.

Management Role of the Tax Department

The functioning of the tax department in this unique role is enhanced to the extent that it is an integral part of the management operating team. Nothing is more ineffective, futile, or indeed dangerous than a totally reactive tax department—one that acts defensively (late) rather than offensively (early). For it is usually too late to prevent a major tax disaster at the time an improperly conceived and executed transaction reaches the tax return. The tax department has a role to play from the moment the germ of a plan appears. Indeed, tax requirements often are the source of new operating ideas to corporate management. Very early in the life of any transaction or business plan, only the tax department can speak for the government partner, to prevent a plan from straying too far from acceptable norms and to propose avenues for accomplishing reasonable corporate goals through routes that will in the end survive—while constantly keeping the corporation's interests in the forefront, and knowing when to resolve so-called gray areas in favor of the corporation.

This dynamic function should continue through the further planning, development, and execution of a transaction, with management receiving clear guidance, direction, and counsel throughout from the collective expertise that should exist in a competent tax department.

With the execution stage of a transaction, the tax department's role has only just begun. Translating a business plan onto the tax return, in a manner that most favorably represents the company's best interests, while keeping within the narrow constraints of statutory and case law, tax regulations, rulings, and published procedures and guidelines, is elementary.

Examinations

Since the large corporation is examined by virtually every level of government for all taxable years, the sensitive task of subsequently negotiating any and all portions of the company's tax liability with government agents looms ahead. This is often a lengthy, drawn-out process, for which a defensive strategy is essential and must be devised. At all times during the continuing negotiations, top management must be kept advised of the progress and must be given reasonable estimates of success for the company's position on the various contested issues as opposed to the government's chances of success.

The process of negotiation continues, often on a daily basis, to settlement, which may be attained at the local district director's level, or pursuant to an appellate hearing in the local area. Most cases will be satisfactorily settled at one of these levels, as both sides weigh the hazards of litigation that otherwise lie ahead.

Other Planning

Assuming an offensive rather than a defensive posture in areas other than specific transaction planning means that the tax department must be deeply involved in, and exert a leadership role in, worldwide dividend planning, establishing intercompany pricing, planning for the most beneficial allocation of expenses between domestic and foreign income sources, planning for the timely application of valuable foreign tax credits (lest they be lost, inadvertently or because of inability to recommend unique tax-oriented maneuvers designed to use "excess" credits), and determining when a particular corporate structure should be altered.

Tax Legislation

The effective tax department is also active in legislative activities at every level of government. To the extent that early notice of adverse or favorable measures or trends can be gleaned, the company will be forewarned and better prepared to take decisive action at the precise moment it is needed. To the extent that unfavorable legislative action can be averted or altered because of this early knowledge, the tax specialist can significantly affect ultimate profits.

Internal and External Contacts

The tax department does not operate solely within the confines of its headquarters. Internally, it maintains two-way communications with field financial personnel at home and abroad, often visiting their locations. In the case of tax examinations at other domestic or overseas locations, the department is directly involved, either in negotiating the examination on site or, sometimes, prudently supervising its conduct by local personnel from behind the scenes.

Externally, the tax department secures its early knowledge of legislative, regulatory, and audit trends by forming and maintaining associations with collegues in other companies within and without its industry. Activity with outside associations designed for this purpose is not only beneficial but quite necessary and, if properly used, clearly cost-effective.

Accordingly, a well-staffed and well-trained tax department, having in its hands fundamental responsibility for disbursement or retention of up to 50 percent or more of net profit, is a key center for future corporate profitability and growth.

Becoming Tax-Oriented

Ideally, management should possess great tax awareness. Usually, however, this is not possible, because the company's executives ordinarily have their greatest skills in sales, production, distribution, finance, or management. Yet business decisions cannot be made without practical awareness of the tax considerations. The solution is for management to discuss all its business plans and objectives with its tax staff, which will advise specifically how and where tax planning may be applied. Only constant and thorough liaison with the tax specialists will allow management to perform its real role: decision making in business matters.

Failure to follow this obvious course can be very expensive to the corporation and to management. If excessive taxes follow from management's choice of the wrong alternative, someone is likely to accuse the directors or officers of mismanagement: a well-managed company would not have paid unnecessary taxes. And there is ample precedent for realizing that if the corporation pays taxes that a well-managed corporation would not have had to pay, the members of the management team may be found by a court to be responsible *personally* to the company for its loss. In this day of the professional minority stockholder, that is a very real hazard, which only good liaison with the tax department can avoid.

☐ *Richard Ise* (*and Robert S. Holzman, the original author of this now substantially revised section*)

STATE AND LOCAL TAXES

State taxation is of major concern to any business engaged in interstate commerce. Many decisions with respect to methods of selling or the location of a warehouse, a branch office, or a stock of goods may have significant tax consequences. Before establishing an office, plant, or warehouse or making sales or soliciting business in a state, a potential taxpayer should review the local laws and regulations that determine taxability.

The factors that may render a foreign seller liable for taxation or may give a state jurisdiction to assert tax liability vary from state to state. It is therefore usually desirable to obtain professional advice with respect to a specific problem. A final decision often requires thorough examination of all the facts and circumstances in the particular case, and research into all applicable statutes, regulations, and cases.

The following criteria are employed in most states to determine taxability and can be used as guidelines: maintaining an office, including a listing in the telephone directory, listing the local office on a letterhead, or placing the company name on an office door; making contracts; employing capital; owning or leasing property; delivering goods; maintaining a stock of goods; furnishing technical assistance or installation; having one or more employees, agents, or officers; qualifying to do business; entering the state to sue; and holding cash, accounts receivable, securities, or other valuables.

It should be noted that a state's ability to collect taxes depends upon its ability to obtain jurisdiction over the taxpayer. A taxpayer may be able to ignore the claims of a state so long as he maintains no property or facilities within that state. However, when such a taxpayer does find it desirable to locate within the state at some future date, he may be faced with large claims for delinquent taxes, penalties, and interest.

Types of Taxes

A great variety of taxes is used by the states and their subdivisions. Some taxes are measured by income, others by value of capital stock, and still others by gross receipts, sales price, rent paid, or similar factors. Those most frequently applied to businesses selling goods in interstate commerce are described in the following paragraphs.

Income Taxes

In 1959 the U.S. Supreme Court ruled in the joint *Northwestern-Stockham* case (Minnesota and Georgia cases) that a net income tax could be imposed on profits earned exclusively in interstate commerce. Subsequent decisions by the Supreme Court made it appear that almost any type of activity within a particular state would cause the income of a business to be subject to taxation by that state.

Recognizing that these new rules placed an unreasonable burden on interstate commerce, Congress enacted the Interstate Income Tax Law, which provides that a state cannot tax income derived solely from interstate commerce if the only activity in the state is the mere solicitation of orders. Simultaneously, Congress provided for a study of the whole problem of state taxation of multistate business activities.

After four years of investigation and public hearings, a House Judiciary Subcommittee concluded that the present system of state taxation creates serious problems that it would be appropriate for Congress to attempt to resolve. Some of the more important reasons given were as follows: (1) the multiplicity of nonuniform state tax laws; (2) the possibility that the same income will be taxed by more than one state; (3) the cost of compliance (often in excess of tax liability).

In 1965 the subcommittee introduced as a bill the Interstate Taxation Act. Similar bills have been introduced in subsequent years, but in each case Congress has adjourned without acting. As a counterproposal to the possible federal legislation, which might restrict state and local taxing powers, several states enacted their own laws. Some states adopted the Uniform Division of Income for Tax Purposes Act, others adopted the Multistate Tax Compact, and some adopted both.

The Interstate Taxation Act provides for all income to be allocated by a two-factor formula, an average of the property and payroll factors.

Under the Uniform Division of Income for Tax Purposes Act, nonbusiness income is generally apportioned according to situs, and business income is to be apportioned using a three-factor formula. This formula is commonly known as the Massachusetts formula and is computed as follows:

$$\frac{\text{Property in state}}{\text{Property everywhere}} = \underline{\hspace{1cm}} \text{ percent}$$

$$\frac{\text{Payroll in state}}{\text{Payroll everywhere}} = \underline{\hspace{1cm}} \text{ percent}$$

$$\frac{\text{Sales in state}}{\text{Sales everywhere}} = \underline{\hspace{1cm}} \text{ percent}$$

$$\text{total percent}$$

$$\text{Allocation factor} = \frac{\text{total percent}}{3} = \underline{\hspace{1cm}} \text{ percent}$$

The Multistate Tax Compact provides that a taxpayer may elect to allocate in the manner provided by the laws of the state or in accordance with the provisions of the Uniform Division of Income for Tax Purposes Act. In addition, it provides for an optional "short form" computation on the basis of a percentage of sales for any taxpayer who (1) is required to file a return; (2) is engaged in the state ony in making sales; (3) does not own or rent real estate or tangible personal property in the state, and (4) has gross sales in the state not in excess of $100,000.

Both the Multistate Tax Compact and the Uniform Division of Income for Tax Purposes Act have provisions, commonly known as the "throwback rule," that treat as sales within a state any sales effected through that state that are made to a state in which the corporation is not subject to tax. Thus, under either act, 100 percent of all sales are likely to be included in the allocation factor.

In the past few years, Supreme Court decisions in *Mobil, Exxon, Washington Stevedoring,* and other cases have upheld the principle that once tax jurisdiction with a state is present (beyond contacts exempted under the Interstate Income Tax Law), it can result in imposition of a state tax on an apportioned percentage of worldwide income. The thrust of several of these cases is toward a unitary concept for all income received; thus nonbusiness income will become extinct. Accordingly, state taxes are likely to become greater administrative and financial burdens on corporations than at present.

Sales and Use Taxes

The constitutionality of sales and use taxes has been established beyond any doubt. The foreign seller who makes contracts and delivers goods within the taxing state is clearly liable for the sales tax. If the goods are delivered outside the state, the sales tax generally does not apply except where the order was obtained within the state. A sales tax levied by the seller's state will apply whenever delivery is made within that state. A purchaser in a taxing state can ordinarily avoid the sales tax where the order is approved by the seller outside the state and delivery takes place outside the state.

Sales that cannot be reached by the sales tax are often subject to the use tax. The use tax is usually at the same rate as the sales tax and is imposed on the storage, use, or consumption of goods within a taxing state. Ordinarily, the seller is liable for collecting the use tax; but if he fails to do so, the purchaser becomes personally liable therefor.

A problem commonly arises when a buyer takes delivery and pays a sales tax on an item that he then transfers for use in another state where he must pay the use tax. Many states have enacted provisions to prevent such a burden on commerce, for example, granting a complete exemption or granting a credit where a sales or use tax has previously been paid.

Exemptions from sales tax are often provided for goods that are sold for resale, or for machinery and equipment used exclusively in manufacturing, processing, or assembling. Most states have myriad rules and regulations governing the enforcement and collection of sales and use taxes. Reporting requirements often result in significant expenditures by taxpayers for record keeping, training, return preparation, and professional fees. Substantial additional time may be required for audits performed by the taxing jurisdiction.

Capital-Stock Taxes

Many of the taxes applied to the value of capital stock require a division of the tax base among states by methods similar to those used for income taxes. Some states have both a corporate income tax and a capital-stock tax and use identical procedures for apportionment. In a number of states, a capital-stock tax is imposed as a minimum alternative to the income tax.

The proposed Interstate Taxation Act previously discussed would require apportionment under the two-factor formula. It also provides that a domestic corporation can be taxed on its capital, without apportionment, so long as the measure of tax includes no element of retained earnings.

In some cases, the tax on capital may be levied annually. Other states may require payment of a tax based on capital stock at the time the corporation qualifies to do business in the stage and at the time of any subsequent increases in capital stock employed in the state.

Gross-Receipts and Gross-Income Taxes

Taxes on gross receipts and gross income are very similar to sales and use taxes, being measured by total sales price either on an individual-sales basis or in the aggregate. A gross-receipts tax is defined as "a tax, other than a sales tax, which is imposed on or measured by gross volume of business in terms of gross receipts or in other terms, and in the determination of which no deduction is allowed which would make the tax an income tax."

Apparent overtaxation of interstate commerce results from these taxes when a tax is imposed on production activities in the state of origin and on in-shipments by the state of destination; both types of taxes are generally upheld by the courts. As a result of these situations that produce taxation at both ends of a sale, the interstate company is subject to multiple gross-receipts taxation.

The gross-receipts tax is ordinarily used only in special and limited circumstances—that is, where another, perhaps preferable tax cannot be effectuated or in a situation where the tax may be competitively and lucratively imposed on exports from the state. The primary criticism of the tax is that its burdens fall indiscriminately and unfairly. One major inequity usually stressed by critics is that variations in ratios of profits from one business group to another are not taken into account. Another criticism is that it hinders the entry of new businesses, since they tend to have lower profit margins and are in a less favorable position competitively to pass the tax on in the form of higher prices.

Other Taxes

Other taxes which may be imposed by the states and their subdivisions include qualification, privilege, and license fees, occupancy and rent taxes, real and personal property taxes, taxes on unincorporated businesses, and taxes on the value of intangible assets.

Administration

Many states have established full-time appointive commissions charged with the administration of the tax laws of the state, such as the Department of Taxation and Finance of New York.

Most states have transferred to the administrative body all revenue functions formerly vested in elected officials. However, corporate organization or qualification fees are usually administered by the secretary of state. All tax administrative bodies maintain offices in the state capital for the state concerned, and correspondence concerning tax matters should be addressed to the director of tax administration.

Deficiency notices resulting from audits are ordinarily issued in a manner similar to federal procedures. The taxpayer is usually given an opportunity to file a protest, to agree with the findings, or to request a conference (frequently through a protest). When the issue is one of law rather than fact and must eventually be settled by court action, it may be expeditious to bypass the procedures for hearings with the various levels of the tax administrative bodies.

☐ *Irwin Klepper and J. D. Mach (and Marilyn J. Gowin and Richard W. Saunders, the original authors of this now substantially revised section)*

PRESENTATION AND INTERPRETATION OF OPERATING RESULTS

Financial considerations permeate all areas of operations within an enterprise. The success or failure of both the enterprise as a whole and its individual structured segments can be measured in financial terms. Consequently, usage over a long time has made it clear that operating results and financial results are perceived and used as interchangeable expressions.

Each profit-oriented enterprise is directed by a management, which is charged with the ultimate well-being of that enterprise. Operating results reflect the stewardship of that management.

Role of Management

As Figure 2-33 illustrates, the term *management* has both a broad as well as a narrow connotation, which can be schematically portrayed as levels of a management pyramid. This pyramid is composed of levels of authority and spheres of influence, each of which constitutes management.

The job of management can be described as consisting of diagnosis and action. In this context, diagnosis involves becoming aware of conditions, events, or opportunities and identifying and defining issues, whereas action involves planning, organizing, and controlling. For management to function properly, the organization structure must be developed along lines of responsibility, whereby the reporting of operating results is directed to those key people at the appropriate level who can initiate and take required action.

Operating Results versus Performance Results

Operating results and performance results are not necessarily interchangeable terms. Although certain overlap may exist, there is a distinction between the two in that operating results are enterprise-oriented while performance results are individual-oriented.

For an enterprise to succeed, each level of management must ensure that the goals and objectives established for the enterprise are met. To effectively measure the performance of a manager, then, these goals or objectives as related to

Figure 2-33. The management pyramid.

the manager's responsibilities should be agreed upon in the form of key result areas and then gauged and reported on periodically for progress status. How well a particular level of management performs can be judged and measured in many instances by the specific operating or financial results applicable to that specific level. In other instances, however, factors other than financial results are involved, such as share of market, labor or public relations, environment impact, and other nonfinancial elements. The remaining portion of this section does not address itself to such nonfinancial reporting but rather discusses operating results as they affect the enterprise and its segments.

Source of Data for Operating Results

A primary responsibility of financial management is to provide a system of financial reporting that ensures availability of appropriate data for external and internal reporting. The collection and reporting of the operating results normally are part of the accounting stream of an enterprise's information system. The information system can be manual or computerized, depending on size and stage of sophistication of the organization. The generation of accounting data is governed by generally accepted accounting principles which have been developed by both government and private-sector bodies. Thus these data are highly formalized and structured and carry significant weight with external users. For internal reporting, management has the prerogative to define the rules to a certain extent and can occasionally sacrifice precision in order to gain time, as in the case of "flash" reports. For example, once actual sales data are available, standard costs and budgeted expenses, as opposed to actual costs, might be used to obtain a quick view of what profits were for the reporting period.

Presentation Methods

Operating results can be presented in a variety of reporting formats. They can be presented orally, in visual displays, as written reports, or by a combination of these methods, depending on requirements at the time of presentation. Further, such reports may be for either external or internal purposes, or may be summary reports focusing on the enterprise as a whole or segment reports focusing on one or more areas within the enterprise.

Formats for external reports are usually well standardized, since these reports are subject to careful policing by independent bodies. While there is some degree of standardization for internal reports, their formats will depend a great deal on the prevailing management philosophy as well as the cost system currently in use at the enterprise. For our purposes, reports concerning operating results can be categorized as: (1) summary reports, (2) control reports, and (3) special-purpose reports.

Summary Reports

Summary reports of operating results can focus either on the entire enterprise or on its reportable segments and internal profit centers. These summary reports are normally made up of the statement of operations, the balance sheet, and the statement of changes in financial position.

The statement of operations, perhaps better known as the income statement or profit and loss statement, was at one time considered the most important operating statement. However, in recent years the balance sheet and the statement of changes in financial position have become equally prominent because of the emphasis on cash flow.

The distinction between the various statements lies in the time covered and the elements being reported. The statement of operations details revenues, expenses, and resulting net income or loss to reflect operating results over a specified accounting period such as a month, a quarter, or a year. The balance sheet is a summary of assets, liabilities, and equities, and reflects the net gain in value from operations along with other changes affecting the capital status of the enterprise as of a given point in time such as end of month or end of fiscal year. The statement of changes in financial position, also called a statement of sources and

Figure 2-34. Statement of operations (000 omitted).

	Segment			Consolidated		
	A	B	C	Current	Current	Prior Year
	Actual	Actual	Actual	Actual	Plan	Actual
GROSS SALES	175,500	95,600	74,400	345,500	355,500	325,400
Allowances and Deductions	3,900	2,100	1,600	7,600	8,900	8,100
Transportation	11,300	6,200	4,700	22,200	25,400	22,700
Total	15,200	8,300	6,300	29,800	34,300	30,800
NET SALES	160,300	87,300	68,100	315,700	321,200	294,600
Standard Direct Cost of Sales	101,711	60,450	49,453	211,614	214,985	201,920
(Gain) Loss Direct Cost Variances	(300)	700	(700)	(300)	–	300
ACTUAL DIRECT MARGIN	58,889	26,150	19,347	104,386	106,215	92,380
Advertising and Promotion Expenses	13,236	1,600	2,100	16,936	17,000	15,000
DIRECT MARKETING MARGIN	45,653	24,550	17,247	87,450	89,215	77,380
Selling and Warehouse Expenses	4,300	2,550	2,050	8,900	9,000	8,100
PRODUCT CONTRIBUTION	41,353	22,000	15,197	78,550	80,215	69,280
Other Specific Period Expenses						
Manufacturing	11,740	4,800	4,612	21,152	19,950	17,600
Administrative	2,482	1,225	1,155	4,862	4,865	4,750
Research	1,450	1,120	1,105	3,675	3,680	3,590
Total	15,672	7,145	6,872	29,689	28,495	25,940
Other (Income) Expense	200	(150)	11	61	100	150
SEGMENT CONTRIBUTION	25,481	15,005	8,314	48,800	51,620	43,190
Corporate Allocation						
Overhead	2,670	1,505	1,325	5,500	5,520	4,790
Interest	411	400	189	1,000	1,000	600
Total	3,081	1,905	1,514	6,500	6,520	5,390
PRETAX PROFIT	22,400	13,100	6,800	42,300	45,100	37,800
Income Taxes	10,020	6,450	3,330	19,800	21,100	18,300
NET EARNINGS	12,380	6,650	3,470	22,500	24,000	19,500
Earnings per Common Share	–	–	–	4.50	4.80	3.90
Return on Capital Employed	19.0%	22.0%	16.1%	18.6%	19.6%	19.0%

uses of funds, shows the flow of funds into and out of the enterprise over a speci-fied accounting period. Basically, the statement of changes in financial position provides the same information provided by the balance sheet and the income statement but from a dynamic rather than static point of view.

Summary reports can be for both external and internal purposes. Internal re-porting usually demands more detail than external reporting. The examples pro-vided as Figures 2-34 through 2-37 illustrate internal reports. For external-reporting formats, refer back to "General Accounting and Financial Statements." Figures 2-36, 2-37, and 2-38 reflect the operation of an enterprise consisting of

Figure 2-35. Balance sheet (000 omitted).

	Segment				Consolidated		
ASSETS	A	B	C	Corporate	This Year	Plan	Prior Year
Cash	250	100	150	3,000	3,500	3,000	2,000
Receivables–Net	9,600	7,850	10,200	50	27,700	28,225	26,000
Inventories	15,300	7,200	11,200	–	33,700	34,000	31,900
Prepaid Expenses	150	50	250	10	460	500	390
Current Assets	25,300	15,200	21,800	3,060	65,360	65,725	60,290
Other Assets	1,250	350	200	10	1,810	1,830	1,860
Property and Equipment	73,960	35,750	30,190	8,060	147,960	148,960	128,820
Less Accumulated Depreciation	23,210	13,100	18,240	5,860	60,410	60,410	56,480
Net Property and Equipment	50,750	22,650	11,950	2,200	87,550	88,550	73,240
Total Assets	77,300	38,200	33,950	5,270	154,720	156,105	134,490
LIABILTIES AND EQUITY							
Notes Payable			400		400	–	–
Accounts Payable	5,600	5,300	8,900	400	20,200	19,600	19,500
Accrued Taxes	3,000	1,700	1,000	10	5,710	6,000	4,700
Other Accrued Expenses	3,500	1,000	2,500	1,090	8,090	8,165	7,500
Current Liabilities	12,100	8,000	12,800	1,500	34,400	33,765	31,700
Long-Term Debt	–	–	–	12,500	12,500	12,500	10,000
Deferred Taxes	–	–	–	13,300	13,300	13,300	11,000
Intersegment Accounts	12,720	6,000	3,310	(22,030)	–	–	–
Segment Equity	52,480	24,200	17,840	(94,520)	–	–	–
Common Stock				5,000	5,000	5,000	5,000
Capital Surplus				25,000	25,000	25,000	25,000
Earnings Reinvested				64,520	64,520	66,540	51,790
Stockholder's Equity	–	–	–	94,520	94,520	96,540	81,790
Total Liabilities and Equity	77,300	38,200	33,950	5,270	154,720	156,105	134,490
				Statistics			
Current Ratio: Actual	2.1	1.9	1.7	2.0	1.9		1.9
Plan	2.0	1.9	1.9	2.0	1.9		2.0
Collection Period: Actual	20	30	50	–	29		30
Plan	19	25	55	–	29		29
Days of Inventory: Actual	55	43	83		58		58
Plan	55	42	80		58		58

Figure 2-36. Statement of changes in financial position (000 omitted).

	Segment				Consolidated		
	A	B	C	Corporate	Current Year	Plan	Prior Year
Sources of Funds							
From Operations:							
Net Earnings	12,380	6,650	3,470	–	22,500	24,000	19,500
Depreciation	3,600	1,820	1,530	350	7,300	7,300	6,900
Increase in Deferred Items	–	–	–	2,300	2,300	2,300	1,500
	15,980	8,470	5,000	2,650	32,100	33,600	27,900
Sales and Retirement of Property	250	50	100	90	490	490	1,500
Increase in Long-Term Debt	–	–	–	2,500	2,500	2,500	5,000
Changes in Other Accounts	35	10	5	–	50	30	50
Total Sources	16,265	8,530	5,105	5,240	35,140	36,610	34,450
Application of Funds							
Expenditures for Property, Plant, and Equipment	13,340	6,285	3,375	–	23,000	24,000	19,000
Dividends Paid	–		–	9,770	9,770	9,250	9,000
Changes—Intersegment Accounts	1,775	2,315	990	(5,080)	–	–	–
Increase in Working Capital	1,150	(70)	740	550	2,370	3,370	6,450
Total Applications	16,265	8,530	5,105	5,240	35,140	36,610	34,450
Summary of Changes in Working-Capital Components							
Current Assets							
Cash	–	–	–	1,500	1,500	1,000	500
Receivable—Net	860	470	370	–	1,700	2,225	2,300
Inventories	690	(100)	1,200	10	1,800	2,100	3,000
Prepaid Expenses	50	10	5	5	70	110	50
	1,600	380	1,575	1,515	5,070	5,435	5,850
Current Liabilities							
Notes Payable	–	–	(400)	–	(400)	–	–
Accounts Payable	200	(400)	(200)	(300)	(700)	(100)	950
Accrued Taxes	(550)	(300)	(160)	–	(1,010)	(1,300)	(200)
Other Accruals	(100)	250	(75)	(665)	(590)	(665)	(150)
	(450)	(450)	(835)	(965)	(2,700)	(2,065)	600
Net increase (Decrease) in Working Capital	1,150	(70)	740	550	2,370	3,370	6,450

three internal reportable segments, indicated as A, B, and C. This particular enterprise has a standard direct cost system and uses budgets in the development of its business plan. For this purpose, the presentation format is a consolidating one, but statements for individual segments are provided to appropriate segment management, as illustrated by Figure 2-39. Certain current-month data that would normally be provided as part of the statements have been omitted.

Control Reports

A control report provides an even finer focus on the details of the operations of an enterprise. Generally it focuses on a specific area of interest. The report

Figure 2-37. Statement of operations, Segment A (000 omitted).

| | Current Month | | | | | | Year to Date | | | | | |
| | Last Year | | Plan | | Actual | | Actual | | Plan | | Last Year | |
	Amount	%	Amount	%	Amount	%	Amount	%	Amount	%	Amount	%
GROSS SALES	11,000	110.0	13,000	110.6	13,600	107.7	175,500	109.5	172,500	110.6	160,000	110.0
Allowances	260	2.6	330	2.8	300	2.4	3,900	2.5	4,300	2.8	3,700	2.6
Transportation	740	7.4	920	7.8	900	7.3	11,300	7.0	12,300	7.8	10,800	7.4
Total	1,000	10.0	1,250	10.6	1,200	9.7	15,200	9.5	16,600	10.6	14,500	10.0
NET SALES	10,000	100.0	11,750	100.0	12,400	100.0	160,300	100.0	155,900	100.0	145,500	100.0
Standard Direct Cost of Sales	6,410	64.1	7,520	64.0	7,920	63.9	101,711	63.5	99,635	63.9	93,410	64.2
(Gain) Less Direct Cost Var.	10	—	—	—	(50)	(0.4)	(300)	(0.2)	—		150	0.1
ACTUAL DIRECT MARGIN	3,590	35.9	4,230	36.0	4,530	36.5	58,889	36.7	56,265	36.1	51,940	35.7
Advertising & Promotions	850	8.5	970	8.3	1,030	8.3	13,236	8.2	13,000	8.3	12,900	8.9
DIRECT MARKETING MARGIN	2,740	27.4	3,260	27.7	3,500	28.2	45,653	28.5	43,265	27.8	39,040	26.8
Selling & Warehouse Expenses	300	3.0	350	2.9	360	2.9	4,300	2.7	4,400	2.9	4,100	2.8
PRODUCT CONTRIBUTION	2,440	24.4	2,910	24.8	3,140	25.3	41,353	25.8	38,865	24.9	34,740	24.0
Other Specific Period Expenses												
Manufacturing	760	7.6	825	7.0	900	7.3	11,740	7.3	9,900	6.3	9,100	6.3
Administrative	195	2.0	205	1.7	205	1.6	2,482	1.5	2,485	1.6	2,350	1.6
Research	105	1.0	120	1.1	120	1.0	1,450	1.0	1,450	0.9	1,250	0.8
Total	1,060	10.6	1,150	9.8	1,225	9.9	15,672	9.8	13,835	8.8	12,700	8.7
Other (Income) Expenses	(130)	(1.3)	20	0.2	30	0.2	200	0.1	150	0.1	50	—
SEGMENT CONTRIBUTION	1,510	15.1	1,740	14.8	1,885	15.2	25,481	15.9	24,880	16.0	22,190	15.9
Corporate Allocation												
Overhead	200	2.0	225	1.9	220		2,670	1.7	2,680	1.7	2,440	1.7
Interest	30	0.3	35	0.3	35		411	0.2	400	0.3	350	0.2
Total	230	2.3	260	2.2	255	2.1	3,081	1.9	3,080	2.0	2,790	1.9
PRETAX PROFIT(Loss)	1,280	12.8	1,480	12.6	1,630	13.1	22,400	14.0	21,800	14.0	19,400	13.4
Income Taxes	600	6.0	650	5.5	730	5.9	10,020	6.3	9,700	6.2	9,100	6.3
NET EARNINGS	680	6.8	830	7.1	900	7.2	12,380	7.7	12,100	7.8	10,300	7.1
Return on Capital Employed							19.0%		18.5%		18.1%	

Figure 2-38. Control reports: interlocking overview by management level (000 omitted).

Current Month			Period Expenses	Year to Date		
Amount			(Excludes Direct Expenses)	Amount		
Budget	Actual	Variance		Variance	Actual	Budget
			Chief-Executive Level			
135	130	5	Executive Office	12	1,548	1,560
715	710	5	Other	9	8,516	8,525
850	840	10	Administrative Expenses	21	10,064	10,085
315	312	3	Research Expenses	5	3,675	3,680
2,150	2,143	7	Selling Expenses	164	25,836	26,000
1,685	1,810	(125)	Manufacturing Expenses	(1,200)	21,450	20,250
5,000	5,105	(105)	Total Period Expenses	(1,010)	61,025	60,015
			Manufacturing Level			
25	24	1	Manufacturing Office	2	298	300
1,312	1,446	(134)	Processing	(1,212)	17,062	15,850
185	180	5	Maintenance Control	0	2,200	2,200
163	160	3	Quality Assurance	10	1,890	1,900
1,685	1,810	(125)	Total Manufacturing Expenses	(1,200)	21,450	20,250
			Processing Level			
20	20	0	Processing Office	0	240	240
450	449	1	Production Department	5	5,425	5,430
455	595	(140)	Finishing Department	(1,242)	6,892	5,650
245	245	0	Packaging Department	15	2,925	2,940
142	137	5	Inspection Department	10	1,580	1,590
1,312	1,446	(134)	Total Processing	(1,212)	17,062	15,850
			Finishing-Department Level			
135	199	(64)	Labor	(395)	1,995	1,600
15	14	1	Supervision	1	184	185
53	71	(18)	Fringe Benefits	(135)	760	625
15	74	1	Supplies	10	150	160
130	130	0	Depreciation	0	1,540	1,540
197	167	(60)	Repairs	(723)	2,263	1,540
455	595	(140)	Total Finishing Department	(1,242)	6,892	5,650

itself may cover as broad an area as do summary reports, but it is distinguished by the fact that it is keyed to other control reports that magnify the details.

One approach often taken is to provide an interlocking system of routine control reports for appraisal purposes. These routinely prepared control reports are keyed to each other to correspond to organizational responsibilities, and details of one level of responsibility appear in lesser detail as summaries at a higher level of responsibility. Such routine control reports permit diagnosis, control, and planning.

Figure 2-39. Product contribution statement, Segment A, Product X10 (000 omitted).

| | Current Month | | | | | | | | | Year-to-Date | | | | | | | | |
| | Last Year | | | Plan | | | This Year | | | This Year | | | Plan | | | Last Year | | |
	Amount	%	Per Unit	Amount	%	Per Unit	Amount	%	Per Unit	Amount	%	Per Unit	Amount	%	Per Unit	Amount	%	Per Unit
Units Sold	80			100			104			1,588			1,560			1,428		
Gross Sales	869	110.1	10.86	1,144	110.7	11.44	1,184	109.4	11.38	18,166	109.6	11.44	17,815	109.9	11.42	15,365	110.0	10.76
Allowances	21	2.6	.26	29	2.8	.29	26	2.4	.25	416	2.5	.26	455	2.8	.29	363	2.6	.25
Transportation	59	7.5	.74	82	7.9	.82	76	7.0	.73	1,175	7.1	.74	1,150	7.1	.74	1,034	7.4	.73
Total	80	10.1	1.00	111	10.7	1.11	102	9.4	.98	1,591	9.6	1.00	1,605	9.9	1.03	1,397	10.0	.98
Net Sales	789	100.0	9.86	1,033	100.0	10.33	1,082	100.0	10.40	16,575	100.0	10.44	16,210	100.0	10.39	13,968	100.0	9.78
Standard Direct-Cost	501	63.5	6.26	660	63.9	6.60	686	63.4	6.60	10,608	64.0	6.68	10,358	63.9	6.64	8,870	63.5	6.21
Direct-Cost Variance	5	0.6	.06	—	—	—	(10)	(0.9)	(.10)	(250)	(1.5)	(.15)	—	—	—	100	0.7	.07
Actual Direct Margin	283	35.9	3.54	373	36.1	3.73	406	37.5	3.90	6,217	37.5	3.91	5,852	36.1	3.75	4,998	35.8	3.50
Advertising	30	3.8	.37	38	3.7	.38	40	3.7	.37	1,000	6.0	.63	982	6.1	.63	800	5.7	.56
Promotions	39	5.0	.49	48	4.6	.48	50	4.6	.49	700	4.3	.44	687	4.2	.44	538	3.9	.38
Total	69	8.8	.86	86	8.3	.86	90	8.3	.86	1,700	10.3	1.07	1,669	10.3	1.07	1,338	9.6	.94
Direct Marketing Margin	214	27.1	2.68	287	27.8	2.87	316	29.2	3.04	4,517	27.2	2.84	4,183	25.8	2.68	3,660	26.2	2.56
Sales Expense	12	1.5	.15	12	1.2	.12	13	1.2	.13	155	0.9	.10	156	1.0	.10	150	1.1	.10
Warehouse Expense	13	1.6	.17	17	1.6	.17	16	1.5	.15	195	1.2	.12	187	1.1	.12	158	1.1	.11
Total	25	3.1	.32	29	2.8	.29	29	2.7	.28	350	2.1	.22	343	2.1	.22	308	2.2	.21
Product Contribution	189	24.0	236	258	25.0	2.58	287	26.5	2.76	4,167	25.1	2.62	3,840	23.7	2.46	3,352	24.0	2.35

Figures 2-38 and 2-39 are simplistic examples of such interlocking overviews. In Figure 2-38, expenses are compared with budget to disclose variances, which in turn call attention to the possible need for corrective action. In Figure 2-39, the profit contribution of a specific product to a particular internal profit center is analyzed in detail, showing each cost and revenue component. Problem areas can be identified by comparisons with plan and prior periods. Summarization upward for Figure 2-39 is not provided, but when all products are combined, the end result flows into Figures 2-34 and 2-37.

Special-Purpose Reports

Reports reflecting operating results may uncover an area or areas that require further analysis. For example, in Figure 2-35, the negative variances for the finishing department are very large, indicating the need for more detailed analysis. The results of such an analysis will be presented in a special report to the appropriate management. Such reporting normally occurs at irregular intervals and is tailored to the specific needs of the situation.

Interpretation of Operating Results

Over the years, financial guidelines have been developed to help assist in the analysis and interpretation of operating results. These guidelines allow internal comparisons with goals, plans, objectives, and standards. Many of these financial guidelines have taken the form of financial or operating ratios that express relationships between single or group items on the balance sheet and the income statement.

The following financial parameters are used by one successful agribusiness enterprise:

Return on average capital employed. This ratio is the result of dividing net operating profit after taxes, which expresses the total earnings available to the investors in the business, by average capital employed, which expresses the average amount of capital invested in the company. This after-tax rate of return permits a direct comparison with the after-tax cost of total capital.

Net operating profit after taxes. This is equal to the sum of net earnings and minority interest income plus the after-tax interest cost of all interest-bearing debt (including imputed interest in rental payments) and deferred charges. It is, therefore, the after-tax profit from operations before all financing and long-term deferred charges but after depreciation and amortization.

Average capital employed. This is computed as follows: Total assets less current liabilities are averaged for the beginning and the end of the year. This is the same as the sum of stockholders' equity, minority interest, deferred items, capitalized leases, and long-term debt. Then average short-term debt incurred during the year is added. The average of beginning and ending operating leases is also added as if these leases were capitalized as debt on the balance sheet. The sum represents the total average capital used in the business during the year.

Return on equity. This is simply net earnings divided by ending stockholders' equity. This ratio defines the yield the stockholder earns on his book investment and is affected by the amount of financial leverage used in the firm's capital structure. This rate should be compared with the cost of equity capital rather than with the cost of total capital.

Total average debt as a percentage of average capital employed. This is the result of dividing average total debt by average capital employed as defined above. Average total debt is the average of beginning and ending long-term debt and capitalized leases plus average short-term debt used over the year. This ratio defines the amount of financial leverage in the firm's capital structure and is one of the factors that influences the firm's average cost of capital. It is of importance to stockholders in determining the value of the company.

Total debt to capitalization. This is the result of dividing total consolidated short- and long-term debt by the total capitalization of the company. Total capitalization is defined as total consolidated debt plus minority interest plus stockholders' equity. This ratio is one of the measures used by the financial community for determining debt capacity and the risk associated with a given level of debt.

Fixed-charges coverage. This ratio is the result of earnings before fixed charges less equity in unconsolidated earnings divided by fixed charges. Fixed charges are defined as total consolidated interest plus one-third of rental payments and amortization of bond discounts. The ratio expresses the number of times earnings before fixed charges will cover the fixed charges due to debtors and lessors and is an important indication to lenders of a company's ability to service its debt. For certain debt covenants and rating-agency purposes, the coverage ratio is calculated for the aggregate of three years.

Current ratio. This ratio is calculated by dividing current assets by current liabilities. The ratio is intended to indicate the liquidity of a company by determining the number of times short-term assets cover short-term liabilities.

Working capital. Working capital is the net of deducting current liabilities from current assets. Working capital is supposed to indicate how much capital is required in the business to finance the excess of current assets over current liabilities.

Cash flow as a percentage of total debt. Cash flow—the sum of net earnings plus annual depreciation and change in long-term deferred liabilities—is divided by total consolidated short- and long-term debt to determine the coverage of the latter. This ratio indicates how quickly a company could repay all its debt, assuming that debt repayment was the only use of cash funds.

New-investment rate. This is the rate at which a company invests funds in excess of its depreciation back into the company relative to the net operating after-tax profit that is generated by existing capital. The rate is calculated by dividing the sum of working-capital changes plus capital expenditures less depreciation by net operating after-tax profit.

Other financial ratios. The following list summarizes a number of other commonly employed financial ratios, along with how they are calculated and used.

Name of Ratio	*Calculation Formula*	*Purpose or Use*
Acid test	$$\frac{\text{Cash + marketable securities + receivables}}{\text{Current liabilities}}$$	Measures immediate solvency.
Daily sales outstanding	$$\frac{\text{Average accounts receivable}}{\text{Average daily sales}}$$	Measures effectiveness of credit department and signals changes in credit status.
Days of inventory	$$\frac{\text{Average inventory}}{\text{Average daily cost of sales}}$$	Measures effectiveness of inventory control and signals changes in conditions.
Assets turnover	$$\frac{\text{Net sales}}{\text{Total assets}}$$	Measures turnover of total assets— low ratio could mean excessive investments.
Turnover of capital employed	$$\frac{\text{Net sales}}{\text{Average capital employed}}$$	Measures how well average capital employed is being used.
Return on sales	$$\frac{\text{Net profit}}{\text{Net sales}}$$	Determines profitability of sales.
Return on assets	$$\frac{\text{Net profit}}{\text{Total assets}}$$	Determines how well assets are put to use.

Dun & Bradstreet annually publishes tables of ratios for more than 70 types of businesses.

To be used effectively, financial ratios should be compared with a par of some sort, which can be a goal established by management, an industry norm or average, a competitor's performance, or the performance of another segment of the business.

Although operating results can be analyzed and consensus conclusions reached, any interpretation of these results ultimately is subjective and individual. In a profit-oriented enterprise, the primary objective of all operating statements is to provide relevant and timely information for making rational economic decisions concerning profitability and solvency of the enterprise and its segments. While analysis can aid in the decision-making process through comparisons, trend establishment, highlighting significant factors, and the like, in the final analysis, each individual must interpret the performance data according to his or her own criteria and frame of reference.

Summary

Every firm has a financial-information system, however simple or informal it may be. The information it provides is the basis for many management activities, whether the information is received by word of mouth or in written form. Management success or the lack of it will in large part be a direct function of the quality of information gathered, presented, and interpreted. Specifically, to improve the presentation and ultimate interpretation of operating results, the user should always be kept in mind, organizational lines of responsibility should be followed, important elements should be emphasized, significant ratios should be included, and significant trends should be isolated.   □ *Donald A. Sullivan*

INTERNAL AUDITING

It is difficult to define the role of the internal audit department. Its range of activities goes from the simple testing of transactions for verifying the effectiveness of internal controls to in-depth reviews of operating functions. The scope and emphasis depend to a great extent on the size of company, type of business, philosophy of management, and interest or concern of the chief executive and the board of directors. In a very small business, the owner-manager, to a limited extent, performs the role of the internal auditor through continuing surveillance of all activities. In a large company, an audit staff of dozens of professionals is not unusual.

Most larger companies have either a formal audit charter or a policy statement defining the unit's purpose, authority, and responsibility. It can detail the scope of assigned activity and the performance expectations of management. The statement is of particular value in clearly outlining the support by senior management for the audit objectives.

After World War I, the responsibilities of internal auditors began to broaden. Corporate structures became more complex, and internal auditors traveled to subsidiary or branch locations to confirm the similarity of accounting records and controls to those at the home office. This led to the need to systematize accounting procedures. The auditor was the most knowledgeable individual to recommend changes in financial processing and control activities.

With the stock-market debacle in 1929 and evidences of "creative accounting," corporate management and the auditing profession were viewed with suspicion. This led to the Securities Exchange Act of 1934, which designated the Securities and Exchange Commission as the monitor for corporate financial reporting. The new thrust for internal auditing was the verification of financial statements, as well as the continued testing of transactions. World War II led internal auditors into the assurance of compliance with government regulations. The boom that followed, with the growth of conglomerates and international subsidiaries, required auditors to review the adequacy of corporate procedures and practices in operational evaluations, along with performing the financial audit.

Internal auditing became a growth activity. The use of computers brought about a new way of life, and management information systems produced current data at high speed, that promptly alerted management to control problems, but also created new problems in the control of masses of data. Both the speed and the volume of computer-generated data brought new opportunities for auditing. The Commission on Auditors' Responsibilities (the "Cohen Commission") was formed by the American Institute of Certified Public Accountants (AICPA) in 1974, and its resulting report recommended, among other considerations, that a company's annual report include comments on the status of internal controls. The Financial Accounting Standards Board was established, and the Foreign Corrupt Practices Act of 1977 was passed. These actions have legislated a standardization of financial reporting and a code of business conduct. The internal audit function is positioned to ensure corporate performance under these requirements.

Foreign Corrupt Practices Act

The importance of internal control was emphasized by the Foreign Corrupt Practices Act (FCPA), which became effective December 19, 1977. The title of the act does not communicate its scope fully. The FCPA takes its name from the act's first section, which prohibits domestic business enterprises from engaging in the use of bribes or payments to foreign officials and others. The second part of the act relates to accounting standards. The act is applicable to all companies subject to the Securities Exchange Act of 1934 and supports the objectives specified in the AICPA Statement on Auditing Standards #1.

Specifically, the FCPA imposes new legal requirements for companies to devise and maintain a system of internal accounting controls sufficient to reasonably ensure that (1) transactions are authorized by management; (2) transactions are reported in conformity with generally accepted accounting principles; (3) accountability of assets is maintained; (4) access to assets is controlled within management authorization; and (5) recorded assets are periodically compared to existing assets. The internal auditor can play a vital role in helping ensure that a company is in continual compliance with all requirements of the FCPA.

Responsibilities of the Audit Department

The responsibilities of the internal audit department are to evaluate the effectiveness of financial and operating controls, confirm compliance with company policies and procedures, safeguard assets, and verify the accuracy and consistency of the company's external and internal reports. Its activities produce written and verbal reports to management with recommendations for corrective action, where necessary. The audit reviews are intended to assure that cash, inventories, accounts receivable, capital, and other assets are properly recorded and safeguarded. The reviews will also confirm that contracts are enforced and that liabilities are legitimate and properly recorded.

Financial audit reviews are generally of a protective nature and are conducted in areas such as, but not limited to, accounts receivable, accounts payable, payroll, contracts, capital assets and expenditures, electronic data processing, inventories, research and development, purchasing, advertising, insurance, construction in progress, and financial reporting. During these reviews it is important to evaluate the segregation of duties in operating units to lessen the possibility of errors or undetected irregularities. Audit units perform some surprise audits, particularly of petty-cash funds. Most audits, however, are carefully planned, with a predetermined scope and discussions in advance of the audit with the department or unit to be reviewed. Audit assistance is also essential in the review of financial data and controls of companies that are potential acquisitions, and in the follow-up to assure compliance with parent-corporation policies and procedures after the acquisition is accomplished.

The vast majority of companies do not assign internal auditors to line responsibilities. In the past, the limited regular exceptions frequently related to bank reconciliations. It is not unusual that internal auditors will be assigned to special nonaudit activities, due to their availability, independence, and discipline. Although this use of their expertise should be encouraged, continuing special assignments can hinder progress with the audit plan. Internal auditors generally coordinate their activities with those of the external auditors, to assure the necessary breadth of audit coverage and to eliminate unnecessary duplicate effort. They also participate with external auditors in the year-end audit. The work of the internal unit can have a direct effect on the extent to which outside services are required. Operational audits and management appraisals are frequent audit assignments, with some companies assigning more than 50 percent of the audit time to nonfinancial reviews. In many companies the internal audit chief is also required to stay abreast of proposed new accounting rules and standards and to confirm the compliance with such changes. Some companies assign full-time auditors to a major activity, such as a construction project or the location filming of a motion picture. It is also common to have auditors perform post-audits on capital projects to review costs against appropriations and test the attainment of the benefits used to justify approval of the project.

The thrust of financial audits will depend to a great extent on the type of business and the interests of management. Banks and other financial institutions devote extensive audit time to the continual checking of transactions, protection of cash, and interface with branch operations. Service operations are concerned with payroll reporting, aging of accounts receivable, control of materials, and consumer relations. With the Foreign Corrupt Practices Act in effect, auditors have found it necessary to reemphasize the prevention and detection of fraud and theft, the determination that an adequate system of internal controls is in place, the testing of those controls, and the installation of new controls.

Operational Audits

Control systems are not limited to financial functions. Administrative and operational controls are as necessary as financial controls for the safeguarding of a company's assets and efficiency of its operations. An operational audit can be undertaken either in conjunction with a financial audit or as a separate endeavor. The audits are less structured. They require more experienced auditors than financial audits. The operational auditors must have a knowledge of operating practices and conditions, and frequently EDP, statistical, or management-consulting skills that are not necessarily present in an audit staff. Among the objectives of an operational audit is an evaluation of how effectively management uses its resources. An operational audit will frequently highlight the need for new controls and procedures, changes in managerial emphasis, and, at times, the advisability of making management changes. These audits can lead to profit improvement through such accomplishments as staffing reductions, new purchasing procedures, revised inventory controls, work schedule changes, and elimination of unnecessary reports or activities.

There are many advantages to a detailed pre-audit review of the scope of an operational audit plan with the management of functions to be audited. Those audited have some degree of anxiety. The prior consultation can reassure the operating management of the audit objectives, point out the successful conclusions reached in similar audits in other areas, and confirm to direct management that all findings will be reviewed with it as they are developed. Auditors should keep the operators informed of the audit's progress and enlist their assistance to expedite the review. Frequently, deficiencies found during an audit can be corrected prior to the completion of the audit. A draft of the audit report should be reviewed with operating management so that changes can be made to correct factual errors, if any, and ascertain that the conclusions are proper and the recommendations reasonable. It is important that the auditor cite control strengths and positive attainments, as well as indicate deficiencies that require correction.

Auditors are frequently invited to report on the adequacy of performance of individual employees in their assigned jobs. This is generally accomplished in an oral report or a written report separate from the operational audit report. Internal auditors can find great satisfaction in undertaking operational audits, since they are generally broader in scope, produce measurable accomplishments, can generate profit improvement, and position the auditor as a problem solver rather than an accountant.

Data Processing Audits

Computers have become the standard tool for recording transactions and accounting for assets. Telecommunications equipment permits instantaneous transfer of cash, transmission of data, and the ability of a headquarters unit to extract for review and audit data stored at division or regional locations. It is essential that an internal audit department have detailed knowledge of EDP. With the rapid growth in computer technology, audit departments have found it difficult to hire qualified EDP auditors, and often have found it necessary to develop internal training programs. As the size of an audit staff increases, the percentage of the staff concentrating on EDP audits usually rises rapidly.

EDP has generally been more concerned with servicing users than it has been with establishing controls. The auditor must program audit checks into the system. Some assistance is available through CPA firms and others who have developed software packages that aid in auditing through EDP. When new computer systems are being developed, it is advisable for an auditor to work with the systems analysts to program controls into the system, and to test the effectiveness of such controls before the system becomes operational.

A key factor in the audit of EDP is the need to point out noncompliance with established policies and standards. Audit reviews should assure that controls are established to prevent unauthorized access to corporate data. Continual monitoring of the listing of those individuals who are authorized to have access to each computer program or application is advisable. An individual who has access to a system can often cause significant disruption or violation of controls in the time between the decision to terminate him and his actual departure. Another significant audit responsibility is to ensure backup facilities in the event of disaster, safe availability of duplicate historical and operating data, and adequate recovery procedures.

In this auditing process, the auditor must be continually alert to the changing corporate environment and business requirements. The reviewer can confirm effective use of the systems and equipment. Auditors can evaluate terminal usage and determine where terminals are in excess. Auditors can review the cost-effectiveness of reports and recommend where computer access could be devoted to a more meaningful application. They can monitor passwords and internal controls to ensure effectiveness of the security system. They should continually evaluate the overall operation of the data center and the use of the external control points. They should review the proposed project schedules of the computer systems department to assure that applications are consistent with business requirements, necessary controls are programmed into the system, and the payoff is reasonable.

The availability of computers means that an individual can have records available at a terminal for manipulation. Computer fraud is more difficult to detect than fraud with simpler accounting records, because fraudulent transactions are hidden in a computer's data bank and can be adjusted with a few seconds of computer time. Although banks and other financial institutions are most vulnerable in the magnitude of a defalcation, the use of a computer by a small business with insufficient operating controls can easily lead to sloppy accounting and an environment that can be tempting to a knowledgeable employee.

Fraud

The procedures, policies, and controls of a company provide the primary assurance against fraud. The internal audit function is present to monitor those practices and recommend new controls when situations warrant. Internal auditors should take "due care" in their examinations, particularly in areas that are conducive to possible wrongdoing on the part of employees and suppliers. Discovery of fraud resulting from collusion is difficult to detect and frequently requires a variety of audit paths when irregularities are suspected. When collusion exists, the very best system of internal controls can be circumvented. Whenever an auditor suspects wrongdoing, he should recommend further investigation. Although unnecessary time may be spent in areas such as the auditing of potential conflicts of interest, the visible investigation by an internal audit function is often a successful deterrent to possible fraud. After legislation of the FCPA, many companies redesigned their policy and procedure statements and redirected the audit staff back toward fraud prevention and the testing of internal controls.

Reporting Relationships

Independence and reliability are key characteristics of the internal audit department. It should have free access to senior management and to the audit committee of the board of directors. Most boards do have audit committees, usually consisting of outside board members. The New York Stock Exchange requires that all listed companies have such a committee. The internal audit unit should report to the most senior management position that will effectively enforce audit planning and compliance with audit reports. In the past, the audit head reported to the financial organization, both administratively and functionally. Since auditing had traditionally been viewed as a financial or accounting requirement, and since auditors talked the same language as accounting and control personnel, this was a comfortable assignment. The difficulty in this relationship, even if the audit head reported to the chief financial officer, is properly reporting the need for corrective action in functions under the stewardship of the superior. Even though the CFO may not directly relate to day-to-day accounting or treasury activities, his corporate position can influence or temper internal audit surveillance.

With the advent of the FCPA and the greater concern for accounting controls, the reporting relationship of the audit unit has tended to move to a higher level in the organization structure. It has become more common of late to have the audit head report functionally to the audit committee of the board of directors. A majority of companies are not yet willing to do this, however, and many have assigned the audit department's functional reporting to the chief executive officer. Administratively, the unit generally continues to report to the CFO, unless the chief executive feels the importance of personal involvement in the complete audit program and can devote sufficient time to the activity. Even if the auditor does not report to the audit committee, that group should have direct access to the internal audit chief, as it does to the external auditor, with or without the presence of other members of management.

Staffing

The internal audit chief should be a seasoned executive, a good manager and planner, and able to communicate well both verbally and in writing. An internal audit department should be staffed with professionals. Generally, this has meant individuals with educational background or work experience in accounting or finance. Probably the most common sources of internal auditors are public accounting firms. Since the basic audit requirements are in the areas of financial reports, controls, and procedures, accounting knowledge is essential to the audit department. However, with the growth of EDP and the payout from operational audits, many larger audit staffs have balanced the accountants with individuals from other disciplines. EDP systems analysts can bring to the audit function important computer expertise and can be taught the necessary accounting techniques. Statisticians, engineers, and especially individuals with advanced training in management techniques can all be assigned within an audit function that is engaged in operational and management audits. It is essential, however, that the activities of these specialists be coordinated within an audit plan, and that the function does not lose sight of its basic responsibilities.

The audit department should maintain a balanced staff with sufficient experience at the managerial or senior level to develop new personnel and professionally undertake the continuing responsibilities. The auditor is in a position to obtain a broad view of company operations and an intimate view of many aspects of those operations. Since auditors are frequently excellent candidates for positions in financial and operational management, the internal audit department can be used as a development step for individuals with great promotable potential. However, auditing can be a satisfying career, and many people find the function a career in itself. It is important that the staff be subject to ongoing training within the company and that educational opportunities be available to sharpen skills and learn new techniques. Some companies set aside one week each year to brief auditors on management plans and practices, review new developments with the external auditors, discuss current requirements, and debate audit-report findings and recommendations.

Audit Plans and Reports

A comprehensive audit plan and informative audit reports are essential. The audit plan should be prepared annually and updated as priority assignments arise or estimated audit man-hours change. The audit plan can be developed from a review of basic audit responsibilities, results of prior audits, and the need to investigate new areas of possible concern. In developing the plan, it is often helpful to discuss with operating and staff managements the availability of the audit function to assist in reviewing the effectiveness of controls and procedures. Frequently, auditors are able to develop excellent additions to the audit schedule by performing a "walk-through" of functions. This could consist of following selected transactions through an entire system in order to understand the types of tests that can be performed. It could also be an organizational orientation, in which functions are visited to determine the location and reporting relationships of control points. It is also helpful to review the internal audit plan with the external auditors so that the two functions can most efficiently coordinate their activities.

Audit reports should be concise and understandable. They should be supported by work papers that are well organized and readable. There should also be included in the file all necessary supporting documents or materials and, after the report has been issued, a copy of all responses, plans, and resolutions. The audit reports should be formatted to convey to management the audit findings and recommendations in sufficient detail to be clearly understood. In many instances, it may be preferable to present highlights to senior management, with the more detailed findings furnished to the management of the areas audited and the units directly responsible for controls and procedures. The audit should generally be addressed to the executive in charge of the functions audited, with information copies as required. That executive should be required to respond within a predetermined period of time. It is usually a preferred practice to review a draft of the proposed audit report with individuals directly responsible for the function audited. In this way, any misunderstanding or misinterpretation can be corrected. Many companies also furnish the external auditors with a copy of each internal audit report.

As important as the issued reports are in conveying the recommendations to management, the internal auditor's involvement should not stop there. Specifically, there should be a continual monitoring of the actions taken to correct the deficiencies noted in the audit reports. This monitoring function can be achieved by requiring that all audit reports be formally responded to with a clear and documented management action plan. In addition, specific follow-up audits should then be scheduled to verify implementation of corrective actions.

Year-End Audit

The most significant responsibility of public accountants is the annual year-end audit and certification of the reasonableness and accounting consistency of the corporate balance sheet and earnings statement. The internal audit department can assist the public accountants in this responsibility. This use of the internal audit function has a number of advantages. First, it is generally less costly to use the corporate staff for a portion of the work than to employ additional outsiders. Second, the internal unit will be available to follow up on any discrepancies noted. Third, the external auditors are often able to pinpoint areas of concern that may be added to the internal audit plan.

This joint endeavor, under the direction of the public accounting firm, frequently leads to an interdependence and understanding of the internal and external functions that are of value throughout the year. It is not unusual for the public accountants to use work papers produced by the internal unit to expedite necessary audit reviews and thereby limit audit fees. In some instances, it is advantageous to team up an internal and an external auditor on a project, with each reviewing a different aspect of the matter.

Audit Committee

Deliberations of the audit committee of the board of directors will vary from company to company depending upon the size and type of business, the concerns of the board, and the effectiveness of corporate operating management. The primary responsibility of the audit committee is to protect the shareholders by overseeing the effectiveness of the company's accounting and operating procedures and controls through the activities of the internal and external audit services. In addition to reviewing the public auditor's reports and annual management letter, an effective audit committee will relate directly to the activities of the internal audit unit. The committee should be alert to the position of the internal audit unit within the management structure. Specifically, it should ensure that the reporting relationships of the internal audit unit permit easy access to senior management. The committee should be cognizant of the audit plan and the relationship with the external audit group. It should review audit reports to evaluate the completeness of the findings and the appropriateness of the recommendations. It should follow up with management to confirm that corrective actions have been taken. The internal audit chief should have direct access to, and be acquainted with, the audit committee.

Evaluating the Audit Function

Quality-assurance reviews of internal audit reports are a continuing responsibility of corporate management. In addition, an independent evaluation of the audit function may be helpful in reassuring corporate management and the audit committee of the unit's competence in handling its responsibilities. The evaluation can be conducted from within the corporate organization or by outsiders. The evaluation made from within the organization might not be considered an impartial one. In a large company, with separate audit units for headquarters and divisions or subsidiaries, the staff unit can evaluate divisional performance. The staff unit itself can be reviewed by a management committee team that includes individuals with prior audit experience.

A "peer review" by an external organization is generally more acceptable to the audit committee. The external auditors employed by the company would be the most obvious source for such a review. They are familiar with the corporate organization, understand the audit plans, and are knowledgeable about the corporate matters. They could probably perform the review quickly and efficiently and at a reasonable cost. If a more independent view is desired, external auditors from a different assignment in the audit firm could be used. Using a different accounting firm is generally more expensive, since a great deal of time will be spent on familiarization. A peer review by an internal audit unit from a different company is not recommended, because it could lead to the disclosure of confidential information and might be conducted on questionable standards.

□ *Nicholas C. Gilles*

THE EXTERNAL AUDIT

The primary objective of the external audit is to add credibility to the financial statements of management. The role of the external auditor is to render an independent professional opinion on the fairness of financial statements to the extent this is required by generally accepted auditing standards.

Financial Statements

The annual report to shareholders is the principal communication used to present financial information to the owners of a business. For publicly owned companies, audited financial statements are required in these annual reports.

Although these reports are addressed to shareholders, the financial statements are often of interest and use to many other groups, including credit grantors, security analysts, rating agencies, regulatory authorities, taxing authorities, labor unions, and employees. The interests of these groups may at times be opposed, but the financial statements should be of general use to all, even though they are prepared primarily with the needs of investors and lenders in mind.

Audited financial statements in the annual report normally include a comparative balance sheet as of the end of the last two fiscal years, and comparative income statements and statements of changes in financial position for the last three fiscal years. In addition, notes to financial statements (which may be extensive) are considered to be an integral part of financial statements. Most of the information in the notes is required by generally accepted accounting principles or Securities and Exchange Commission disclosure rules.

Responsibility for Financial Statements

Financial statements are the representations of management. In fact, management is responsible for the financial statements and all other information in the annual report, except for the report of the independent auditor, which is solely his representation.

It had been commonly believed that many users of financial statements did not understand the separate responsibilities of independent auditors and corporate managements regarding audited financial statements. This misunderstanding apparently arose from the fact that management did not specifically report on the financial statements, whereas the independent auditor did. In the late 1970s, in an attempt to counteract this misunderstanding, corporate managements began a voluntary movement to include in annual reports a report by management on the financial statements. The objective of the management report is to inform financial-statement users of management's responsibility for those statements, the various means by which that responsibility is fulfilled, and the role of others with respect to those statements.

Typically, these reports contain a representation on internal accounting control and its limitations, a description of the duties of the audit committee of the board of directors, and a discussion of the role of the independent auditor.

Although the primary responsibility for financial statements rests with management, that is, executive and financial officers of the company, the responsibility for approval of financial reports rests with the entire board of directors. There is a growing belief among investors, analysts, regulatory agencies, and corporate managements that an audit committee of the board can help fulfill this board responsibility.

Responsibilities of audit committees may vary considerably among corporations. It is commonly recommended that the audit committee

- Be composed of three to five outside directors.
- Nominate the independent auditors for submission to the full board of directors and in some cases to the stockholders.
- Discuss with the independent auditor the scope of audit work before the audit is begun.
- Review reports of the independent auditor on internal control and determine whether management has taken appropriate action on the auditor's recommendations.
- Review with the independent auditor the annual financial statements prior to their issuance.
- Give both the external auditor and the internal auditor free access to the committee, without the presence of management, to discuss any matters they believe the board of directors should know about.

The report by management should clarify the role of the independent auditor. That role, which is to render an independent opinion on the financial statements, does not in any way limit management's responsibility for the financial statements and all the other information, whether audited or unaudited, in the annual report.

Nature of Financial Statements

The responsibilities of management as well as of the external auditor are influenced greatly by the nature of financial statements and the underlying accounting process. The information in the financial statements must be prepared in accordance with generally accepted accounting principles, which must be applied in a manner to achieve fairness in presentation of the information.

Generally accepted accounting principles (GAAP) consist of some broad rules, many specific rules, and some commonly applied conventions concerning the measurement, classification, and disclosure of financial events and transactions. In the United States, generally accepted accounting principles are established in statements of financial accounting standards issued by the Financial Accounting Standards Board. The board is a freestanding body in the private sector, supported by the accounting profession and industry. FASB has also embraced as authoritative the pronouncements of predecessor private-sector standard setters, including the former Accounting Principles Board and the Committee on Accounting Procedure of the American Institute of Certified Public Accountants.

Although these bodies have issued extensive pronouncements, which have been indexed and codified, they do not deal with many areas of accounting. Therefore, in addition to these sources of GAAP, some principles can be found in scholarly writings, textbooks, and published financial statements. For example, there are few authoritative standards for accounting for inventories and fixed assets, two of the most important assets of industrial companies. As a result, diverse accounting practices exist among companies, all of which may be presenting financial statements in accordance with GAAP.

The Securities and Exchange Commission is also a source of GAAP for public companies. The SEC has taken the position that the annual report to shareholders shall be the principal communication vehicle for conveying financial information to shareholders and the public. The stated SEC policy is to rely on the FASB to establish financial accounting and reporting standards, but the SEC feels free to address areas where GAAP are not explicit and reserves the right to reject an FASB standard it finds unacceptable.

Income-tax rules often have an effect on GAAP, even though in many instances accounting for income-tax purposes may differ from accounting in financial statements issued to shareholders. Nevertheless, managements frequently prefer to have conformity between tax and financial accounting unless there is a significant reason for a difference. In one case, the LIFO method of valuing inventories, the tax law requires conformity of the method in financial statements as a prerequisite to its use for tax purposes.

Just as there is no accepted definition of GAAP, and there is no single listing of specific principles embodied therein, there is also no conceptual framework that underlies or gives guidance to the development of GAAP. The FASB has been working for years in trying to develop a conceptual framework that could be agreed upon, but it still has a long way to go on the project.

Yet there are some concepts that do underlie the preparation of financial statements and that are accepted in practice. Their acceptance and use are assumed, and disclosure is made only if they are not followed. They include:

- *Going concern.* The enterprise is viewed as one that is continuing in operation, rather than one that is contemplating liquidation.
- *Accrual basis.* Revenues and costs are recognized in financial statements as they are earned or incurred. This is contemplated in the concept of matching costs and revenues, wherein costs are included in the income statement in the same period as related revenues.
- *Consistency.* The accounting principles are applied consistently in each accounting period, making the statements comparable from year to year.

Financial statements are expressed in monetary terms and therefore give an impression of accuracy that may be unwarranted. The financial statements include factual information and also many estimates and judgments by management with which the independent auditor concurs. Not all measurements are precise. Some require judgments as to the outcome of future events, such as the life of machinery and anticipated warranty costs. Selection of an accounting method must be made where alternative methods are available. How much to disclose is also a matter of judgment. Underlying all these judgments is the consideration of materiality. There is no precise definition of materiality in financial statements; yet materiality is a consideration in accuracy of information presented, the detail of information shown, and the nature and extent of supplementary disclosures.

Notes to financial statements are an integral part of financial statements. Management must present a summary of significant accounting policies. Details of some financial-statement items must be presented. Additional required information includes such disclosures as terms and conditions of long-term debt, contingent liabilities, and stock options. Both the FASB and the SEC require many specific disclosures in the notes to financial statements.

The Auditor

The external auditor is expected to adhere to the ethical and professional standards of his profession. Ethical standards for certified public accountants are set forth in the rules of conduct of the Code of Professional Ethics of the AICPA. The rules are enforceable against CPAs who are members of the AICPA.

A member shall not express an opinion on financial statements of an enterprise unless he and his firm are independent with respect to that enterprise. He cannot have a financial interest in the enterprise or be a director, officer, or employee, or engage in a specified list of restricted transactions. The member shall possess integrity and objectivity and shall not subordinate his judgment to others.

A member shall comply with the general standards of competence. He shall (1) undertake only those engagements which he or his firm can reasonably expect to complete with reasonable competence; (2) exercise due professional care in the performance of an engagement; (3) adequately plan and supervise an engagement; (4) obtain sufficient relevant data to afford a reasonable basis for conclusions or recommendations in relation to an engagement; and (5) not permit his name to be used in conjunction with a forecast of future transactions in a manner that may lead to the belief that the member vouches for the achievability of the forecast.

A member must comply with generally accepted auditing standards when he is associated with financial statements. When financial statements are presented in accordance with generally accepted accounting principles but contain a departure from an FASB standard, he must describe the departure and its effects.

A member shall not disclose any confidential information obtained in the course of a professional engagement except with the consent of a client.

Independent auditors have been held to be liable to third parties that could prove reliance on audited financial statements that contained material errors.

Generally Accepted Auditing Standards

Generally accepted auditing standards were adopted by the membership of AICPA in 1948 and 1949. In summary, they require:

General Standards
1. Adequate technical training and proficiency as an auditor.
2. An independence in mental attitude by the auditor.
3. Due professional care in the performance of the examination and preparation of the report.

Standards of Field Work
1. Adequate planning of work and proper supervision of assistants.
2. Proper study and evaluation of the existing internal control as a basis for reliance thereon and for determination of the extent to which auditing procedures are to be restricted.
3. Sufficient competent evidential matter through inspection, observation, in-

quiries, and confirmations to afford a reasonable basis for an opinion regarding the financial statements.

Standards of Reporting

1. The report must state whether the financial statements are presented in accordance with GAAP.
2. The report must state whether such principles have been consistently observed in the current period in relation to the preceding period.
3. Informative disclosures in the financial statements must be regarded as reasonably adequate unless otherwise stated in the report.
4. The report must contain either an expression of opinion regarding the financial statements or an assertion to the effect that an opinion cannot be expressed and an explanation of why not.

These standards to a great extent are interrelated and interdependent. The elements of materiality and relative risk underlie the application of all the standards, particularly the standards of field work and reporting.

Two standards probably require the most time in an audit and probably give rise to the greatest confusion about what an auditor does. They are the study and evaluation of internal control and obtaining sufficient competent evidential matter.

Internal Control

The purpose of the auditor's study and evaluation of internal control is to establish to what extent he can rely on those controls and to determine the nature, extent, and timing of audit tests to be applied in his examination of financial statements. The study made for this purpose frequently provides the basis for constructive recommendations to clients for improvements in internal control.

Internal control is usually regarded as a part of an overall managerial control system. Internal control can be further divided into administrative control and accounting control. The Auditing Standards Board (and its predecessor committees) of the AICPA found this distinction useful in providing guidance to auditors for interpreting the internal-control standards.

The board defines administrative control as the plan of organization and the procedures and records that are concerned with the decision processes leading to management's authorization of transactions. It defines accounting control as the plan of organization and the procedures and records that are concerned with the safeguarding of assets and the reliability of financial records, and consequently are designed to provide reasonable assurance that:

- Transactions are executed in accordance with management's general or specific authorization.
- Transactions are recorded as necessary (1) to permit preparation of financial statements in conformity with generally accepted accounting principles or any other criteria applicable to those statements and (2) to maintain accountability for assets.

□ Access to assets is permitted only in accordance with management's authorization.

□ The recorded accountability for assets is compared with the existing assets at reasonable intervals, and appropriate action is taken whenever there are differences.

After acknowledging the responsibility of management for administrative as well as accounting controls, the Auditing Standards Board confines the responsibilities of auditors to accounting controls. The concept of reasonable assurance recognizes that the cost of internal control should not exceed the benefits to be derived.

Internal accounting control systems usually depend on the competence and integrity of personnel, the independence of their assigned functions, and their understanding of prescribed procedures. These factors are sometimes achieved by segregation of functions so that no one person is in a position both to perpetuate and to conceal errors or irregularities in the ordinary course of his duties. The systems usually require independent evidence that authorizations are issued by persons acting within the scope of their authority and that transactions conform with the terms of the authorizations.

Regardless of how comprehensive the system of internal accounting controls may be, there are inherent limitations on its effectiveness. The possibility of errors arises from a misunderstanding of instructions, a mistake in judgment, distraction, fatigue, or carelessness. Circumvention or collusion can reduce or destroy the effectiveness of control procedures that depend on segregation of duties. Also, senior management may override control procedures that would otherwise monitor the occurrence of errors or irregularities. Of special concern is the increasing dependence of companies on computers for operational effectiveness and for financial reporting; in many cases, general managers have a limited understanding of electronic data processing operations, and data processing management is insufficiently aware of internal accounting control requirements.

The subject of internal control became increasingly important to both management and independent auditors when Congress passed the Foreign Corrupt Practices Act of 1977. The law has two sections: one section prohibits bribery of foreign officials and applies to all companies, and the other section amends the Securities Exchange Act of 1934 and incorporates into law almost verbatim the professional auditing standards of internal accounting control cited here. This has greatly troubled corporate managements, for the law has no materiality standard, and a weakness in control of minor importance might be construed as a violation of the law. The independent auditor must consider not only his traditional technical responsibilities but also whether his client might be in violation of the law.

Further, the SEC proposed but later withdrew regulations that would have required managements to report publicly on the adequacy of internal accounting controls, and would have required independent auditors to report on the consistency and reasonableness of management's report. Since the withdrawal, the SEC has been monitoring voluntary reports on internal control. Comments on internal control in reports by management have been widely adopted, whereas only a few separate reports on internal control by independent auditors have appeared. In most instances, in order to report publicly on internal control, the auditor would be required to greatly expand the scope of his study and evaluation of internal control over his study made as part of his audit of the financial statements.

Evidential Matter

In carrying out his audit, the independent auditor must obtain and evaluate competent evidential matter concerning assertions made in the financial statements. The assertions are representations made by management. For example, management asserts that sales in the income statement represent the exchange of goods or services with customers for cash and other considerations and that costs in the income statement represent the related costs of those goods and services. Similarly, management asserts that assets shown on the balance sheet represent things owned stated at appropriate costs or values and liabilities represent obligations of the company.

The auditor needs to examine corroborating evidence to support these assertions. He examines underlying books and records, vouchers, invoices, checks, contracts, and minutes of meetings. He will observe physical inventory counts to determine that inventories included in the balance sheet physically exist. He will obtain written confirmations from independent sources outside the entity being audited to assure that bank balances are correct, customer balances are properly stated, and inventories at outside locations exist.

The auditor will test accounting transactions to determine that particular components of the financial statements are properly classified, described, and disclosed. He does not examine all transactions, but he selects sufficient substantive tests for a sample of transactions to achieve his audit objectives. He must decide how much reliance to place on the system of internal accounting controls, taking into account the risk of errors or irregularities that would be material to the financial statements. If internal controls are weak, he may choose not to rely on them at all but to extend his tests of evidential matter instead. The auditor also must consider a rational relationship between the cost of obtaining evidence and the usefulness of the information obtained.

The Auditor's Report

Upon completion of the audit, the auditor must issue his report in accordance with the four standards of reporting referred to earlier. Ordinarily, any differences between the views of management and the independent auditor are resolved to their mutual satisfaction so that the latter can issue a standard unqualified opinion, such as the following:

> In our opinion, the aforementioned financial statements present fairly the financial position of ABC Company at December 31, 19X2 and 19X1, and the results of its operations and the changes in its financial position for each

of the three years in the period ended December 31, 19X2, in conformity with generally accepted accounting principles applied on a consistent basis.

The standard report is expected, and the auditor's report takes on added significance if there is a variation from this standard. Three broad deviations from the auditor's standard report are qualified opinions, disclaimers of opinion, and adverse opinions.

The auditor's opinion may be qualified because of a departure from generally accepted accounting principles, a limitation on the scope of the audit, major uncertainties, or a lack of consistency of accounting principles. Qualified opinions that state that the financial statements are presented fairly "except for" departures from GAAP or "except for" scope limitations are seldom seen, because the SEC refuses to accept such reports and insists that the qualifications be removed and the financial statements and auditor's opinion be reissued. The auditor's opinion may be "subject to" the outcome of an uncertainty or contingency that is so material that its potential effect on the financial statements is pervasive. When a change in accounting principle is made in the financial statements, the auditor must note this change in his report and state that he concurs with the change. Qualified opinions usually refer to a note, which contains a full explanation of the reasons for and effects of the qualification.

When an auditor is unable to form an opinion, either because of a scope limitation or a contingency too great to permit a qualified "subject to" opinion, he must state that he has no opinion. If a departure from GAAP is so significant that he thinks the statements are all wrong, the auditor must issue an adverse opinion in which he states that the financial statements are not presented fairly.

Supplementary Financial Information

Both the FASB and the SEC require certain supplementary information in the annual report in addition to the audited financial statements and notes. The supplementary information may be presented outside the statements and notes, or it may be included in the notes and labeled "unaudited."

The FASB requires supplementary information on the effects of changing prices. The SEC requires selected interim financial information. Both the FASB and the SEC require certain supplementary information on oil and gas reserves.

Ordinarily, the independent auditor will not need to expand his report on the audited financial statements to refer to the supplementary information. He will expand his report if the required supplementary information is omitted, if the supplementary information departs from the applicable guidelines, or if he is unable to complete limited prescribed procedures.

The annual report may contain other information not included in the audited financial statements or the required supplementary financial information. The independent auditor has no responsibility for this other information; however, he should read it. If he believes the other information is materially inconsistent with the financial statements or contains a material misstatement of fact, he should discuss it with the client in an attempt to eliminate the inconsistency or misstatement. If the matter is still not resolved, he should consult legal counsel as to further action.

Additional Services by the Independent Auditor

The independent auditor has the professional competence to provide many additional services not required in performing the audit. Frequently during the course of the audit, he may become aware of opportunities to improve the efficiency or effectiveness of the client's accounting procedures. Recommendations of this nature are often included in the auditor's report to management on internal controls.

Independent accounting firms also have specialists in income taxes, management advisory services, and specialized industry matters. Clients frequently engage their auditing firms to carry out special projects. The firm will be well prepared to carry out this work because of the base of knowledge already obtained through the audit. In turn, the firm's ability to audit may be enhanced by knowledge gained through special assignments.

Although nonaudit services have been an important part of public accounting practice since the inception of the profession, some critics contend that the performance of nonaudit services may jeopardize an auditor's audit independence or at least the appearance of independence.

At one time the SEC required companies to disclose in proxy statements whether each nonaudit service provided by the auditor was approved by, and the possible effect on the independence of the auditor was considered by, the audit committee or the board of directors before the service was performed. The SEC also required disclosure of the fee for each nonaudit service, expressed as a percentage of the audit fee. In 1982 the SEC withdrew these requirements but promised to continue to observe self-regulatory means of monitoring nonaudit services.   □ *Leonard M. Savoie*

MANAGEMENT OF PENSION FUNDS

A major advantage of a qualified pension plan or profit-sharing plan is that an employer's contribution is a deductible expense. To qualify, the benefits must be funded, and there are several decisions that must be made under the general heading of *funding policy.*

The first decision is to choose a *funding agency.* This can be an organization or an individual that accumulates or administers the assets to be used to pay benefits under a pension plan. Typical funding agencies include life insurance companies, corporate fiduciaries, and individuals acting as trustees.

These funding agencies have several different contracts or instruments for funding pension benefits. For example, insured pension plans may be funded through group deferred annuities, deposit administration contracts, or even individual policies. The various contracts are called *funding instruments.* A funding instrument is an agreement or contract governing the conditions under which assets are accumulated or administered by a funding agency to pay benefits under a pension plan.

Funding instruments are trust agreements with corporate fiduciaries or contracts with life insurance companies or individuals acting as trustees. In a plan where all assets are being accumulated in a group pension contract, the insurance or annuity contracts are viewed as the funding instrument. In many large companies where several investments firms or mutual-fund companies are managing the pension assets, a bank often acts as the "master trustee." The master trustee bank does not have to be one of the investment managers.

The Employee Retirement Income Security Act of 1974

This act (ERISA) affects all employee benefit plans, but its most pronounced impact is on qualified pension plans. The definition of a "fiduciary" has been broadened and includes, for example, plan administrators as well as plan trustees. Essentially, the "prudent man" rule applies to the investment of plan assets, but investment in an employer's securities must be limited to 10 percent of the plan's assets. The limit does not apply to stock-bonus, thrift, or profit-sharing plans that explicitly permit such investments in employer securities.

The list of transactions prohibited for plan fiduciaries is increased, and ERISA states explicitly that fiduciaries "act solely for the benefit of covered employees." Greater documentation of plan procedures and policies is required.

Plan sponsors (that is, companies with pension plans) are legally liable for imprudent investment practices. To a large extent, ERISA prompted plan sponsors and beneficiaries to actively question pension asset management practices and to demand justification of investment risks and costs.

Setting Investment Policy to Meet Objectives

An investment objective is inadequate if expressed only in terms of return. In its simplest terms, the investment objective of a pension fund is to meet promised benefits at a cost acceptable to the plan sponsor. Whatever the original statement of objective, essentially it can be converted to one of earning an adequate return on current and future assets. An objective is something we wish to accomplish, and risk is the potential for not meeting the objective.

But a policy is something tangible, and links objectives to risk. Thus an investment policy is inadequate if it is a statement of desired returns without reference to the likelihood of meeting the objective, that is, to the risk.

The plan sponsor must recognize that the pension fund exists in the same economic universe as the corporation. Therefore, the company must have consistent economic and financial analyses of capital markets for its corporate planning and its pension fund, all assessed in the light of the plan sponsor's unique characteristics. This means that planning of investment policy must be integrated with the plan sponsor's actuarial and economic policy.

The objectives of an ideal pension-fund investment policy might be characterized as (1) minimum fluctuation of annual total pension costs; such annual pension costs expressed as a percentage of covered payroll; (2) maximum security of employee expectations; (3) maximum long-term investment performance; (4) minimum short-term asset volatility; and (5) discharge of ERISA duties. Furthermore, the policy should be understandable by the board of directors, employees, and analysts and should satisfy common sense.

Obviously, those idealized criteria are not internally consistent. In choosing among these ideal characteristics, it is essential for a plan sponsor to fulfill the ERISA mandate to plan participants; base investment decisions on independent analysis; take the asset-mix decisions from an implied forecast of stocks, bonds, or other asset classes to a carefully considered business planning decision; avoid extreme market-oriented decisions; and express the uniqueness of the company.

Investment policy guidelines might include minimum quality ratings for stocks or bonds, or specification of a desired range of volatility and diversification for the equity portfolio. For example, one approach to setting guidelines for the asset mix might be based on the following framework:

1. For most plans, most investments can be held for long-term results, as there is generally little need to retain a great portion of a pension fund in a liquid or stable market-value condition for the purposes of paying benefits. In other words, current contributions plus current investment income generally will exceed the expected benefit payments for a number of years in the future.

2. Therefore, in making long-range planning decisions on asset mix, it is important to avoid overemphasizing the recent past, whether it has been favorable or unfavorable. A review of the investment performance at the end of 1974, for example, was disappointing for all investors. Not only were absolute rates of return low, but equity investors received little or no premium over the rate of return provided by long-term bonds. Furthermore, the rate of inflation exceeded the gross rate of returns on both bonds and stocks, resulting in negative real rates of return. A continuation of this experience would destroy our nation's capital structure, and was not a credible reference point for determining future investment policy in 1974.

3. Assuming the continued strength of our nation and the ability of the U.S. economy to produce goods and services at a reasonable profit and to assure capital formation in amounts necessary to sustain this economic growth, we can expect future investment results that give investors a positive real rate of return. Inflation will probably still be with us, but the bond investor should have a total return, including coupons and changes in capital value, that exceeds the rate of inflation, on average *and* over the long term. Common-stock investors, also over the long term, should receive a total investment return that exceeds the bond investor's return. This equity risk premium will be a compensation for the greater volatility of common-stock market values and a recognition of the fact that equity returns over shorter time periods—which can extend for several years—may fall significantly below bond returns.

This illustrative background statement might suggest an investment policy that has a majority commitment to equities, say 50–75 percent in common stocks. Whatever the investment policy, it should be written down by the plan sponsor and not be delegated to the investment manager or managers. The investment policy should be reviewed periodically, together with several other dimensions to the analysis:

1. Liquidity requirements to cover benefits payments must be assessed.
2. Funding and fiduciary requirements of ERISA have to be taken into consideration.
3. The relationships between investment policy and actuarial policy have to be studied.

The plan sponsor should not only state the investment policy in terms of guidelines for each asset class (say, 50–75 percent in common stocks), but also express explicitly the expected annual variation implied by such a policy. For example, if we think common stocks and bonds will be as volatile each year as in the past, we could say that a 50–75 percent guideline in equities implies an annual variation of plus or minus 16 percent around some kind of annual return objective. This plus or minus 16 percent annual variation is sometimes known as "standard deviation" and is acceptable for many plan sponsors because the bottom line is the earnings stream, not the market value of the pension fund on a year-to-year basis.

A strong version of this line of reasoning is that *the plan sponsor cannot control investment return, but can control variability through its investment policy.*

Selection of the investment policy is selecting the risk-return exposure of the fund and is the cornerstone of any pension plan. Risk can be specified in terms of accepted variability of return and degree of diversification. Asset-mix guidelines should be in writing. The simplest example would be the policy statement, "The ratio of equity to fixed income shall be maintained at 60:40." Another investment policy guideline might be, "Equities shall be at least 30 percent, and fixed income at least 30 percent, of the portfolio at all times, with the remaining 40 percent to be applied at the discretion of the manager."

Investment Strategy Formulation

The last guideline just cited suggests that while the plan sponsor should set investment *policy*, professional money managers should be responsible for investment *strategy*. Think of investment policy as the average, normal, or basic portfolio plan. Think of investment strategy as a deviation from this basic portfolio plan.

Once the company decides on investment policy, it, being the plan sponsor, decides who will have the responsibility for investment strategy and management of the pension funds. With the assistance of a consultant, small companies usually contract with a bank or an insurance company to handle this responsibility. As pension-fund assets increase in size, greater use is made of independent investment managers, in-house investment people that are on the company payroll, or a combination of investment managers.

Essentially there are three levels of involvement available to the company:

■ Direct involvement. The company shifts assets from one manager to another as the attractiveness of the style of investment management and the asset categories changes.

- Semidirect involvement. The company allocates new cash flow and selects new managers on the basis of its asset allocation decisions. Generally, specialized managers are selected for each asset category (for example, stocks, bonds, real estate, oil and gas, venture capital) and each specialty product. Examples of specialty products within the common-stock environment are small-capitalization common stocks, growth or income stocks, index funds, mutual funds, and international equities.

- Indirect involvement. The plan sponsor generally hires balanced investment managers, who make the asset-allocation decisions for the company, including in many cases which specialty product the fund should own. The asset-allocation decisions usually involve allocating new cash flow among these managers (unless the company has hired a single investment manager) and selecting new talent as needed. Investment managers are normally retained until they no longer meet the company's goals.

In practice, few companies accept the responsibility for directly shifting assets from one manager, asset category, or specialty product to another as market conditions change. Semidirect involvement is growing. Indirect involvement has been predominant in the past.

Whatever level of involvement the company takes in asset-mix decisions, by the very act of hiring managers to make these decisions and delegating the responsibility to them, the company still has made an asset-mix decision. This is because the company should know beforehand the investment philosophies of these managers and what kind of asset-mix changes they are likely to make.

In making investment strategy decisions, plan sponsors as well as their investment advisers understandably find it most difficult to ignore recent events. Therefore, it is most helpful for a plan sponsor to articulate its own investment time horizon (such as a market cycle period of five years or less) if it differs from the investment adviser's perspective.

The following checklist of questions was prepared to assist the company in having more meaningful dialogs with investment people on the investment strategy (deviation from the basic portfolio plan):

1. What is the investment manager's essential investment strategy?
2. How does the investment manager determine the probability of an imminent upturn or downturn in the market?
3. Has the investment manager's investment strategy changed during the past five years? If so, how and why has it changed?
4. How does the investment manager's investment strategy contrast with that of other investment managers?

Selecting External Managers

Investment managers can be classified as primary, secondary, and tertiary on the one hand and by investment style on the other.

Primary investment managers. These are institutions that manage assets of more than $2 billion and that have a major in-house research capability. Principals themselves are not involved directly in money management—the responsibility is delegated to others. These institutions may also have in-house expertise in fixed-income securities and real estate investment. Their portfolios would be characterized by common-stock issues of large capitalization and low volatility. This class would generally cover the major banks and insurance companies and some very large investment counselors.

Secondary investment managers. This class covers the institutions with assets under management of between $500 million and $2 billion. They have some of the characteristics of both the primary and the tertiary managers. The institutions included in this class would be major investment counselors, investment bankers, mutual funds, and brokerage-house affiliates.

Tertiary investment managers. These are institutions managing assets of less than $500 million. These institutions are characterized by principals being directly engaged in money management and research. The portfolio has a significant number of common-stock issues with small capitalization and high volatility. They might be especially adept at discovering emerging companies. This class primarily covers smaller investment counselors and some mutual funds.

Investment styles. Another way to think about selecting the investment managers for the pension fund is to more precisely define investment styles. This classification system is based on the belief that the market sector and individual issues are the key components of risk, in that order, and, by implication, of returns as well.

The company focuses on how the investment managers approach market timing and sector emphasis or rotation. This approach, usually applied to classifying equity managers, can also be applied to the balanced and bond asset categories. To most investment managers, the market and sector elements are the most important factors in their portfolio structuring process. Some investment managers make great changes in asset mix but little in sector emphasis; others believe in significant shifts in sector emphasis but not asset mix. The company should understand that the investment managers do this by a predisposition to a style of management that rarely changes materially over time.

The investment-style characteristic that needs to be defined by the plan sponsor within each category (for example, balanced, equity, and fixed income) is *flexibility:* (1) The investment manager's *flexibility in sector allocation,* such as changing industry or sector concentration to reflect the perceived economic, market, or interest-rate cycle. (2) The investment manager's *flexibility in asset allocation,* such as shifting between bonds and stocks in a balanced account, or between cash equivalents and either common stocks or fixed-income securities in an equity- or bond-oriented account, respectively.

■ *Equity managers.* In the late 1970s, most equity-oriented investment managers were moderate asset allocators and moderate sector allocators. Moderate equity asset allocation may be defined as an investment style that lets a portfolio's cash-equivalent content reach a maximum of between 26 percent and 50 percent of the equity portfolio. Moderate equity sector allocators are investment managers who are responsive to economic or market cycles, but use moderation in shifting portfolio concentrations by sector or stock-characteristics groups. (In up markets, the minimal asset allocators often do best, while in down markets the active asset allocators/active sector allocators often do best. In the five years ending in 1980, for example, with only one down year, the minimal asset allocators/moderate sector allocators, particularly the bottom-up managers, did best.)

Top-down equity managers develop a market or economic overview, identify sectors that should prosper within that scenario, and then select securities to conform with sector guidelines. Bottom-up equity managers select common stocks on the basis of fundamental, valuation, or technical attractiveness. They do not explicitly manage by sector-weighting strategies.

 ▪ *Balanced investment managers.* Most balanced managers today are moderate asset allocators, who change equity exposure by less than 50 percent but more than 25 percent.

 ▪ *Bond managers.* Bond managers are fairly evenly divided among active, moderate, and minimal asset allocators. There are few active sector allocators. An active bond manager is one who frequently varies the portfolio's maturity distribution between long-term, intermediate-term, and short-term maturities, so that more than two-thirds of the portfolio may at some time consist of long-term bonds and at another time of short-term bonds.

There are a number of consultants in the field of aiding corporate management in the selection of investment managers and constructing portfolios using mutual funds to achieve the objective.

Measuring Investment Performance

To measure investment performance, a plan sponsor should be familiar with *capital asset pricing theory* (the relationships between risk and reward if investors behave rationally and optimally). This is the basis for what is now called modern portfolio theory (MPT). MPT is the systematization of common sense, as was "fundamental" security analysis, which Benjamin Graham talked about in the 1930s.

One simplistic but perhaps helpful way to think about MPT as it is used for measuring common-stock performance is that MPT treats stocks like bonds in the sense that a selection of bond portfolios composed of lower-grade bonds rationally should provide more reward for the risk taken than a higher-grade bond portfolio. One of the best known offshoots of MPT is index funds. Common-stock index funds are big pools of stocks so well diversified that their performance, practically speaking, duplicates that of market indices such as the Standard & Poor's 500.

By moving away from an "indexed" portfolio of common stocks, you are taking a chance that you will underperform the market instead of beating it. So the first simple step in MPT breaks investment risk into (1) the risk that the stock market will go down relative to cash equivalents ("market risk") and (2) the risk that you will do better or worse than the market (called, logically enough, "nonmarket" risk). Using computers, MPT seeks to measure these risks as precisely as possible. The technical term for this market risk is "beta." A highly volatile stock is said to have a high beta. The market as a whole has a beta of 1. When the stock market does poorly relative to short-term investments, you probably would prefer to have a common-stock portfolio composed of low-beta stocks rather than high-beta stocks.

Today, betas are constructed from a complex recipe of facts and figures. For example, a company's beta will tend to be high if it has a high debt-to-equity ratio or if its industry tends to be cyclical.

Now, there is the other kind of risk—the risk of trying to construct a common-stock portfolio of the best stocks. When you are trying to outguess the market, you are shooting for a high nonmarket risk—for a high "alpha," in MPT lingo. Suppose, for instance, you think the stock market has undervalued ABC relative to other stocks. ABC has a beta of 1.7, but you think that a 10 percent rise in the stock market could boost ABC, say, 40 percent—far more than you would expect from the beta. Even if you think the market stays level, you believe ABC is due to rise. ABC is said to have a "positive expected alpha." Here is where the limits of MPT come in; the computer cannot tell you what a stock's expected alpha is. You have to tell the computer, on the basis of your own analysis, which stocks are under- or overvalued.

What is the use of this modern portfolio theory (MPT)?

Fundamentally, a plan sponsor should know the risks taken as best it can. For instance, you probably would want to avoid a high-beta portfolio if you think the market was likely to fall. Nor would you want to take a big risk of underperforming a rising stock market by overloading on a group of "covarying" companies unless you had reasons to believe that a capital-goods boom was coming and that the stock market had not yet anticipated the fact.

For all its potential drawbacks, modern portfolio theory is trying to do in a very sophisticated way what money managers have been trying to do for centuries. It really is a cost accounting system. If you are in a manufacturing business and do not know the different costs of making your product, you are not likely to be profitable or competitive. The same goes for portfolio management. *The cost of producing investment returns is taking risks. So MPT is investment-management cost accounting.*

Modern portfolio theory has won a permanent place in the pension manager's investment-performance-measurement tool chest—just as Benjamin Graham's ideas have. But reading Benjamin Graham does not make a good money manager, and neither will learning the cost accounting system of MPT.

However, modern portfolio theory is a set of analytical tools and disciplines, based upon relationships between risk and reward if investors behave rationally and optimally. MPT thus should enable plan sponsors to systematically and unemotionally process information useful in establishing and monitoring risk levels and return objectives.   □ *Gordon L. Mills*

INVESTOR RELATIONS

Investors pay a premium for certainty and discount for uncertainty. While investing ranks low among the sure things in life, this dictum nevertheless is the underlying justification for a formal and organized investor relations program. The financial officer of a corporation is in a unique position to influence the overall content, nature, and scope of the company's program.

One school of thought holds that dealing with the investment community is one of the major curses of public ownership and that the inquiries of analysts, portfolio managers, or even the company's shareholders are an intrusion on management's privacy, at best, or, at worst, a means by which confidential information becomes available to competitors. Somewhere in between lies the concept that "the less they (investors) know, the better off we (management) are."

At the other end of the scale is the philosophy that by adhering to the principle of full and meaningful disclosure and engaging in an active investor relations program a company is pursuing a course of enlightened self-interest. Those who advocate this approach do so in the belief that over the long run it will maximize the value of the company's shares in the marketplace.

From this latter perspective, companies that fail to fund and support an ongoing investor relations program are failing to carry out their responsibilities. First, they are failing the corporation itself, failing to do a vital part of the job for which they are compensated by the shareholders. Second, they are failing free enterprise by their lack of participation in a process so important to the survival of the very system which sustains them.

Aside from such lofty notions, what is investor relations, what are its purposes and objectives, what are the principal elements of an effective investor relations program, by whom should such a program be run, how can the results be measured, and what is the role of the financial executive in these efforts?

Goals and Objectives of an Investor Relations Program

Investor relations is the communications function that links the public corporation with its relevant investment markets. It is concerned with the communication of relevant and timely financial information to all relevant investment markets so that investors can make intelligent investment decisions (buy, hold, or sell) based on realistic evaluation of risks and rewards.

More simply stated, investor relations is designed to keep the public and the investment community informed fully and in a fair and timely fashion.

All too often companies place too much stress on simply complying with the disclosure requirements of the SEC instead of undertaking programs geared to the needs of investors for pertinent and useful information.

Such an approach may well satisfy the regulators, but it will hardly contribute to raising capital, a function of particular interest to the financial executive. Carl H. Seligson, managing director of Merrill Lynch White Weld Capital Markets Group, stated the case well in a recent issue of *The Financial Executive:*

> A firm's success in raising new capital depends, among other things, on stimulating the interest of potential investors. This can be achieved by developing a comprehensive finance plan and disseminating this information . . . through an investment relations program. These two factors go

hand in hand, and are essential for all companies, and for those companies that are capital intensive—utilities, for example—they can be crucial.

Seligson goes on to recommend that financial officers consider the investment community's needs when formulating a financial plan. The ideal plan, he writes, should focus on the company's track record, earnings history, return on common equity, plans for a higher proportion of debt or equity, expectations of new capital costs, anticipated yield on the book value of its common stock, dividend records and regularity of future payouts, and contingency plans in the event its calculations prove wrong.

"It would be a mistake to come up with a sound estimate of the company's future and not use [these data] to the fullest advantage," he advises, while at the same time conceding that "the idea of communicating financial projections . . . unfortunately is tantamount to treason in many companies."

Other widely held goals of an investor relations program were defined in a "two-way mirror" research survey reported in *Financial Analysts Journal*. The survey covered two groups, corporate members of the National Investor Relations Institute (an organization of investor relations practitioners) and sell-side chartered financial analysts (CFAs).

Asked to list the principal goals or objectives of their companies' investor relations programs, 187 NIRI members replied as follows:

1. Provide solid understanding of company—fair valuation.   57
2. Maintain "fair" stock price.   40
3. Increase investment community interest.   31
4. Keep investment community informed.   29
5. Broaden (diversify) shareholder base.   26
6. Increase price-earnings ratio, maximize stock price.   16
7. Meet needs of, and provide information to, shareholders.   14
8. Improve, maintain liquidity (trading volume).   11

Asked to state what they believe should be the principal goals and objectives of the investor relations programs of those companies they follow on a regular basis, 150 CFAs replied as follows:

1. Disseminate information ("timely," "reliable").   81
2. Make business understandable; provide insight and interpretation; explain corporate philosophy.   26
3. Encourage an honest, unbiased, and balanced (both positive and negative) view of company.   18
4. Open up "access" to management, insight into management philosophy.   14
5. Inform shareholders specifically.   8
6. Forewarn financial community of significant new developments and fundamental changes in business.   7
7. Provide reliable contact for inquiries.   7
8. Cultivate high (also stable) stock prices.   5

While the NIRI members understandably place greater emphasis on the price of their stocks than do the CFAs, it would not be difficult to construct a compatible set of broad goals for an investor relations program from these two lists.

While there is general agreement on the general goals of investor relations programs, each company should tailor its program to achieve specific objectives based on its own needs. For example, is the objective to broaden holdings of individual investors? Or is the program aimed at institutions, and if so, what type?

Increasingly, companies are turning to marketing techniques to solve their investor relations problems. While it is not likely that companies will offer "cents-off" coupons to introduce a new issue of common stock, there is a rising trend toward setting objectives on the basis of attitude studies of both individual and professional investors. Such well-known survey organizations as Yankelovich, Skelly and White, Opinion Research, and Lou Harris Associates are active in this area, along with a few specializing in the field, such as Financial Marketing Services.

Surveys generally seek to develop information on the demographics of the company's shareholders, what their attitudes are toward the company and its management, the size of their portfolios, their household income, activity in the market, why they bought the stock, how long they've held it, their expectations as to capital gains, dividends, and stock splits, and the like.

Similar attitude studies of registered representatives, analysts, and portfolio managers, especially when conducted regularly over a number of years, can measure change in the perception of the company and its management. Such surveys are indeed a highly effective—and objective—way to measure the effectiveness of an investor relations program. An extremely useful technique is to measure attitudes in a group survey that compares results among companies in a given industry.

The Place of Investor Relations in the Organization

With the goals of the investor relations program defined, it is possible to develop an investor relations program designed to capitalize on the perceived (and hopefully real) strengths of the company and to correct either the misconceptions about the company or the problems themselves. The latter is especially critical: not even the best investor relations program, executed by the most competent people and employing large resources, will succeed over the long run or cover up poor performance.

Even given the best of performances by a company, an investor relations program also cannot succeed without the full support of a company's top management. Anything short of this is mere window dressing. Equally important, investor relations must be part of the top policy-making level of every major corporation. In the words of Robert H. Savage, retired vice president of investor relations for International Telephone and Telegraph Corporation: "The investor relations executive cannot just serve as an output device. He must also have a say in the corporate decision-making process. . . . [He] has a responsibility not only to express top management's point of view to the investment community, but equally to represent and speak for the financial community within the company."

There are as many ways to ensure that the investor relations executive is "wired into" the office of the chief executive as there are tables of organization. Some corporations house investor relations in the financial or treasury department, reporting to the CFO, with perhaps indirect reporting responsibility and working relations with the CEO. Others have separate investor relations departments, sometimes headed by a vice president, reporting directly to the CEO. And still others incorporate investor relations in the company's corporate-communications area.

With an admitted bias based on personal experience, the latter approach affords the distinct advantage of ensuring full coordination of all of the company's communications—with professional investors, shareholders, employees, and government and regulatory agencies. Such a structure will go a long way toward ensuring that the company conveys a consistent message to all its constituencies.

The effective management of such a coordinated communications program requires a skilled communicator who has some training, knowledge, and experience in financial matters. It also requires close coordination with the company's CFO and his staff to ensure the accuracy and availability of appropriate financial data. Because the CFO and his staff are in close touch with the financial community and sensitive to its needs and concerns, they are in a unique position to influence the content of the financial information provided by the company. The financial staff also can make an important contribution to improving the effectiveness and timeliness of the information by providing internal management reports—usually monthly—that are consistent with the format of the company's quarterly public reports.

Basic Elements of an Investor Relations Program

While there are as many effective investor relations techniques as the mind has the ability to concoct, most well-conceived programs will include the following fundamental elements:

- *A carefully planned and professionally executed program of written communications, in which the annual and quarterly reports play a key role.* The annual report should be in tune with the company's investor relations goals. Increasingly, quarterly reports have been expanded to include news and feature stories on the company's activities as well as detailed information on operating results, the income statement, and the balance sheet. Some companies publish newsletters for shareholders, and others send specially prepared material to account executives employed by brokerage firms. Analysts should be sent 10-Q and 10-K reports automatically.

- *An organized mailing program to members of the investment community, analysts, portfolio managers, registered representatives, and investment advisers.* This material— quarterly and annual reports, news stories, product literature, and so forth— should be tailored to meet the needs of the particular audience and should not commit the sin of overkill by inundating the audience with useless information.

- *Management meetings with members of the investment community.* Presentations may be made to analyst societies operating in most major cities in the United States; "splinter groups" of analysts specializing in a particular industry; meetings organized by brokerage firms, investment bankers, or the company itself; and meetings with registered representatives, sometimes attended by their customers. Other sessions may be held with portfolio managers at a large bank or institution, or they make take the form of small private luncheons or dinners involving top management and representatives of large institutional shareholders or potential shareholders.

■ *Meetings with investment professionals at company headquarters.* These typically take the form of briefings by the investor relations executive and meetings with senior management, including the CFO.

■ *Plant tours.* These can be particularly effective to demonstrate a new manufacturing technique, introduce a new product, or simply educate analysts on the nature of a company's business. Another version of this approach is a tour of the company's research facility.

■ *Special services for individual shareholders.* These include free "800" telephone numbers for questions, regional information meetings in addition to the annual meetings, welcome letters to new shareholders and "regrets" letters to departing shareholders (sometimes both communications include surveys), and product samples or discounts.

■ *Dividend reinvestment plans.* Many companies pay both fees and brokerage commissions under such plans, providing the shareholders the opportunity to reinvest dividends without cost; many plans permit investment of additional funds per quarter up to a set limit such as $3,000, while others offer a 5 percent discount from market.

■ *Financial-press relations.* A well-conceived investor relations program should make effective use of the media to help broaden interest among potential investors and to keep shareholders and the investment community informed of the company's activities.

■ *Corporate (financial) advertising programs.* Although such programs can be costly, if properly conceived and executed, they can help broaden the recognition and knowledge of a company. As with other forms of communications, the one-shot approach will not work and is a waste of money.

■ *A "stock watch" program.* This should involve both daily monitoring of transfer sheets and a systematic analysis of stock-market activity to detect trends in ownership as well as potential takeover activity.

■ *"Marketing" surveys.* As discussed earlier, these can be critical to setting goals and measuring progress.

Although these are some of the most frequently used techniques of the trade, they cannot succeed, no matter how cleverly conceived or brilliantly executed, unless the company and its investor relations program have an abundance of one critical commodity: credibility. In simple terms, this means being truthful, having a willingness to reveal and discuss bad news as well as good, avoiding "surprises," and treating everyone on an equal basis.

Credibility is an asset in good times, but it is critical when a company is having problems. It takes time to build and can be shattered in an instant. The financial executive is in a unique position to make sure that his company goes forth to Wall Street with its credibility working for it and not against it.

Costs versus Benefits

Having said all this, we get down to the question near and dear to the heart of the financial executive: "How much will an effective investor relations program cost, will it get results—and if so, how can I measure them?"

Depending on the size of a company, its capitalization, and its shareholder base, an effective investor relations program, including annual and quarterly reports, will cost from $500,000 to $1 million, although the job can be done for considerably less by small companies. A financial advertising program will add significantly to this total.

While there is little empirical evidence showing what the bottom-line impact of an effective program is—or even indicating what the measure of benefits should be—there are many examples of successful programs. One handy measure is a company's price/earnings multiple compared with that of the Standard & Poor's 500 or other leading companies in the same industry.

For most companies, it is fair to say that all other things being equal, an effective investor relations program is worth one or two multiple points over not having any program, and even more in those situations where companies have a negative image among investors.

This flies in the face of examples of companies that treat the investment community in a cavalier manner, but sell at attractive multiples. These are the exceptions that prove the rule.

The efficient market theory notwithstanding, most managements are not willing to entrust the value of their company's stock to chance. For better or worse, investor relations is a key part of management's charter; the task is to make it work for you and your shareholders. □ *Marvin L. Krasnansky*

Index

Italicized names indicate contributors.

ABC inventory control method, 141, 147
absorption costing, 117, 125-128
accelerated cost recovery system, 150
accounting, 5
  replacement cost, 10-11
  standard-cost, 121-125, 130
accounting, cost
  absorption costing, 117, 125-128
  computers and, 116-117
  for defense contracts, 128-133
  direct (marginal) costing, 117, 125-128
  job-order cost, 120-121, 130
  process cost, 117-120, 130
  standard cost, 121-125, 130
accounting, general, 105-115
  administration of accounting system in, 106-107
  chart of accounts in, 107-109
  defined, 105
  financial reporting function, 109
  function of, 105-106
  internal audits and, 171-179
  internal control function, 109
  see also financial statements
accounts payable, bank services for management of cash flow, 89-93
accounts receivable
  bank services for management of cash flow, 80-89, 96-97, 104
  credit collections, 98-105
  days-sales-of-receivables-outstanding, 7, 101
  financing of, 72, 104
acid test, 170
administrative and general services
  budgets for, 37-38
  as a percentage of sales, 7
advertising, in investor relations function, 200
alpha in modern portfolio theory, 195
American Institute of Certified Public Accountants (AICPA), 105, 110, 172, 181

ethical standards of, 183
generally accepted auditing standards of, 183-184
internal-control standards of, 184-185
annual (short-term) planning, 30-43
  cash forecasts in, 30, 40-41
  consolidated corporate plan in, 30, 41-42
  forecasts in, 9, 30, 40-41
  objectives in, 32
  operating-profit plan, 30, 34-38
  plan approval and communication in, 42-43
  plan development in, 32-33
  strategic plan relationship to, 30
  time horizon for, 21
annual reports to shareholders, 180-182, 187-188
  in investor relations program, 199
assets
  affordable growth of, 29
  on balance sheet, 110-113
  return on, 170, 175
  turnover of, 7-8, 170
audits and auditing
  audit committee and, 15-16, 176, 178-179, 180-181
  audit department in, 172-173, 176-177
  bank services in, 81, 93-97
  of capital expenditures, 10, 60-61
  of data processing systems, 174-175
  external, 16, 173, 178, 179-188
  internal, 13, 15-16, 171-179
  operational, 16, 173-174
  plans for, 174, 177
  post-, in capital expenditures programs, 60-61
  pre-award, for defense contracts, 131-132
  reports on, 174, 177-178, 186-187
automated clearing house (ACH) depository transfer check, 88

Automatic Data Processing, 88, 94
average capital employed, 168
average cost method of inventory valua-
    tion, 119-120, 135

Baker, Kenneth A., 57-69
balance sheets, 106, 110-113, 162-163
    financial ratios from, 7-8, 11-12
    purchasing department use of, 96, 97
    for reporting operating results, 152-153
bank loans, 70-71, 72
bankruptcy, trends in, 99
Bankruptcy Reform Act of 1978, 99, 102
bank services
    and accounts payable management,
        89-93
    and accounts receivable management,
        80-89, 96, 97, 104
    in audit control, 81, 93-97
    in cash management, 80-98
    in collection process, 80, 81-84
    concentration-system design, 85-89
    as criteria for bank selection, 97-98
    in disbursement process, 81, 89-93
    funds mobilization, 81, 85-89
    loans, 70-72
    as master trustees of pension funds, 189
Bank Wire Transfer System, 86
Beehler, Paul J., 78-98
benefit cost (B/C) ratio, 63-64
beta
    for determining cost of common stock,
        66
    in modern portfolio theory, 194-195
Boisi, Geoffrey T., 53-57
bonds
    expected returns on, 190-191
    industrial-revenue, 74
    investment managers of, 193, 194
    tax considerations on redemption of,
        150
breakeven analysis, for wire transfer ser-
    vices, 85-86
Brody, Kenneth D., 53-57
budgets and budgeting, 9, 30-43
    for administrative and general services,
        37-38
    budget development in, 32-34
    capital expenditures in, 21, 30, 38-40,
        67-68
    control reports in, 164-168
    inventory, 35-36
    production, 36-37

    in standard-cost accounting, 121-125
    variable (flexible), 44-45
    see also annual planning
business-direction planning, 19, 22-25

Caldwell, C. Dow, 133-148
CAP (capital-asset-pricing) model, 66,
    194-195
CAP (cash asset percentage), 49
capacity buying in material requirements
    planning, 145-146
capacity-requirements planning in material
    requirements planning (MRP), 145
capital, on balance sheet, 113
capital asset pricing (CAP) model
    for cost of common stock, 66
    for measuring investment performance,
        194-195
capital budgets, 21, 30, 38-40, 67-68
capital expenditures, 57-69
    analysis of, 10
    budgets for, 21, 30, 38-40, 67-68
    capital rationing in, 67-68
    central considerations for, 69
    cost of capital in, 65-66
    evaluation methods for, 61-65
    in evaluation of results, 59-60
    installment plan financing of, 73-74
    net present value (NPV) analysis of,
        61-64, 65, 67-68
    plans for, 27-28
    requirements of program for, 58-61
    risk analysis in, 62, 68-69
capitalization, defined, 11
capital-stock taxes, 158
capital structure
    bonds in, *see* bonds
    common stock in, *see* common stock
    defined, 75
    tax considerations of, 149-150
captive subsidiaries, finance, 104
carrying costs, 139, 142
cash asset percentage (CAP), 49
cash flow
    accounts receivable collections in,
        103-105
    in acquisition/divestiture decisions, 26
    dividend policy and, 29
    forecasts of, 30, 40-41, 69, 103
    in merger/acquisition evaluation, 26, 56,
        59, 61-64
    as percentage of total debt, 169
    planning of, 69-78

statement of, 41
in strategic financial analysis reporting, 49
see also discounted cash flow valuation
cash management, 78-98
as bank selection criterion, 97-98
borrowing against or selling accounts receivable, 103-105
cash-flow method of forecasting receivables, 103
objectives of, 79-80
techniques of, with bank services, 80-97
casual loans, 70
certification, of financial analysts (CFA), 197-198
chart of accounts, 107-109
Chaudhuri, Asok K., 57-59
chief executive officers (CEOs)
audit department reports to, 176
chief financial officer and, 6, 10
inventory management role of, 148
in mergers, acquisitions, and divestitures, role of, 53-54
chief financial officers (CFOs), 6-17
audit department reports to, 176
corporate communications role of, 17, 199, 200
financial administration by, 12-17
financial policy setting by, 6-12
in mergers, acquisitions, and divestitures, role of, 10, 54, 57
Commerce Clearing House, 129
commercial paper, 71
common stock
cost of capital determination and, 25, 66
earnings per share, 56-57
expected returns on, 190-191
financing with, 77
investment managers of, 193-194
merger and acquisition impact on, 56-57
tax considerations on redemption of, 150
communication
in capital expenditure programs, 58-59
chief financial officer's role in, 17, 199, 200
coordination of corporate, 199-201
compensating balances, 70-71
compensation, executive
compensation agreements in, 150-151
compensation committee role in, 58-59
computers
bank services through use of, 93-97

cost accounting systems and, 116-117
and data processing audits, 174-175
fraud with, 175
internal-control standards and, 185
in materials requirements planning (MRP), 140-146
in modern portfolio theory applications, 194-195
consolidated corporate plan, 30, 41-42
consultants, merger strategy and, 55
contracts, cost, 129
controller, function of, 13-14
controls and controlling
in credit systems, 101
internal, in accounting system, 109
in material requirements planning, 36, 140-146
see also budgets and budgeting
conversion costs, 134-136
convertible preferred stock, 77-78
cost-benefit analysis, 63-64
cost centers, 117
cost (reimbursement) contracts, 129
cost of capital
in capital expenditures programs, 65-66
determination of, 25
as discount rate in present value analysis, 62
in strategy development, 19, 25
cost of goods sold
on income statement, 114
cost of sales/service plan, 35-37
credit
collections on, 80, 81-84, 98-105
granting of, information for, 99-101
crime
computer, prevention of, 175
internal audit function and, 175-176
current assets, 110
current liabilities, 113
current ratio, 169
cycle counting, 144, 147

daily sales outstanding, 170
Dalton, Arthur Mark, 17-51
damaged goods, 147
days-sales-of-inventory-on-hand, 7, 170
days-sales-of-receivables-outstanding, 7, 101
debentures, 76, 78
debt
bonds, 74, 150, 190-191, 193, 194
cash flow as percentage of, 169

debt *(continued)*
    cost of capital determination and, 25,
        65-66
    debentures, 76, 78
    financing with, 75-76
    loans as, *see* loans
    management of, in setting financial
        policy, 11-12
    ratings on, and lease financing, 73
debt-to-capitalization ratio, 11
debt-to-equity ratio, 11
decision making
    federal taxes and, 149
default on defense contracts, 132-133
Defense Acquisition Regulations (DAR),
        128-129, 131
defense contracts, 128-133
    accounting for, 129-132
    termination for, 132-133
    types of, 129
deferred charges, 113
deferred income, 113
depository transfer checks (DTC), 86-89
depreciation methods
    accelerated cost recovery system, 150
    straight-line, 150
direct (marginal) costing, 117, 125-128,
        130
directors, boards of
    annual plan approval by, 42-43
    audit committee of, 15-16, 176, 178-181
    chief financial officer and, 6, 10, 11,
        15-16, 17
discounted cash flow valuation, 56
    for capital expenditures, 61-65
    of cost of common stock, 66
discounts, management of, in disburse-
        ments, 89
dispatching in manufacturing, 90
dispatch list in material requirements plan-
        ning, 145
distribution requirements planning (DRP),
        145
dividends, 12, 75
    in cost of capital analysis, 66
    policy development for, 28-29
    reinvestment of, 200
    yields on, defined, 66
divisionalization
    corporate and division controller rela-
        tionship in, 14
    treasurer function and, 15

"dotted-line" relationships, 14, 15
drafts, sight, 101
Dun & Bradstreet, 100, 170

earnings
    accumulated-earnings taxes on, 152
    on defense contracts, 131
    dividend policy and, 28-29
    in product/service mix selection, 27
    sustainable growth rate of, 8-9
earnings per share
    dilution of, in mergers and acquisitions,
        56-57
economic order quantity (EOQ) rule,
        141-143, 146
economic trends, chief financial officer
        and, 10-11
employee benefits, chief financial officer
        role in, 12
equipment financing, 104-105
equity, return on, 169
equivalent units in process cost accounting,
        118-119
ERISA (Employee Retirement Income Se-
        curity Act of 1974), 189-191
escalation clauses, 129
ethical standards, of external auditors, 183
evidential matter in auditing, 186
external audits, 16, 173, 178, 179-188

factoring, 72, 104
Federal Reserve, 86, 88, 91-93
FIFO (first in, first out) inventory valua-
        tion method, 120, 135-136
finance
    accounting in, *see* entries beginning with
        "accounting"
    capital expenditures and return on in-
        vestments, 57-59
    cash flow planning, 69-78
    cash management and bank relations,
        78-98
    chief financial officer responsibilities in,
        6-17
    cost accounting and analysis, 115-133
    credit collections, 80, 81-84, 98-105
    external auditing, 16, 173, 178, 179-188
    general accounting and financial state-
        ments, 105-115
    internal auditing, 13, 15-16, 171-179
    inventory and, *see* entries beginning with
        "inventory"

investor relations, 195-201
operating results presentation, 159-171
planning, budgeting, and forecasting,
    17-51
role of, in general management, 5-6
finance companies
accounts-receivable financing by, 104
captive, 104
financial accounting, *see* accounting, general
eral
Financial Accounting Standards Board
    (FASB), 181-182, 183
establishment of, 172
inflation accounting and, 10-11
supplementary financial information
    for, 187
financial planning
annual, 30-43
budget-development process and, 19-21
business-direction planning in, 22-25
data relationships in, 49-51
performance reporting in, 43-49
scope of, 18-19
strategy development in, 25-30
financial ratios, from balance sheets, 7-8,
    11-12
financial statements, 6-7, 110-115
defined, 110
external audits of, 16, 173, 178, 179-188
internal audits of, 13, 15-16, 171-179
management responsibility for, 180-181
nature of, 181-182
in presentation of operating results,
    161-168
statement of changes in financial position,
    tion, 115, 162-164
statement of retained earnings, 114-115
see also balance sheets; income statements
    ments
financing
of accounts receivable, 72, 104
equipment, 104-105
foreign, 12
government, 74
import, 84-89
installment, 73-74
intermediate-term, 71-74
of inventory, 72
long-term, 74-78
project, 72-73
short-term, 70-71
finished goods, 133

fixed assets, 113
fixed-charges coverage, 169
fixed-price contracts, 129
float
collection services to reduce, 80-84,
    98-105
disbursement techniques for management
    ment of, 89-93
funds mobilization to reduce, 85-89
measurement of, 96
forecasts and forecasting
cash flow, 30, 40-41, 69, 103
environmental, in business-direction
    planning, 23-24
by external auditors, 183
in short-term planning, 9
time horizon for, 21
Foreign Corrupt Practices Act (FCPA), 6-7,
    14, 15, 172, 173, 176, 185
foreign financing, 12
fraud
computer, 175
internal audit function and, 175-176
funds, sources of
external, 28-29
internal, 28

GAAP (generally accepted accounting
    principles), 181, 182, 187
Gantt, Henry L., 106
General Electric Company, 88, 94
generally accepted accounting principles
    (GAAP), 181-182, 187
generally accepted auditing standards,
    183-184
Gibbons, Robert P., 133-148
Gilles, Nicholas, C., 171-179
goals, defined, 24
Goodwin, Paul R., 57-69
government contracts
allocable costs in, 130
allowable costs in, 130, 131
government financing, 74
government regulation
on inflation accounting, 10-11
of inner controls, 6-7
of securities markets, 76, 77, 171, 172,
    185
Gowin, Marilyn J., 155-159
Graham, Benjamin, 194, 195
gross margin (marginal contribution)
defined, 126

gross margin *(continued)*
  inventory valuation method based on,
    136-137
gross profit
  defined, 126
  on income statement, 114
gross profit percentage, 7
growth
  affordable, 29
  sustainable, formula for, 8-9
  tax considerations in, 152

Hammar, Lester E., 133-148
HIBOR (Hong Kong Interbank Offered
  Rate), 71
Holzman, Robert S., 148-155
Hong Kong Interbank Offered Rate
  (HIBOR), 71
Howe, W. Asquith, 115-133
human resources, in financial department,
  16-17

income statements, 106, 113-114
  financial ratios from, 7
  for reporting operating results, 162-163
indirect costs, defined, 130
industrial-revenue bonds, 74
inflation
  accounting for, 10-11
  in compensation decisions, 42
  escalation clauses in contracts and, 129
  incentive financing as ledge for, 78
  in present value analysis, 62
installment financing, 73-74
insurance, preauthorized checks for pay-
    ment of, 83, 84
Interactive Data Corporation, 94
interest, in cost of capital analysis, 65-66
interest-rate future contracts, 76-77
intermediate-term financing, 71-74
internal audits, 13, 15-16, 171-179
internal control, 109, 184-186
internal rate of return (IRR)
  of capital expenditures, 64-65, 67-68
  defined, 64
  in investment/divestiture decisions, 26
Internal Revenue Service, 134, 148-154
International Trade Commission, 13
interstate commerce, tax considerations in,
    156-159
Interstate Income Tax Law, 156, 157
Interstate Taxation Act, 156, 158

inventory, 133-148
  carrying costs on, 139
  cyclical, 144, 147
  days-sales-of-inventory-on-hand, 7, 170
  defined, 133
  financing of, 72
  physical, 147-148
  tax considerations in, 150
  turnover of, 137-138
  valuation of, *see* inventory valuation
inventory budgets, 35-36
inventory management and control,
    139-148
  ABC inventory method in, 141, 147
  cycle counting in, 144, 147
  economic order quantity (EOQ) for,
    141-143, 146
  open-to-buy method, 146-147
  reorder-point method, 139-140
inventory valuation, 134-137
  average cost method, 119-120, 135
  cost of specific lot, 136
  FIFO (first in, first out) method, 120,
    135-136
  gross-margin method, 136-137
  LIFO (last in, first out) method, 136,
    150, 182
  selecting method of, 134, 137
  specific lot method of, 136
  standard cost method of, 135
investment bankers, merger strategy and,
    55
investments
  on balance sheet, 110
  bank services in, 94-95
  mix of, in pension fund portfolios,
    190-192
  performance appraisal of, 194-195
  see also specific types of investments
investor relations, 195-201
  basic elements of, 199-201
  costs and benefits of, 201
  goals and objectives of program for,
    196-198
  role of, in organization, 198-199
invoices, service charges on past-due, 101
involuntary conversions, 151
Ise, Richard, 148-155

job-order cost accounting, 120-121, 130
journals, 107

Kanaban method, 144
key factors
    defined, 45
    reporting of, 45-48
Klepper, Irwin, 155-159
Krasnansky, Marvin L., 195-201

leases and leasing, 12
    debt ratings and, 73
    financing, 73-74
    leveraged, 73-74
    operating, 73
Ledbetter, J. Lee, 115-133
ledgers, 107
legal lists, 29
liabilities, accounting, 113
LIBOR (London Interbank Offered Rate),
    71
LIFO (last in, first out) method of
    inventory valuation, 136
    financial/tax use of, 182
    tax impact of using, 150
lines of credit, 70-71
loans
    bank term, 72
    from foreign banks, 71, 72
    short-term bank, 70-71
lockbox services, 81-83, 96
long-term debt, 113
long-term financing, 74-78
long-term planning, 9, 18
    capital investment plan in, 38-40
    models in, 9, 49-51
    time horizon for, 21
Lund, Harry A., 69-78

McDonald's, 97
Mach, J. D., 155-159
management, finance role in, 5-6
management information systems (MIS),
    16
management structure
    in divisionalization, 14, 15
    levels of management in, 160
managers, credit, 99-102
manufacturing, production planning in,
    35-36, 145
marginal accounts
    defined, 99
    risk reduction in, 101-102
marginal (direct) costing, 117, 125-128
marginal income, 126

marketing plan, 34, 37
markets, securities, government regulation
    of, 76, 77, 171, 172
Massachusetts formula, 156-157
material requirements planning (MRP),
    36, 140-146
materials planning and control, simulation
    in, 36, 140-146
mergers, acquisitions, and divestitures,
    53-57
    cash flow as consideration in, 26, 56, 59,
        61-64
    chief financial officer role in, 10, 54, 57
    evaluation in, 56
    organization for, 53-54
    planning in, 55
    in product/service mix selection, 27
    strategy in, 54
    structuring the transaction for, 56-57
    tax considerations in, 151, 152
Miller, Donald E., 98-105
Mills, Gordon, L., 188-195
mission, defined, 24
models, in long-term planning, 9, 49-51
modems, 25
money managers
    investment strategy formulation by,
        191-192
    measuring performance of, 194-195
    selection of, for pension plans, 192-194
MRP II (manufacturing resources plan-
    ning), 143-144, 145
multinational corporations
    inner controls of, 6-7, 14
    subsidiary control and, 261-262
    tax planning of, 15
Multistate Tax Compact, 156-157

National Data Corporation, 88, 94
National Investor Relations Institute,
    197-198
net income after taxes as percentage of
    sales, 7, 8
net operating profit after taxes, 168
net present value (NPV)
    in capital expenditure decisions, 61-64,
        65, 67-68
    in investment/divestiture decisions, 26
new investment rate, 169

objectives
    defined, 24

objectives *(continued)*
  formulation of, in planning process,
    24-25
  investment, of pension funds, 189-190
obsolescence, product, 147
open-to-buy inventory control system,
    146-147
operating budgets, 58-60, 64
operating-profit plan, 21, 30, 34-38
operating results, 159-171
  interpretation of, 168-170
  management role in, 160
  performance results compared to,
    160-161
  presentation methods for, 161-168
  source of data for, 161
operational audits, 16, 173-174
opportunity costs, in capital rationing, 67
organization, in mergers, acquisitions and
    divestitures, 53-54
organization charts, for financial function,
    12-13
organization structure, chart of accounts
    responsibility and, 107
overhead
  in cost accounting systems, 118-121,
    124-125, 126-128
  in inventory valuation, 133, 135

PACs (preauthorized checks), 83-84
PADs (preauthorized debits), 84
past-due invoices, service charges on, 101
payable-through drafts (PTD), 91-92
payback analysis
  in capital expenditure decisions, 61, 64
  in investment/divestiture decisions, 26
peer reviews of internal audit function,
    179
pension plans, 188-195
  chief financial officer role in, 12
  external manager selection for, 192-194
  investment policy of, 189-191
  investment strategy of, 191-192
  measuring investment performance of,
    194-195
performance appraisal
  capital expenditures in, 59-60
  in financial planning, 43-49
  investment, measurement of, 194-195
  operating results compared to, 160-161
  pension fund, 194-195

performance reporting, 21, 43-49
  key-factor reporting, 45-48
  by product line, 45, 46
  responsibility reporting, 43-44
  strategic plan monitoring, 48-49
  variable (flexible) budgeting, 44-45
physical distribution, planning in, 145
physical inventory, 147-148
planning,
  for audits, 174, 177
  of distribution requirements, 145
  in mergers, acquisitions and divestitures,
    54-55
  production, 35-36, 145
  research and development, 37
point-of-sale systems, 146-147
policy
  financial, and chief financial officer, 6-12
  investment, of pension funds, 189-191
Pollack, Shepard P., 5-6
position assessment, 24
post-audits in capital expenditures pro-
    grams, 60-61
preauthorized checks (PACs), 83-84
preauthorized debits (PADs), 84
preferred stock
  cost of capital determination and, 66
  financing with, 77-78
pretax income as a percentage of sales, 7
price and pricing, determination of, 35
price/earnings ratio, investor relations pro-
    gram impact on, 201
Priebe, Robert J., 98-112
prime rate, 70
private placement
  of debt, 76
  of equity, 77
process cost accounting, 117-120, 130
*Production and Inventory Management in the
    Computer Age* (Wight), 143
production planning, 35-36, 145
product-line reporting, 45, 46
product mix
  profitability and, 27
  selection of, 26-28
products/services
  mix selection for, 26-28
  strategy development for, 25-26
profitability
  credit techniques to improve, 101-102
  financial ratios to measure, 7-8, 11-12

inventory decisions in measuring, 138-139
product-line reporting of, 45, 46
in product/service mix selection, 27
profitability index
for capital expenditures programs, 63-64
in investment/divestiture decisions, 26
project financing, 72-73
PTD (payable-through drafts), 91-92
public relations, investor relations and, 195-201

Quigley, Joseph M., 69-78

RCA Corporation, 81
remote-disbursement techniques, 92-93
reorder-point method, 139-140
reorganizations, tax-free, 151
replacement cost, accounting for, 10-11
reports and reporting
audit, 174, 177-178, 186-187
"roll-up," 43, 44, 46
research and development, planning in, 37
responsibility, accounting function and assignment of, 107, 109
responsibility reporting, 43-44
retained earnings, statement of, 114-115
return, internal rate of, 26, 64-65, 67-68
return on assets, 170-175
return on average capital employed, 168
return on equity (ROE), 169
return on investment (ROI), formula for, 8, 138
return on sales, 7, 8, 170
revenue plan, 34-35
risk
in modern portfolio theory (MPT), 194-195
reduction of, in credit decisions, 101-102
in setting pension fund investment policy, 189-191
risk analysis
in corporate expenditure programs, 62, 68-69
in granting of credit, 100-101
"roll-up" reporting, 43, 44, 46
ROP (reorder point) inventory system, 139-140
routing in material requirements planning (MRP), 144

salary
in compensation agreements, 150-151
deductibility of, for federal taxes, 149
sales
affordable growth of, 29
credit department link to, 99, 102
daily outstanding, 170
financial ratios regarding, 7-8
forecasts of collections on, 103
management of, 144
pretax income as a percentage of, 7
sales and use taxes, 157-158
sales budgets, 34-35
sales plans (budgets), 34-35
Saunders, Richard W., 155-159
Savage, Robert H., on investor relations, 198-199
Savoie, Leonard M., 179-188
scheduling, in material requirements planning (MRP), 145
secured loans, 70
Securities and Exchange Commission
audit committee requirements of, 15-16
disclosure of nonaudit services by auditors, 188
formation of, 171
inflation accounting and, 10-11
internal control regulations of, 185-186
registration of debt offerings and, 76
registration of equity securities and, 77
Regulation S-X, 110-113, 114
as source of generally accepted accounting principles, 181-182
supplementary financial information for, 187
Securities Exchange, Act of 1934, 171, 172, 185
Seligson, Carl, on importance of investor relations, 196-197
service charges
for accelerating collection of receivables, 103-105
for late payments, 101
Shanahan, John T., Jr., 98-105
short-term financing, 70-71
SIBOR (Singapore Interbank Offered Rate), 71
sight drafts, 101
in materials planning, 36, 140-146
in risk analysis of capital expenditures, 68-69

SKU (stock-keeping units), 146
specific lot method of inventory valuation, 136
Stamm, Charles F., 133-148
standard-cost accounting, 121-125, 130
    material and labor variances in, 123-124
    overhead variances in, 124-125
standard cost method of inventory valuation, 135
standard deviation in pension fund investment policy, 191
startup costs, 152
statement of changes in financial position, 115, 162-164
statement of retained earnings, 114-115
stockholders, mergers, acquisitions, divestitures and, 54, 55
stock-keeping units (SKU), 146
straight-line depreciation, 150
"straight-line" relationships, 14, 15
strategic operating plan, 27
strategic planning
    monitoring function in, 48-49
    plan development in, 29-30
    time horizon for, 21
strategy
    investment, for pension funds, 191-192
    in mergers, acquisitions and divestitures, 54-55
strategy development, 19, 25-30
    annual planning and, 30
    funding/financing strategy, 28-29
    product or service mix in, 26-28
    of product or service strategy, 25-26
    strategic plan in, 29-30
strategy memorandum, 25, 29-30
subsidiaries, captive finance, 104
surveys, in investor relations function, 197-198

tax department, 152-154
taxes, 5
    deferred, in capitalization, 11
taxes, federal, 148-155
    decision-making limitations and, 149
    growth considerations in, 152
    potential savings of, 149-152
    tax department responsibilities in, 152-154

taxes, state and local, 155-159
    administration of, 159
    types of, 156-159
tax planning, 15
termination of defense contracts, 132-133
term loans, 72
Thornhill, William T., 105-115
time sales, 104-105
total average debt as a percentage of average capital employed, 169
total debt to capitalization, 169
trade credit, 70
treasurer, function of, 13-15
trends
    in bankruptcy, 99
    economic, 10-11
Tsinikas, Byron A., 17-51
turnover, asset, 7-8, 170
turnover, inventory, calculation of, 137-138

underwriters
    debt financing through, 76
    equity financing through, 77
Uniform Division of Income for Tax Purposes Act, 156-157
Urban Development Action grants, 74

variable (flexible) budgeting, 44-45
variances
    in annual planning, 31-32
    in standard cost-accounting, 122-125
    in variable budgeting, 44-45
volume (capacity) variances, 125
Vos, Hubert D., 6-17
Voss, Thomas H., 105-115

warrants, debentures with, 78
Wasch, Richard S., 17-51
Wiesner, Richard H., 98-105
wire transfer of funds, 85-86, 89-91
working capital, 79-80, 169
work in process, 133, 148

Yoder, John, 133-148

zero-balance accounts (ZBAs), 89-91
zero coupon debt, 76